ZAMBOANGA TIMES

Tales of Jim Tuck
Book 2

DAVID A. ROHE

This is a work of historical fiction.

Ordering Information:

Prime Seven Media
518 Landmann St.
Tomah City, WI 54660

Printed in the United States of America

Table of Contents

Acknowledgements

First of all, this book would not have been completed without the encouragement and technical assistance of someone with as strong, maybe stronger vested interest in its completion than I have. That person is Douglas Chowns. His veneration for Jim provided the intermittent kicks up my bum required to finish. I couldn't stop because it was as important to get this story told for him as for me, and I didn't want to disappoint either one of us. Also, Douglas is an artist, with the genius for design that created the book cover. Well done.

Next in line is my long-time friend, confident and loving editor, Kelly Budd Wesselman in Albany, Georgia. She assisted, from a distance, with her efforts to eliminate my use of passive voice, as well as my more cryptic prose. She actually praised a few of my phrases from time to time. Well done, Kelly. You are a gem.

Besides Doug and Kelly, I have Margaret and Irene Tuck to thank for information and documents that helped inform the story; Margaret is Jim's widow and a good friend, and Irene is Jim and Margaret's daughter. Imagine my surprise when my scepticism with Jim's story about his relationship with a newspaper in Zamboanga was supported with the copy of the page from the paper, dated May 28, 1938 that is on the cover, as well as copies of Jim's many passports. Margaret supplied that document. Irene also gave me access to a trove of letters and documents that she had saved.

Finally, my wife, Sharon Robinson, with her wit and subtle support, as in "Did you do any writing today?" kept me constantly aware over a 10 year period that she was patiently watching. That's a long time to keep the faith, and she did.

Thank you all.

DAR

Forword

This is intended to be the second book of four that I am writing about Jim Tuck. Whether it is or not depends on my longevity since it is the first one of the four written, and I am not making rapid progress.

Jim was a real man who I really met in Augusta, Georgia, probably in 1982. He died in Augusta in October 1989, age 73. Between these two events, meeting and dying, I became privy to myriad stories from his past, mostly long past, but a few current ones. I am a good listener and Jim, particularly with a tumbler of cheap red wine with an ice cube, was, to put it mildly, talkative. His network outside Augusta, Georgia was vast while it seemed to me that his local group was excessively restricted. His house, at the time on the outskirts of Augusta, was constructed of wooden power poles so it looked like a two-story log cabin, set off the road in the trees. His family in Augusta consisted of his wife Margaret and daughter Irene (Book Four) and a black dog I suspect was a lab; his daughter by his deceased wife was Xochitl who lived in England. Wall space in the house was dedicated to bookshelves, nearly all the wall space. The kitchen was spacious as Jim liked to show off his cooking skills. Indeed, he taught me to cook a turkey, which I have made each Thanksgiving since. (It is now 2021 and I am in New Zealand.)

So, Jim was a storyteller. He was also a story embellisher. As the stories became more fantastic, I became sceptical. But, I still listened, with my glass of wine in hand, and my scepticism did not diminish the fascination of listening. I spoke at Jim's memorial service and noted that after careful consideration I decided it did not matter whether the stories of his exploits were factual. Once I relaxed and simply enjoyed the tales I realized that I needed to write them, somehow. Thus Zamboanga Times eventually came about. Once I began the research and writing, I found that the basis of the story, Jim in Zamboanga, was actually backed up by documented evidence. You could have tipped me over with a feather.

Jim always said, and wrote elsewhere, that he was the editor of the Zamboanga Times newspaper. Well, he wasn't. He was the manager as of May, 1938, according to the scrap of newspaper masthead I have, and the paper was the Mindanao Herald. His favourite newspaper was the New York Times, which I suspect he then remembered as his paper in the Philippines. So, he got his job title and the name of the paper wrong. He was working on a newspaper in Zamboanga in the Philippines just before the outbreak of WWII, having already flown for the Chinese in their current fight with the Japanese. Perspective, Dave Rohe, perspective.

Jim was outrageous in many ways, causing more than one person to lose a bit of perspective. His personality was large, as was his life, which was winding down in, of all places, Augusta, Georgia, U.S.A. when I met him. It had coursed through the States, Mexico, South America, Asia, Europe and God knows where while he earned income variously as a merchant seaman, pilot, boxer, writer, promoter and marketer for anything and everything. Prior to scampering from the States to Spain, he was remodelling decrepit tenements and brownstone buildings in Manhattan, then renting or selling them. This last scheme is what got him into hot water and required the scampering to Spain, described in Book Four. I am not like Jim, would not care to be, but writing as much of his stories as well as I can is a compulsion I have to abide. Here they are.

DAR
Auckland, New Zealand

CHAPTER ONE

From California to In-the-Drink

He is warm, wet, weightless, rocking back and forth. Whumph, splash! "Cough! Ugh!"

And salty. "What the Hell!?" He notices that he is floating, the brain fog starts lifting, allowing the memory of why. His head is throbbing. Well, at least it's not from a hangover.

He had awakened from a splash in the face, damned near drowned from it. The Mae West is keeping him up pretty well, but no telling how long the life preserver can last. Besides, the collar is chafing his neck and the crotch straps are cramping his balls. But he's floating, enough to get awakened by a splash in the face. Stuff tastes nasty.

If he were just about anywhere else, the stars overhead would be beautiful. "Where's the plane?" Things are beginning to shift into focus.

He had been flying his DC-3, from Yap, Micronesia to Manila. "Damned Yap gas! Never should have put that goddamned crap in the tank!"

Twenty-one years old and floating in the South Pacific. "And I thought it was dangerous getting shot at in China. Huh!"

Now he starts to examine his position. No plane, probably sank with all on board. How the Hell did he get out? Can't see the co-pilot or the three passengers.

"Hey, Mike! You out there?" No reply, but yelling sure aggravates the headache. His slightly gravelly voice does not carry far.

So, what has he got to work with? Is he going to get out of this one? Inventory. Got my senses, pretty good bump on the left side of the forehead, his hat is gone – "I'll miss that hat." Parachute's attached, unopened. It has the emergency kit on the front. Hmm, feel for the flares, Yep. Anything else? More lumps, which could be the compass, combat knife, bit of water and packaged food, and a length of nylon string. That's about all that should be there. Chute is getting heavy, better jettison it and keep the kit.

Detach the kit, carefully, buckle it to his belt, "Crap!" Can't look down to do it, too much chop. Too much salt water to drink. Feeling his way, he takes the kit off the chute harness and fastens it to his web belt in front.

Quick release of the chute harness and it drifts away slowly, then sinks out of sight. Now he floats a little higher in the water, fewer salty drinks. Tequila shots it ain't.

"Better. Now, what are my chances?"

Reviewing the final moments of his flight: Flying from Palau - the last stop between southern Micronesia and the Philippines - to Manila had been the last leg of this circuit. Bouncing as usual at 10,000 feet, fighting a head wind, the starboard engine coughs, coughs again, and sputters. Starboard engine cuts out, then restarts, then cuts out completely. Can't just be water in the fuel, although there is bound to be some. Filter is likely clogged, but can't get to it. So that's it for the starboard engine.

So the fuel in the starboard engine can be shifted to the port engine to add to its flying time, but if dirty fuel shut down the starboard engine, does he want it feeding the port one? It's all the same stuff, put into both tanks, port and starboard. Its rough fighting the yaw from one operational engine, but it's better than walking.

Coughing, sputtering port engine.

"Hell! Mayday, mayday, EZ639 170 miles out, inbound from Palau to Manila. Engine failure." Sputter, silence. "Mayday, mayday!" Cough, cough, engine restart sounds on the port side. "Mike, keep calling it in!"

He starts a more controlled descent to 5,000 feet, 4,000, 2,000, finally down to 500 feet, cough, sputter, 200 feet with lots of noise from the back, people yelling, screaming, Mike repeating position to Manila, making sure handle is down so wheels are up. Complete silence from the port engine at one hundred feet, no readout from the altimeter, but he can see the black, choppy water easily enough as it rises.

"Never did this before, first time for everything. This goddamned thing glides like a rock."

He slides the side window open, keeps pulling back the yoke.

"You Sonofabitch!" he screams.

Whump! Skip. Whump! Maps flying, salt spray spewing into the open window. It hurts everywhere. Hands are aching from gripping the yoke?

"Stay level, you old whore!"

Whump, whump, bump, bump, bump, whish, as the tip of the starboard wing catches a swell. Crack! His head strikes the window frame to his left. Fade to black.

He looks around again. "Mike!" Quiet except for the wind from the northwest. "I must have gone out the window. Manual said to open it if I had to ditch. Couldn't remember why."

"Who's talking? Man, I'm losin' it, that's my voice.

"It's 0430. When did I start calling in the mayday? Must have been 0330 or so. Hmm, interesting, out for an hour. Need some sleep. Head aches like a sonofabitch." Pound, thump, pound, thump. "Maybe if I just lean back here for a minute, relax."

The eastern horizon is pink when he wakes up again. A few stars still in the west. Checking his watch it's 0515 and there is a slight hum from above, toward the northwest, getting louder.

"Can't see a goddamned thing, which means they can't either.

They could fly right over me at 100 feet and miss me."

Flares. Lean back to raise my waist. There the pouch is mostly out of the water.

"I thought the water was warm but I'm shaking like crazy." The shivering makes undoing the pouch's buttons and zipper flap very difficult. The humming is growing louder all the time. Finally the last button is undone but the zipper is stuck. Never been opened before. A mighty, adrenalin-fueled pull and it slides a bit and sticks again. "Goddammit!" Yank! It slides all the way to the left, but the tab breaks off. Feeling for the flares, Jim still can't tell what's what. He can't look down there. Finally he pulls the pack off his belt and lifts it near his face, but with his hands out of the water he starts to submerge. He lowers his hands quickly just as a choppy wave smashes his face. Spurting water, gurgling, coughing, he recovers enough to pull out an oiled canvas bag of tubes wrapped in waxed paper. "Ah!" The sound from above is no longer a hum, it's a definite plane engine at maybe 5,000 feet, and it's approaching fast. Opening the bag just enough to remove one flare, he is rocked by another wave, instinctively raising his hands to keep the flare dry. He sinks a bit. Down come the hands, the wave is gone and he has the flare out, semi-dry. Rewrap the flares and close the bag tightly, stowing it with the pouch on his chest. The engine sound is now just to the northwest and loud. He pulls the tab and the flare explodes into a blue-white magnesium light, which he raises above his head, waving frantically. He hardly hears the hissing and crackling of the flare due to the engine's roar. He is fixed on looking up, but glances to his left just before a two-meter swell engulfs him and the flare. It's out. It's dark. It's getting quiet, the plane is passing on. It's all shit.

Jim Tuck doesn't do the crying thing: he shouts and rails against malicious gods. He doesn't believe in insanity. It's interesting but he rarely uses the F-word, even in extreme situations. And this certainly is one.

"Bet the idiotic sonofabitch didn't even look out the window. He's still heading toward Palau. I told them I was only 170 miles out. Probably wants to import some of the Palau palm wine while making his cursory search. Well, he's gotta get back to Manila, so he'll be back this way. Damn, it's cold! It's the tropics for chrissake!"

The next several minutes are taken up in trying to close the pouch better to keep the remaining flares inside as dry as possible. It's not easy with shivering hands and no tab on the zipper. Once it's three-fourths closed he takes a break and leans back again, this time to rest. The pouch is up under his chin, about as safe as it's going to get. It's as quiet as it gets on the ocean. Dozing, he wanders back to California and flight school two years ago.

———◆———

The land of fruits and nuts is also the land of opportunity for writers. After Mexico, it's also the most promising for making a buck without having to get bashed for it. Boxing got him enough food and travel money for day to day, but this is the chance to make it big. Screenwriting, in southern California, that's the thing.

At 19 years old and shaving every other day, he lacks the hard-bit-ten look of a veteran of the movie mayhem, but at 5 feet 8 inches and dark wavy hair, a well-sculpted body, and eyes showing experience beyond his years, he turns a few heads. The heads he turns listen to his tales, over a glass of red wine with ice, and begin spreading the word about the new talent in town. Usually it's after getting to know him better, but that's another story.

He writes a freelance newspaper piece about traveling in Mexico that gets him enough money for a new shirt, tie and a creased pair of pants. Food he is able to bum. Even though he now looks respectable, transportation around town is on foot, most of the time, or hitchhiking. He'll pay the rent when he has the next commission in hand.

Finally, he catches a ride with the very attractive Chayo Gonzales, just as he is heading from the Spanish speaking side of town to downtown Hollywood. Nice Packard convertible, powder blue with a white top that's down at the moment. Chayo met him a week ago at a party where there were not that many Spanish speakers and he was not bad to look at, so they hit if off that afternoon. It was a bit of a mystery where he came from, what he's doing and where he was staying, but it was no mystery what he was interested in.

"Jim, how did you get invited to this party?"

"I didn't."

"What do you mean, you didn't?"

"I saw the party tent from the road and it looked like a good time, so I came in. The fellow at the gate thought

I was some of the Latino help and sent me to the back of the house. Here I am."

"Outrageous!"

"Not too, but fun anyway."

She felt a bit sad when she had to leave to head back to the Hills. Dinner was waiting, as was her husband Oscar, but it had been fun, and the conversation had covered more than the usual local and New York gossip. Funny how he seemed to know more New York gossip than California. But his Spanish was good, if Mexican tinged. "Maybe later?" he asked.

"Sure, we'll get together again, soon."

It didn't take long for Chayo to spot Tuck hitchhiking again. The wind is messing with his hair; she is wearing a peach-colored scarf over most of her long black hair. It went with the low-cut blouse and shorts of the same color. The car top's down, like the last time.

"Where you headed?"

"Hollywood, to see if I can get to Zanuck."

"Zanuck?! You must be nuts, nobody gets directly to Daryl F. Zanuck."

"Why not?"

"It's not done. If you get a call, you go. If not, you wait."

"Not the way I do things."

"Look, you want to be a screenwriter, I can get you with some of the folks doing documentaries, short subjects, that sort of thing. No hay problema. But Zanuck! You're nuts!"

"Yeah, maybe. You're not the first to mention it. If I need the small time stuff, I'll get back with you. But first, I have to see Zanuck."

"What do you know about flying?"

"Nothing, why?"

"Se quiere?"

"Sure. As I said, why?"

"I'm scheduled for my regular lesson this afternoon. Why don't you come along, then we can have an early supper. Oscar is in Guadalajara this week and I could use the company this afternoon. Besides, we could have some fun."

"Flying?"

"Que se quiere."

"Why not? Zanuck will still be there tomorrow, I suspect."

The airfield was small, over the hills from downtown. It was home to half a dozen one- and two-engine planes, and a flight instructor named Sam, who wore a white silk scarf no less. He did not look too pleased with the extra company. But since Chayo seemed to want Jim there, what the heck.

She was going up in a single engine four-seater Cessna. "Come on along."

"Sure, sounds good."

"Maria Rosaria (that was her given name, but everyone she knew her called her Chayo), you know my insurance does not allow passengers."

"Bullshit, Sam. (It was cute when she said it. It came out "boolsheet".) I'm paying, you're teaching, he's coming along. Or, do I get another instructor?"

Jim to himself, "Now that's the way it's done."

"OK, OK. Don't get it in a twist."

Flying was the greatest thing since the heights of the mountains in Mexico. Noisy, but way too much fun!

Once on the ground, he was still buzzing, not wanting to leave. This may be way better than screenwriting. How to make a living at it is the question.

"I got another lesson Saturday. Wanna come?"

"Definitely."

"OK, let's get some supper, and we can talk about it. See ya Saturday, Sam. Oh, do you think we can have a longer lesson and you can teach Jim at the same time? I'll pay. Two lessons at each visit."

"I don't know about that one. I'll have to ask the boss."

"I thought you were the boss."

"Well, I am, mostly, but some decisions I have to kick upstairs."

"Kick away, mister. See ya Saturday, two lessons. If you have trouble getting your boss to agree, just let me know ahead of time so I have enough time to change flying schools by Saturday. I don't want to mess up my schedule."

"Yeah, right. It'll be OK, I'm sure."

"Good."

It turned into a routine: flying, a good meal, sex and a cigarette, or three. Bottle of red wine in the room, wherever. She was the most lively, entertaining, energetic woman he had ever enjoyed. Making love in Spanish was always more romantic, somehow. There were just enough close calls with Oscar to liven up the illicit nature of the romance.

And the flying was getting interesting. He now had his private pilot's license, after only three months, and was working on his multi-engine rating. That's where the money is. Sam didn't like him at all, and Jim could see why. He just didn't give a shit.

Multi-engine flying was significantly more complicated than single engines; Jim wasn't having quite as much fun at it but he was persistent. He could do the navigation and the bookwork easily enough, but some of the manual skills were coming slowly. Landing was often an adventure and flying with one engine in a two-engine plane was a bitch. Why he kept creeping toward a stall on takeoff was a mystery, but he enjoyed the abject terror in Sam's eyes every time it happened. So, although repeating the mistake was off-putting to a degree, it had its rewards.

It's Saturday night after a strenuous flight training class for both of them. They are enjoying the merlot with great steaks in the town Santa Clarita, where they stopped on their way back from the aerodrome.

The talk is casual . . . what's the plan for Wednesday, and what to expect in the next lesson. Suddenly who should walk into the restaurant but Oscar with three other men. He is talking animatedly to one of the other fellows walking away toward the bar. One of the them, Alex, glances toward the table and his eyes meet Chayo's, with recognition on both parts. Jim is eating with his mouth full and attending to the steak when he gets a kick under the table and just about chokes. Looking up, he sees the terror in Chayo's eyes, follows her gaze and excuses himself to the bathroom, all in one flowing motion. By the time Oscar's attention is brought toward Chayo's table, Jim is gone, but not his meal.

Oscar stops, turns fully toward the table, and slowly walks. A quizzical look flows up his face, along with the color, and he is about to ask what the fuck is going on when the guy who spotted Chayo in the first place says "Where did she go?" Chayo just looks at Oscar, then tunes in to the other fellow and it clicks, "She got sick and had to go to the restroom. I hope she is OK. Hi, Oscar. Good to see all you fellas. What a surprise! Is this where you were having your meeting tonight?"

"Of course. Aren't you a bit late finishing flying?"

"Not too late and I arranged for Isabella to meet me here afterwards, like she does sometimes. Since you were going to be away we planned to have dinner together."

Oscar says, "She's not back yet. Think you should check on her?" Chayo is examining Alex's face as Oscar is talking, and he has the queerest expression, sort of triumph and disgust all at the same time.

Finally she comes back to the conversation and says, "You're right, I better check on her. I was so surprised to see you that I almost forgot. Be back in a minute." She is up and on her way to the bathroom area in a split second giving Alex a last supplicant's glance on her way out.

Inside the swinging door there are two doors, Mens', Womens' and an exterior door cracked open. She pushes it further and hears "I'm outta here. See you Wednesday. Pick me up at the train station." Hasty footsteps fade, then nothing.

So, now what? Back at the table she explains that Isabella had just left in her car. She had called her doctor to see her urgently since she was worried about the baby, being four months pregnant with her first. "Since my dinner partner is gone, how about if I join you men?"

"Not tonight, dear. This is a highly confidential business meeting. I have a private dining room reserved and we will be late, I'm sure. The information we are sharing is extremely sensitive and must be kept to the four of us. I am very sorry because you look so fetching tonight, with all that extra color in your cheeks. You would be a fine addition, but I am afraid also a distraction and you know how it is with women and sensitive information. They can never keep a secret. So, I'll see you at home. Very sorry, babe." With that, and a buss on the cheek the gentlemen move on; she is sweating impossibly, her heart still thumping, and she is horny as hell.

"Shit!" She can't eat, so she pays the bill and leaves.

Wednesday dawns bright and clear, like nearly every day. And she is off to the train station. Jim spots the Packard as it turns the corner into the drop-off area, top is up.

As he opens his door he says, "Being a bit careful are we? Too nice a day for having the top up, I'd say."

"Shut up and get in."

"Testy. How's Oscar?"

"Oh, shut up. He's muy feo."

"So you think he suspects something?"

"Of course he does. He gets suspicious when there is something happening that he doesn't know about. It makes him muy feo. He won't stop until he knows everything about it, and then he decides how he wants to handle it. As soon as he finds out about you, it won't be a pretty day."

"So his buddies in Mexico might be up here soon to help take care of the situation?"

"If they are, you will not be happy."

"Thought so."

"So, what you gonna do?"

"Today's my last lesson for awhile. I'll probably go back to New York, where I have some of my own buddies who are every bit as nasty and efficient as Oscar's Mexicano ones."

"Well, if you are going, when will you leave?"

"Soon. Gotta have my last lesson, first. I'm about to graduate in multi-engines. I need that ticket."

"I think you should think about going VERY soon."

"Thanks, I'll consider it."

The airfield is bustling when they arrive, planes doing touch and goes, three others doing aerobatics in the immediate vicinity, the twin-engine DC-3 warming up on the ramp, and Chayo's racer being pushed out from the hangar when they drive up. Sam spots them and walks from the hangar over to the car.

"Sam, why don't you take Maria Rosaria up on her own today, while I do a little studying for my written test in your office?"

"I don't like people in my office, but I'll be happy to take her up by herself. It's been awhile, eh?"

"I need the charts on your wall to study from, for the navigation section of the exam. No problem, right?"

"I don't like it…" A pause as Chayo gives him a withering look. "Oh, I guess so. Just stay out of the filing cabinet. We'll be back in 45 minutes."

"Thanks"

Chayo and Sam leave for the plane. It's racing technique today, and the plane won't be very fuel efficient, so time in the air will be limited.

Jim walks slowly and purposefully toward the tower where Sam's office is on the second floor. Looking back, he sees them climb into the cockpit, Chayo in front, Sam in the rear seat, then he is in the building, already a bit nostalgic. Two stairs at a time, he hustles to Sam's office where the filing cabinet is the first place he goes. The lock is a simple one presenting no trouble. Shifting through the files he finds "Kunming flight school" and removes it. It takes about five minutes to copy the essentials and return it to the file. Next, it's the desk drawers and the third one has the stationery he needs. The typewriter is a good one, so he uses it to type the letter of introduction.

A sample of the graduation certificate for multi-engine pilots is on the wall, and he finds blank certificates in the drawer below. With the blank certificate and letter of introduction, and with an example of Sam's signature stowed in a file folder for safe keeping, he is out the door in a total of 15 minutes.

Outside, he hears the buzz of Chayo's plane off to the East, but it's too far away to see it. Outside the gate the shuttle bus to town is just arriving, so he boards and in five minutes is on his way to town. An hour and a half later, he is packed and off to the port where a freighter to Hawaii is completing loading of automobiles for the islands. Passage in exchange for work is arranged easily with his seaman's log book in hand, and he locates the forward compartment to stow his gear before returning to the deck for work.

The week at sea allows him plenty of time to get the certificate looking authentic and even adds a bit of wear and tear to the appearance, just for additional authenticity. The Hawaii stopover is pleasingly short. He has always enjoyed island women, and the captain was able to introduce him to the captain of a ship bound for Hong Kong.

Passage assured, he had three days to work. He helped prepare cargo for the Portuguese freighter, applying as much Spanish as he could to the communication, until he picked up a bit of Portuguese.

———— ◆ ————

Whump! What a wave that was! Choke, cough, retch, "Holy mother!" He looks at his watch, "Out for 35 minutes. Seems like hours. If the plane is going all the way to Palau before returning, then it'll be at least another three hours. It's getting cold, errr!" Inventory check. Pouch still near his face, shift the crotch straps again, neck is beginning to be a problem, especially if it starts to bleed. Sharks will get the scent miles away. Shifting and loosening the life preserver straps a bit, he is able to get the collar of his jacket under the ring of the preserver to protect his neck a bit. "Still hurts like it's been sanded. But maybe the damage will stop here." He moves his legs to keep the circulation going, takes his wrinkled hands out of the water for awhile, just not too high, sings a Mexican lullaby, thinks about Woodstock, NY five years ago when he realized it was time to leave home. Woodstock in 1931, not long after WWI finished. Things were a bit tight financially, but fun was to be had anyway. Shipping companies were ramping up due to the strong orders from Europe, and ships' captains were not too picky about a seamen's qualifications since they were all shorthanded. Jim had finished growing the year before, so he was tall for his age. He easily convinced the recruiter he was 18, instead of 15, not that the recruiter probably cared all that much. Apprentice seaman's book in hand, he was off to see the world. Woodstock was fun, and home, but its consequences could wait.

Now that the pain was receding from his neck and groin, he could rock with the waves. Headache's still there, but now it's about the only thing keeping him from dozing again, except for the cold. The rocking of the waves allows his meditative sense to return and his journey unfolds to the next layer, mercenary in the Chinese Republican air wing, better known as the Flying Tigers. That multi-engine ticket came in handy, for sure. Rocking, drifting, dozing.

———— ✦ ————

Hong Kong to Kunming, western China, home to the Flying Tigers, is 800 miles one way, and the trains are slow as molasses. A bit of gambling and a few clever trades got Jim enough cash to cover the cost of the trip, including ticket and food. The food mostly was good, some of it revolting, but the tastes were all interesting. The wooden slatted bench seat required as much standing as sitting. No room for reclining with the third class car full of people and animals. Chickens in bamboo cages bumped against pigs trussed and lying on their sides in the aisle; goats were tied to the overhead rails. Every couple of hours a few passengers and their cargo were replaced with counterparts from neighboring provinces, but the car stayed full. Since it was October, the temperature was reasonable outside but stifling inside. Lots of body heat to make sure no one was chilly. No personal space either. Your neighbor on the seat needs rest, so your shoulder becomes a ready-made pillow. Every time you get up to relieve your butt, the seat becomes fair game. Thank God you're the biggest one in the car. Facial expressions require no translation.

After two days traveling, Jim had gone through many travel companions and was out of edible food. The chickens in cages were beginning to look good. The rocking, roofed box that doubled as a passenger car passed through an ancient brick and stone wall and after another half hour slowed its rocking as it came into a siding in a substantial city. In his best Mandarin, Jim asked "Kunming?" to affirmative nods. That brought a long sigh of relief and more intense study of the scene outside the window. Chaos never looked so good.

Every conveyance known to God or man was in motion beside the tracks. Human beasts carried most of the loads. Next came loads on bicycles, donkeys or ponies. Last came the two-wheeled carts pulled by people, or if they were lucky, any sort of domesticated animal from bullocks to dogs. They were moving all at the same time in all directions. The noise was amazing, the smells of the dung of animals and people hung in the slightly blue air just waiting to stick to something or someone. Uniformed men of some rank and official station blew whistles, probably to compete with the rest of the shouts and bedlam. The whistleblowing did not seem to have any real effect on the crowd's motion.

Just before the train came to a stop, the first passengers - the ones without cattle - leaped to the station platform and were off. The rest were not far behind, and Jim was suddenly alone in the car that seconds before had been packed. He almost felt lonely or anxious at the new situation, until he realized that the train was starting to move. Suddenly he was in motion and leaping onto the platform with his pack flapping behind. He stopped and checked inside his shirt where the envelope was supposed to be. There were the pointy paper corners wrapped in waxed paper. Relieved, he started the process of finding a way to Wujiaba airfield and Captain Claire Chennault. His envelope was his ticket, and Captain Chennault, head of the flying squadron, would be its recipient.

The only two good things Sam, his reluctant flying instructor, had done for Jim were to try to teach him to fly, with mixed results, and let slip that this wild-man

American was in China as a volunteer, read mercenary, to rebuild the air arm of the Chinese military. In response to the Japanese invasion, Chennault was seeking pilots, flying instructors, and mechanics. If Jim's information was correct, since this air service was to be in the hands of the Chinese Republicans and not the communists, then the U.S. was probably going to subsidize it. Since all the positions were to be voluntarily taken by whomever was qualified, the pay would not be restricted to usual military standards. The sky was the limit, in other words. Those had always been the sweetest words to Jim Tuck's ears, and the fact that it was in China put syncopation in the song.

He had sent a letter to Captain Chennault letting him know that he was on his way as soon as he had discovered the location of the nascent flying school in China. He was arriving a bit ahead of the schedule outlined in the letter since he hadn't anticipated leaving quite so soon. But it is what it is, and he had done quite an acceptable job on the certificate verifying his completion of the multi-engine program, so no need to stay to the bitter end. In this case, leaving early prevented a bitter end, actually.

Using his hands and mouth to imitate flying planes with their noises, planes landing and flying, to at least a dozen different members of Life's audience resulted in sufficient information to set him on his way. It seemed that most considered the distance to the field to be too far to walk, but he had enough cash for a little food, and coffee or tea, for two days. Coffee and tea came with boiled water, the only kind of water he should be drinking for awhile. If he used his cash for transportation, he would end up hungrier than he was right now.

Outside the station were hundreds of carts with every sort of food you could imagine, much of it heated. He bought half a dozen bananas, the perfect fruit, and some mystery meat with rice. He had to drink the tea there since it was from a communal cup. He took his bearings and was on his way.

Away from the station, the view opened up so he could appreciate the mountains to the west. They helped with his bearings since the people he had asked had mostly agreed that the airfield was to the northwest. The temperature was mild now that he was away from the crush of people. It was early fall but the elevation was over 3,000 feet, just north of the Tropic of Cancer, which cooled the air. The city was obviously large, and it took quite awhile to emerge from the congestion of the center. The more residential areas were still packed with people.

By late afternoon, and the 37th individual he had asked for clarification, he topped a rise and noticed an open expanse in the distance. He had not seen any open areas until now. Everything had been covered by people or buildings. As he watched, he noticed a single engine plane come in on approach and, just after it disappeared from view, it appeared again rising rapidly. It was too far to hear an engine and he did not recognize the profile of the plane, but he did recognize a touch-and-go training procedure. It lifted his spirits at just the right time. He was exhausted after two days of little sleep and considerable hunger combined with constant motion.

Off he went, his pace was at least twice what it had been. After an hour he realized that the air at this altitude does interesting things to estimates of distance, and he was not sure at all how far he had to go. Glad that there was no rain on the dusty roads, he turned the corner, and there was a high chain- linked fence enclosure, airfield type support buildings, and the obvious end of a tarmac runway. Hallelujah! Not being a praying man, he naturally thanked any gods for their assistance.

Cough! Ugh! Sneeze, to get the water out of his nose. What had awakened him? He looked around, shivering uncontrollably, hands over his bundle on his chest being occasionally splashed. Tired, tired, tired. That's what he remembered about arriving in Kunming, besides finding his destination. Here he is again, and cold as well, even though each splash is slightly warm on his face. The breeze cools it off, sucks the warmth from his face and hands.

Buzzing is coming from the fully-lit southeast, coming fast, louder by the second. A plane is coming in low and fast. Roused, he tries to open the packet for the flares, but nothing works right. His fingers will barely move, his arms are like lead. He lets out an enormous growl and shouts to all those facilitating gods to get the hell out of the way, and yanks the packet open, getting hold of the bag of flares. "Careful, now. No need to get this close and screw it up." Carefully unrolling the waxed paper wrap, as far out of the water as he can without sinking, he firmly pulls out a flare, stowing the last two back in the pouch. Can't zip it with the broken tab and one hand holding the flare. Just has to be as careful about his body movements and not dunk the pouch while it is still open. Twisting around, he strains to see where the sound is coming from. It is getting significantly louder and suddenly he sees the body of the plane, at no more than 500 feet, coming fast. One pull on the igniter and it slips out of his fingers. They are not working. "DAMN YOUR FILTHY HIDE!" Wrapping the string of the igniter around his finger he gives another mighty pull as he can nearly see into the cockpit of the plane and the flare bursts bright blue, with just enough smoke to add to the effect. He can see the face of the pilot, but with the rubber mask he can't tell if he knows him. The plane flashes overhead and is racing away, with Jim's heart sinking until it climbs and rolls out to reverse direction and flies directly over his frantically waving arm. The wings of the plane rock side to side in affirmation, and Jim's heart soars in gratitude. The plane rises again and rolls to return to the northwest and Manila, waggling again just to be sure he has seen it.

The rest is mostly a blur with the fishing boat coming alongside, the rescue ring just missing his head as it is thrown, the half day on the fishing grounds waiting for the Coast Guard boat while the fishermen fished. He looked interesting, at least, in cut off shorts, ragged T shirt and sandals, all borrowed so he could get out of his soggy flight clothes and rotten boots. He did remember that the boat was manned not by Filipinos, but by Portuguese. From his trip to Hong Kong, he was on the ragged edge of understanding the conversations, but just missed it, even though his Spanish was pretty good. "Obrigado" seemed to work pretty well, but it was limited for much more conversation.

The 17-hour ride to Manila in the Coast Guard boat is nonexistent. He missed the ride, or at least most of it, just sleeping on the stack of sacks below decks.

CHAPTER 2

Out of the Drink and Into the Clink

B ack at Manila is a little different. He is met at the dock by an ambulance, an immigration official, and an aviation official with his policeman sidekick. A few quick questions establish the facts that he doesn't need the ambulance or have his passport with him because it is at the bottom of the ocean. His Pacifica Airlines is not quite registered with the Philippine protectorate authority, and his airline is also at the bottom of the ocean with its passengers and crew, minus one. The aviation official, a fairly short, emaciated fellow with a pencil-thin mustache from Buffalo, New York, out here and not loving any minute of it, is not smiling. When it is time to leave, the Filipino policeman makes sure Jim is firmly and securely in the aviation authority car as it departs for the provincial court.

At the court Jim is booked for manslaughter and for operating an illegal airline. He is taken to one of the least inviting accommodations he has ever used - and he has used quite a variety. In some ways he is nostalgically reminiscing about the pleasant ride from Hong Kong to Kunming and the comfort afforded by the cattle car accommodation during the ride. There are 14 other felons in the cell, below street level, with one rat per resident. It's a wonder the rats have not died from heat exhaustion. The water spigot does not work, thank God, the ragged T shirt fits right in, and all the salt water he soaked up is now flowing out. He can hardly breathe, but the locals who are his cell mates don't seem too concerned by the environment. The stone floor is as warm as the air, so no relief except for his fatigue. "Can't go to sleep in here. Won't wake up intact."

So he sits, stands, bumps along the wall, leans against the bars of the door, sits again. You get the picture. And sweats, and sweats, and tries to force down the panic of not being able to breathe. "Sure could use a cigarette, or nine." Everyone in Manila smokes, except prisoners.

Darkness settles in, like a shade pulled down over a lamp, so very slowly, but without hesitation. Down, down, down it comes and the other faces are harder and harder to see, until a bare ceiling bulb lights in the hall, casting shadows on everyone. The only ones with full faces are facing the barred door. Everyone else has only half a face, which is plenty. Conversation is minimal, and what there is is mostly in Tagalog, which Jim has not acquired at all. One thing for sure, no one is happy and the distaste for the situation is on everyone's faces.

One very large, as in tall and fat, fellow purposely places himself at Jim's side. The heat of the room goes up with the additional body heat, and Jim tries to slip away unsuccessfully. A hand like a meaty claw on his shoulder keeps him firmly in place, sitting on the floor. "You American? You fly plane into the ocean?"

After nearly 12 hours in the cell, this is the first conversation directed at Jim, and the fellow seems to know what's going on somehow. Jim wonders, "How did that information get in here, and how did he get it?" Mysteries of the world abound.

"Why?" asked Jim.

"I know this thing. I just make sure. What plane is it?"

"I don't think I understand."

A firm, not so gentle squeeze on his shoulder produces serious pain in the front, just below the point of the shoulder, causing Jim to wince and King Kong to smile. His large mouth does not indicate humor.

Through gritted teeth, Jim says, "It was a DC-3. I was flying from Palau to Manila and the fuel line clogged in both engines and we crashed." The squeeze lets up slightly.

"Ah. So, who is driving this plane?"

"I was, why?" The grip comes back on, a bit more forcefully, repeating the wince and the grin.

"What the hell do you want?"

"I want go Sarawak, see my dear mother. I have no transport. You take me."

"Sure, sure." The grip slackens. "How?"

The grip returns. "You drive me on a plane."

"My plane is on the bottom of the ocean!" Now the grip is getting serious, and Jim wriggles to get away, which creates a pain he has never had before. "Unh!"

"You like this, eh? You say stupid things so you make me do this more. I want go Sarawak, you take me in plane. You will get the plane and take me. Yes?"

"Unh!" Panting, and squirming, Jim says, "Sure! Unh!"

The grip comes off and a tingle starts in Jim's fingers as the feeling comes back in his arm. This hurts almost as much as the grip, but seems to be slacking off as he can feel his fingers again.

"So, how do we get a plane?" The hand heads for his shoulder, and he says, "OK, OK, I'll find one."

"Good. We free tomorrow, and you will get plane." A few curious sets of eyes follow the conversation with interest. Most are still dull and uncomprehending, but some start sliding across the floor, closer to the two who are talking. One is squirming. One speaks to King Kong in Tagalog and he gets a swift backhand across the side of his head, sending him rolling backward into the corner. A mass reverse migration, like a waning tide occurs with all backs again against the wall. A mighty paw pats Jim on the head, and he suddenly realizes that being King Kong's ride home makes him a valuable commodity. He falls immediately to sleep.

It's light, motes floating in the air are nearly beautiful in their various colors, drifting down from the street above. Street noises are loud, helping rouse him from a very deep sleep. King Kong is awake, staring at his face, as if willing him awake. The cell stinks worse than yesterday. Jim is not getting used to it.

Suddenly there is a clanging of metal latches. The lights flare on and the cell door swings open. In walks the largest person Jim has ever seen, swinging a truncheon and gazing around the room, obviously looking for someone or something.

"You! Stand up!"

He is staring straight at Jim, flicking the truncheon up and down. Jim stands up.

"Come here." As Jim stands and starts toward the jailer, King Kong stands up looking more than a little unfriendly. "Sit down, kaka!" Jim recognizes the Spanish colloquial for shit.

Jim is decidedly indecisive, remains standing but slouching as if to sit. "He stays with me," snarls King Kong. Whack! The truncheon motion was way quicker than the eye and King Kong is on his knees. Whack! Now he is on his face and not moving.

The jailer delivers the invitation, "Anyone else?"

The cell is the quietest it has been since Jim moved in. "Come!" Jim straightens and goes, wondering if he should ask the obvious. He doesn't.

The cell door clangs closed and Jim is motioned to move forward toward the exit door. As soon as the door opens, the cell bursts into cacophony behind him and the bedlam is deafening until the door crunches shut behind him. The half flight of stairs leads to the rear of the entrance hall of the police station/courthouse. Jim follows to the right and down a long hall with multiple wooden doors on the right, none on the left. The air is slightly less dense up here but still hot and humid, and the décor is early neglect. If flaking paint were worth anything, the courthouse would rival the Taj Mahal.

At the third door Jim gets a tap on the shoulder indicating stop. The door is opened by the jailer and Jim feels the point of the truncheon in the small of his back. As he walks in, the door closes firmly and there is the sound of a key turning in a lock. Straight ahead, nine feet max, is a barred window looking down on an alleyway filled with trash. There is glass in the top half of the window, but none below at face level. The glass above only serves to obscure the sky since it is as grimy as a mechanic's grease pit. A pallet is on the floor along the right wall, and a maximum of four feet away is a sink on the left wall. He tries the tap and nothing comes out except a roach. Probably just as well; as thirsty as he is, he probably would have drunk whatever liquid might have come out.

Since all his possessions have been confiscated, he has no idea what time it is. There is moderate traffic noise in the street beyond the alley, and, since there is little sun, he is guessing it is before morning rush hour, maybe six a.m. How long since he arrived back in Manila? Time is becoming a problem to reckon. Not been long though, since he realizes that he only spent one night in the pit downstairs. Hmm, wonder if King Kong made it OK. He did get me a couple hours unmolested sleep. Sleep, what a good idea. The pallet looks pretty good, and as he lies down, a key is inserted into the door lock and turned. The door opens and a tray slides into the room with a thick slice of buttered bread, mug of coffee, and a jug of water on it, and closes again. He doesn't have to be asked twice and drinks the jug empty, leaves the coffee, eats the bread and lies back down. That's the last he remembers until there is a loud banging on the door and the metal peephole slides open.

The door swings open to reveal a man in a khaki uniform, peaked hat and captain's bars on the shoulders of the jacket, carrying a chair into the room. He's wearing the first smile Jim has seen in awhile. As he sets the chair down, he says, "You Jim Tuck?" His hat comes off and hooks over the upright on the back of the chair releasing the tight black curly hair. His high cheekbones and slightly hooked nose make Jim think of the Indians in the mountains of Mexico. About Jim's height, he has an illegible brass name tag on his left breast, just above his battle ribbons. Jim notices there is not a good conduct medal among them.

As he sits up on the pallet, he nods his head. He realizes he doesn't smell too good, and here he is receiving guests. Oh, well. "Who the hell are you and what are you doing here at this hour of the morning? What hour is it anyway?"

"My name is Antonio Arizza, Tony, U.S. Army Air Corps, attaché at the embassy here in Manila, and recently returned from working with Claire Chennault in Kunming." Now Jim notices the wings on the collar of his shirt.

"Well, I'll be goddamned. How'd you find me here?"

"The consul got a call that an American was plucked out of the drink and brought to Manila yesterday. I asked around at the port and found out who met you, and figured there must be a pretty good story in there somewhere. Butterman makes quite a welcoming committee, doesn't he?"

"Who the hell is Butterman?"

"The cute little skinny guy, pencil-thin mustache. He's the one stuck you in here, downstairs, I believe."

"Yeah. Said he was with CAA and had investigative and arrest authority. Seems he was right, doesn't it?"

"Yeah, he has the authority." Tony is sweating now, since there is no moving air in the room, and he has more clothes on than makes good sense in the tropics. Beads have formed on his forehead and are running down his cheeks, but he makes no attempt to wipe them off.

"Why don't you take that jacket off? It's hotter than a whorehouse dance hall in here."

"Won't be doin' that. Gives the gooks pleasure to see us uncomfortable in their environment and can't afford to allow any signs of weakness."

"Suit yourself. So, back to the question, what the hell you doing in here, and at this hour of the day?"

"Just came to ascertain a few facts, if possible, assuming you're willing to give them to me. Gotta know what I'm up against if I'm going to spring you out of here."

"Why would you want to spring me out of here in the first place? I don't know you."

"True, but Chennault does. Once we asked where that DC-3 might have come from, his name came up, and he told us if it was Jim Tuck, to get him outta there. And, if it was Jim Tuck, tell him to keep his goddamn mouth shut."

"Yeah, that sounds like Chennault. So, how did you know it was a DC-3 that went into the drink?"

"Only three planes are scheduled to land at between two and four in the morning. Not a busy time and, I guess, with your airline's status, it's the best time for you. That's the time of day with the least scrutiny of the finer points of aviation protocol - not that those finer points are ever very strictly observed in Manila, especially if there is cash around to obscure the facts," Arizza says."Drives poor old Butterman to drink. Funny, actually, watching him run here and there trying to put order into this chaos they call an airfield.

"Hell, Wujiaba was a model of efficiency and order compared to this place. Hard to imagine Americans are responsible for its operation. Actually, they're not," Arizza continues. "They are responsible for keeping the bars, brothels, and fan salesmen busy. The airfield is entirely run by locals."

Jim responds, "Why do you think I came here in the first place? All I had to do was contact the proper white-faced superior, who everyone knows is on the take to support his expensive habits. I get him paid regularly and he lets the folks down the line know that there is no trouble with Pacifica Airlines. Which he did, and which got me 11 good months of operation."

"So what happened? Two nights ago, I mean?"

"Goddamn Yap gas, that's what happened."

"Fuel line?"

"Right. Both filters clogged completely. Those things fly like a sinker on a fishing line once the engines stop. Got close enough to the water I could belly flop in, but the starboard wing caught a chop and over she went. Don't remember anything else until a wave woke me up. Got any aspirin? I still have quite a headache. Lump is down a bit, but the throbbing is hell."

"None on me. I'll arrange to get some in here with a bottle of water. How was your welcoming committee downstairs?"

"Not bad. They mostly left me alone, until King Kong decided he needed a ride to Sarawak and he started pestering me. Guess he is out of the pestering business for awhile. Couldn't understand most of the others anyway, although a lot of the language has some Spanish in it."

"You do speak Spanish?"

"Course."

"Bueno. That may be very handy later. Can I get you anything else while I'm out?"

"Maybe some clothes. These came from the fishermen who pulled me out of the water. My other clothes have disappeared."

"I'll see what I can do. You look about my size. Thought you'd be bigger. Hmm. Anyone else in the plane when you went down?"

"Co-pilot Michael O'Reilly and three passengers, and about a ton of guano in bags."

"Too bad. You know O'Reilly well?"

"Well enough. Met him in Alma Alta when we were getting ready to ferry DC-3's to Kunming."

"Uh, I suspect that may be what Chennault meant when he told me to make sure you kept your mouth shut."

"Hell, that son of a bitch knows that information is common knowledge. What the hell is he talking about?"

"Common knowledge and acknowledged common knowledge are two very different things, my friend. Our Russian buddies are masters at the subtle use of lying out loud. Where do you think those DC-3's came from? Surely not made in Russia. But the U.S. wants them in China, and through Russia is one of the fastest routes there. Don't fuck it up, buddy. The Russians got themselves a new non-aggression pact with Japan, so they can concentrate on Germany. If they're caught supplying materiel to China, all hell breaks loose"

"Gotcha."

"Clothes and aspirin. Be back this afternoon. Gotta try to get this ball rolling to get you outta here. Hasta la vista." And he was gone, chair and all.

———————◆———————

The pallet still looks pretty good, and since he was awakened early he decides on a nap. No pillow but no worries. He's out like a light. Soon he's floating in the ocean, but then climbing into a cockpit. The ocean disappears and he's flying, oxygen mask in place, at 25,000 feet, the noise of the twin engines drowning out any possibility for conversation except on the radio, which is silent anyway. Chennault's voice is in his ear instead of the radio's static, reminding him over and over that he came from India, not Russia. How that happened given his location and direction was another mystery, but it was to be repeated endlessly while he was preparing for the trip to Alma Ata.

"Remember if this thing works, it'll prove invaluable in a year's time. Invaluable." The word keeps repeating to the beat of the engines.

He's landing at Wujiaba in China. He can see Chennault at the flight buildings, hat on, ascot at the neck, smiling ear to ear. Even before his feet hit the ground, he hears, "Any trouble?"

"Not if you don't include endless arguments among Russians, delays fueling the plane because of electricity, pump failures, no one in the tower speaking English, ground crew needing cash before they remove the chocks, and a few other incidentals. Came off like a dream."

Pointing to the DC-3, Chennault says, "There will be plenty more of these coming through shortly. Let's get some details of the experience on paper including any recommendations you might have. Before that, we'll go over the basics of another slightly unorthodox flight. Been to India?"

"No, and never had an idea that I wanted to. Why?"

"That's the next flight, Assam, India. Heard of it?"

"No, but I'll find it."

"You know, as lousy an instructor as you were, you are that good at improvising. We're lucky we still have enough of your class of Chinese pilots to use the planes we have. Never seen anything like it. You had a higher attrition rate than anyone in the history of aviation training, and, unfortunately, many of those we lost took their planes with them. Guess we have enough things needing done that there are more jobs than pilots, or you'd have been long gone, volunteer or no volunteer. Well paid at that. OK, here's the chart room. Let's look at the possible routes to Chabua airfield."

The walk was not far, but after that many hours in the cramped cockpit space of the DC-3, his legs still felt tired and he desperately wanted to sit down. No one sits if Chennault is not sitting. So, he and Chennault are standing over the chart table, Jim gritting his teeth a bit, not complaining. He knows Chennault does not abide wimps, and actually neither does Jim. But...

"OK, here we are and over here, see on this next sheet across the connector, over the southern Himalayas is Assam, and here is Chabua. We don't have good data on the elevations of these mountains, but they are the Himalayas. We expect that one of your first chores will be to get some data on elevations, as well as the shortest route between Wujiaba and Chabua. This is going to be very important, maybe more than you realize now. The Japs in Burma are heading toward the Burma–China highway and, if I'm right, will interdict it in the next year. Right now, all the supplies we get to Chiang Kai-Shek are coming in through that highway. Once it's gone as a supply route, Japan will have a much easier time with the Chinese army. At some point, we are going to have to fly in more cargo than comes over the road now and we'll need a secure route. Find it, map it, and develop a protocol for its use."

"Glad to be of service. When do I leave?"

"Tomorrow, first light. Use the plane you just came in on. Take Harry as your right seat, and enough ballast to make it a realistic test. Assuming you make it back with the information we need, I'll be able to put forward a convincing argument for the service. If you don't make it back from this one, it means we have to start again and will be that much further behind in developing alternative strategies for resupply."

"Gladdens my heart to have your confidence, concern, and support. I'll bring back a token of my esteem."

"Keep the bullshit to yourself. A map and protocol will do." "Right."

———— ♦ ————

Waking on the woolen pallets, Jim can feel the sun on his face. He continues to look west past the lake toward the mountains while the warmth makes him sweat. He wipes the sweat from his face and listens to the street noises below, his current reality.

"Pretty impressive dream, that was. Haven't thought about those trips to Russia and India in awhile. Hmm, lot of water under that bridge since then."

He splashes water on his face from the bucket in the corner and realizes he needs to pee badly. No facilities in the room, so he must be expected to get out of the room to go somewhere else. Banging on the door, he calls for someone to get him to a toilet. Nothing. "Come on you, sonsabitches, I gotta go!" Nothing. Now it is beginning to be uncomfortable and he bangs harder on the door. Nothing. He's looking around for possibilities. The bucket, but that's his drinking water. No holes in the floor so he'll probably drown himself if he lets go now. Finally, he climbs onto the windowsill and his hips are just at the height of the lower open part of the window. He unbuttons and manages to just get his penis through the bars as it lets fly. The stream is large and long, arching out into the street. Suddenly there is cacophony from below but he doesn't care since he has finally relieved himself.

Finally, he's gotten rid of just about all he can and he can wait for the trip later down the hall. There is a loud banging on the door, and just as the peephole slides open he hits the floor and sits on his pallet. An eye fills the hole in the door, examines his room and him for several seconds, then the hole slides shut. No key-in-the-lock noises indicates he may have dodged a bullet (or truncheon) for now.

For lack of anything else to do, he performs some deep-knee bends, then torso twists, and finally pushups off the wall, just to keep his circulation going. It's been days since he has moved around much and the immobility is starting to turn his mind a bit. He knows he must stay as alert as possible. He starts walking, three steps door to window, two steps wall to wall, three then two then three; after 20 trips or so he starts putting a bit of variety into it, closing his eyes to see if he can anticipate the wall or window, how close he can come without hitting it. Can he vary the length of one step, followed by a compensation from the next, and still get as close without hitting the wall? The game has endless variations and he is well into trying them all when a knock comes at the door and his evening meal arrives. The local fellow who brings it in says nothing, does not establish eye contact, is ready to exit when Jim says, "Hey, can you get me to a toilet?" No response. The fellow starts to back out the door when Jim jumps up, scaring the fellow half to death and asks louder, "Can I go to the toilet?" Blank stare, and out the door he scampers. Jim lunges at the closed door and starts thumping it with the heel of his hand, yelling. The peephole slides open revealing a yellow eye of someone who is obviously bending down to look in. "I need to go to the toilet. Can you help me?"

"Shut up! Bang on door again and this stick cracks your skull."

"Toilet! Banyo! Whatever!"

"Shut up, pig, or I come in there, and you not happy at all." Jim recognizes the voice as the brute who lead him upstairs after he nailed King Kong. The instructions are heeded, but reluctantly because now he really has to go again.

He whispers, "May the fleas of a thousand camels nest permanently in your crotch."

Back in the middle of the room, he notices that he has another pitcher of water on the tray. This he drinks most of, then empties the rest into the bucket and pees into the pitcher. He'll save it until the middle of the night and jettison it out the window when the foot traffic is gone from below. He sets it on the tray, takes up the bread and butter and the banana and is sitting on the pallet when the door suddenly opens. The mute attendant enters and whisks away the tray before he can object, pitcher and all. "Hope they're particular about washing the dishes."

A few more laps and he is ready for bed. It's now dark outside the window, the light in the hall seeps under the door as the only light in the room. Maybe he can catch up on his sleep tonight, maybe. Being alone has some advantages. If he wants to piss in the morning he'll have to get up fairly early to miss the rush hour traffic. Drifting off, he smells the curry and khorma of Assam, and feels the lightheadedness of high flying over and around the Himalayas, hunting for a safe route.

———◆———

Fifteen thousand feet, 18,000 feet, 20,000 feet, and he nearly scrapes the belly of the DC-3 on the mountain. Thrills and chills from near spills over the hump of the southern Himalayan Mountains. And the air currents are fun as well. Over one ridge, and into a deep valley, only to climb like a kite to clear the next ridge. Three major valleys and dozens of smaller ones. The only thing keeping him in line is the compass because he's never been here before. It often feels like he'll likely never make it back. They've turned the plane into a flying gas can, which provides the needed ballast and requisite fuel for this hunting and pecking around the mountain tops. The chart provides little support since much of what he is flying over has not been charted, not in the West anyway.

Up, up, up and over, and suddenly there is flat land as far as the eye can see, with some inconsequential hills here and there, a braided river dead ahead arising from multiple headwaters to starboard, and a small city, of sorts. Chabua is in the northeast so he drifts to starboard searching for straight lines that might be used as runways. Nothing. He has passed the city's eastern side, heading into the emptiness beyond.

"Get the receiver onto the locator beacon's frequency. We gotta have some direction to find this thing." Turning to port, he swings back around, coming across the northern edge of the city. The radio is broadcasting more steadily the more he turns until the reception starts to fall off. He returns a bit to starboard and a steady signal is maintained. The signal holds as they fly straight away from the river until it starts to break up again as he begins his turn south. Harry spots some regular patterns on the ground at the edge of the city, ahead at about two o'clock. Jim backs off the power and drifts down to examine the location. As it passes on the starboard side of the plane, Harry reports that the regular lines are truly etched in the dirt and on the southside of the expanse there are three buildings, two small and one larger, with something like a tower on the top. Jim makes his call identifying himself as Yankee Bull requesting landing instructions and he gets a wonderfully warbled response of indeterminate meaning. He responds reporting his need for landing to which there is a loud burst of warbled shouting in the background then "NO, NO, NO! UP, UP, UP!" He pulls back the yoke and there is a mighty roar as a single engine plane passes from his portside rear out under his starboard wind, rattling his window with the thrust and prop wash. "May the saints preserve us! Shit and goddammit!" His heart is still pounding as he pulls up and left to circle again.

This time he receives a stern English voice in reply to his landing announcement, sounds of an Oxford English origin. "You will land according to our instructions, sir, or you won't be landing here!"

"Fine by me. Just get someone on the mike that I can understand."

"Your cheek, sir, is entirely out of place, given the danger you've created in our airspace. Be quiet and listen carefully to instructions."

Jim: "I'm at your disposal, captain."

From the landing strip, "Lieutenant, if you please. Turn left to orient to the runway, runway 0.9, if you don't mind. Turn now."

Jim: "Right you are, turning now. Descending to 2,000 feet and continuing to turn, 1,800 feet."

From the strip: "You have been given no instructions concerning descent. Return to 5,000 feet and we will restart the drill."

Jim: "1,500 feet, three quarters turned, aligning with runway, 1,000 feet."

Strip: "Discontinue your descent, return to 5,000 feet immediately!"

Jim: "800 feet, now aligned with the runway 0.9, although I only see one runway. But what the hell, 500 feet. I'll —"

Chirp, apoplectic: "RETURN TO 5,000 FEET IMMEDIATELY! DO YOU READ ME? IMMEDIATELY!"

Jim: "Wheels down, approaching runway 0.9, 200 feet. Aah, there we are."

Chirp: "AARGH! Permission refused for landing at this airfield! If you land, your plane will be confiscated and you will be arrested, understood?"

Jim: "Wonder why we have not heard any other instructions from the tower? Odd, really. Usually they talk us all the way onto the ground during a first arrival. Oh, well, touch down in 5, 4, 3, 2…"

Bump, tires screech, brakes applied and slowly heading west into the sun. Buildings are south, so he begins his turn as he lowers the volume on the radio transmitter, not off. "Harry, remove the fuse from the receiver, will ya? Thanks."

Jim pulls the plane up to a low building next to what appears to be a metal-sided, three-story main tower and shuts down the engines. He returns the transmitter volume to normal before he leaves the cockpit. Exiting the rear of the plane, he sees a khaki-clad, sweating mustachioed man waddling over to him with three - much shorter and much thinner - immaculately dressed, unsmiling brown fellows just behind. As Jim steps down from the small rear door of the tail, the overweight and overwrought fellow pulls up straight in front of him, panting and sweating profusely as he bellows, "What is the meaning of this outrageous performance!?"

"Hello, lieutenant. You're the fellow on the radio, right? Jim Tuck from Wujiaba airfield on a fact-finding mission from Captain Chennault, second in the Chinese air corps. So nice to meet you and I actually thought the landing was one of my better ones, except the small close encounter in the air. You really should have your controllers practice a bit of pronunciation, maybe a few drills of typically useful air traffic terms. But I don't want to tell you your business, do I? Nice weather today. Say, it was a bit awkward at the end of the landing when your transmission cut out. Having difficulty with your equipment, are you?"

"Squadron Leader Captain Fitzpatrick, you insufferable boorish oaf! My air control officer was trying to assist your landing on the radio and receiving precious little assistance from your end. Cut out transmission, indeed! Muhammed, check the status of the radio immediately! You, Mr. Tuck, will accompany Mr. Singh here to the tower, where you will await my return and most likely your incarceration!"

"How unsporting of you, sir. But I'll be in the nearest place where I can get a drink, if you don't mind. I have a wicked thirst from the flight. Oh, you can contact Captain Chennault at this number at Wujiaba airfield. He is awaiting your call, I believe. Now, Mr. Singh, if you don't mind."

"Singh! If this gentleman tries to go anywhere other than the tower before I have returned, shoot him! Dismissed!"

"Yes, sir."

Jim, "Damned unfriendly of you, Captain, in light of the poor performance of your staff and your dodgy equipment. I am afraid things will likely go hard on you if you don't adopt a slightly more welcoming attitude, my good man."

"AARGH! Get out of my sight!"

Jim and his co-pilot saunter off in the direction of the three-story tower with Singh in the lead. The day is warm, but not too hot. The terrain is quite stunning, but obviously will present difficult flying conditions in bad weather. The take-off will have to be quite steep, and he still has a tendency toward stalling the plane from time to time. The whole runway will be needed for sure to get maximum velocity before lifting off. The squadron leader is more than a bit excitable, but Chennault will sort him out soon enough. Hmmm, now for a drink.

"Sing, anywhere around here a fellow can get a drop of liquor?"

Mr. Singh stops dead in his tracks, turns and looks at Jim as if he has two heads and says, "Sir, Assam is 98% Muslim religion. There is no alcohol in this area, and never will be. Please to follow me."

"Shit. How do they expect a reasonable man to soberly tolerate a place like this. No wonder the captain is a bit testy. Harry, you still got the item?" Harry pats the breast pocket of his flight jacket and smiles.

They had no more than sat down when they hear stomping rising up the echoing stairwell and the door flies open to the captain's blustering entrance. "So, your receiver is not operational suddenly, is that correct?"

"Seems that way, why?"

"Muhammad tells me that the access port to your receiver has been recently opened and that there seems to be a part missing. There is a tell-tale circular dust-free area that obviously was the location of some part or other."

"Don't know anything about that, Captain. Now, since we are likely to be doing frequent business with one another over the next several months, or longer, perhaps we could make some effort to be more accommodating to one another's needs. I am, at the moment, quite thirsty and in need of liquid refreshment. What do you have to offer?"

"For you, sir, the stockade and a swift trial. I suspect that you will be lucky if you receive no more than an expulsion from my brother, the magistrate. Am I making myself perfectly clear?"

Jim, "Perfectly, so I suspect I should return the favour. The Chinese National government of General Chiang

Kai-shek has, through Captain Claire Chennault, employed me to explore an air transport route over the Hump, Southern Himalayas to you, and I am to report to the authorities upon my immediate return tomorrow. As the Chinese government has made direct overtures to the Indian Raj, who has instructed the governor of Assam province to provide full and exemplary cooperation with this exploration mission, in light of the likely aggressions to come, I am deputized to speak for Captain Chennault in all matters concerning logistics and cooperation. Speaking to me, sir, is the same as speaking directly to Captain Chennault and, by extension, to General Chiang. Am I making myself perfectly clear, or do I need to slow my speech to accommodate your wit? Now, my report can allude to the sorry nature of your administration, manners and equipment, or explain that you are obviously doing the best you can in difficult circumstances. It is up to you. Either way, you will calm down, find me a large glass of red wine with ice, dinner that is palatable and a bed for the night that won't leave me scratching on the flight back. Now, Captain, is better than later!"

The captain's face is blossoming redder by the second. He fumes his way to the telephone where he drops the receiver, retrieves it and violently strikes the cradle repeatedly as if the operator would answer more quickly the harder and faster he hits it. Finally, he is connected to the operator, asks for the adjutant's office and waits, shifting from one foot to the other, a violently menacing look on his pudgy, sweating face. His eyes appear to be popping from his head and he is blowing hard when he suddenly says, "Captain Fitzpatrick here, sir. I have an extremely rude Yank here, sir, a pilot, with a fantastic tale of a mission from Wujiaba to Chabua, an exploration flight preceding an air cargo route between the two locations. Have you any information concerning such an impending program, or should I just clap him in irons and await the magistrate's bidding?"

All the color drains from his face as he suddenly stands more erect but with his shoulders slumped. "Letter, sir? No, haven't seen such a letter, sir. I understand, sir. Yes, sir. No, sir, absolutely not, sir! Yes, he is right here, sir." Turning to Jim, the captain says, "He would like a word with you."

"Hello, Jim Tuck here, recently of Wujiaba airfield. Yes, sir, good to hear your voice as well. Oh no, sir, just a little misunderstanding, probably due to dodgy equipment and a few procedures that could use a bit of tightening up. No, sir, I am in perfect health. Just could use a bit of a relaxing beverage and a meal before turning in. Have quite an adventurous return flight tomorrow,

I expect. Yes, sir, I'll convey your respects to Captain Chennault and I am sure he will pass them on to the General. Yes, sir, he is still here. I'll pass the telephone back over to him. For you, Captain."

"Yes, sir, I understand, sir. My fullest cooperation in all matters, sir. Completely clear, sir."

"Singh, take our guests to the officers' quarters, arrange for a meal and beds as appropriate and introduce them to the charge' who will be able to accommodate their personal needs for liquid refreshment. Any questions?"

"Oh, no, sir. Straight away, sir. Any other orders, sir?

"None at all. Oh, have the charge' ring me here. I'll have some requirements of him as well. Dismissed."

"Very good, sir. This way, gentlemen."

"Nice we were able to get all that sorted out so efficiently, Captain, … Fitzpatrick was it? I'll be sure to include your swift attention to detail in my full report. Good day to you. Oh, and we will be departing at 0600. Could you have your crew assure all the fuel tanks are full in the plane, and perhaps my partner and I could have a chat with a few of your more experienced pilots this evening before turning in, eh, what? Thank you again for your hospitality and assistance." Jim turns on his heel and is gone out the door, not waiting for a response.

Harry says, "You knew you had him by the balls all the time, didn't you? He had me shaking a bit."

Jim responds, "Wasn't sure until I saw the phone in the office. On his own, he probably would have been a bit difficult to deal with. But as long as I could get him to contact a higher up who had a bit of information, I figured we had him, yeah. No need to entirely bust his balls, but incompetents like him need a bit of shaking up from time to time. Now for a drink. Singh, where is the charge', anyway?"

With a small private smile, Singh responds, "This way, sir, a short walk to the rear of the complex."

———— ◆ ————

The sound of a key in the door lock, the peep hole sliding up and shut again wakes him to dim dawn light and a dry mouth, just like the one he had after a bottle and a half of red wine that first night in Chabua. The door opens and a tray with the water jug, buttered bread, coffee and a note are laid on the floor to the right of the door. By the time Jim is sitting and focusing on the door, it is closed again. He hears the lock turn.

The water is just in time to get rid of his dry night mouth. The Manila accommodations are not great, but they sure beat downstairs and are even better than some he has paid for in the past. Having wet his mouth and spit the majority out the window, he downs the bread and drinks what passes for coffee. The caffeine stimulates his kidneys and he takes advantage of the early hour's light traffic to pee out the window. No need to bang on the door and anger Mighty Joe Young with the club, not first thing in the morning anyway.

Just as he is reeling it in off the window sill, there is a bang on the door. The peephole slides open to reveal a yellow eye. The door opens and Tony Arizza enters in his dashing pressed suit.

"Bit early for the embassy crowd to be up and about, isn't it?"

"Old Army habit. Got some news and some questions. Which do you want first?"

"News, of course. I've got some bread, want a slice?"

"No, thanks. I've managed to get some of the real article at the embassy before I came over. OK, news. Seems Chennault has a few strings to pull somewhere in Washington. The ambassador received a reasonably explicit note from the State Department to the effect that you should be freed and out of here at the earliest possible date, with some stipulations."

"What stipulations?"

"The ambassador is drafting a memorandum of understanding, binding in all locations having U.S. influence, which prohibits you from discussing, in any detail, your role at Wujiaba airfield, or any of your volunteer assignments while in China. You'll sign it and then you'll be quietly ejected from the Philippines to the States. I am to verify the areas that are covered on the memorandum by debriefing you concerning your activities in China, while under the direction of Capt. Chennault. I'll compare my information with the information he has provided in a letter to the ambassador. Any new stuff not in the original order will be added so nothing gets out, as in nothing. What I was told is that this data is considered highly classified. I have clearance to receive it, but if any of it surfaces, you will be arrested and incarcerated for an indeterminate time in facilities less enjoyable than these. Seems a bit harsh to me, but them's the facts, man. You want out of here, you're going to have to agree to button your lip for some time to come. Got it?"

"Got it. You got the list of information I am supposed to keep mum about?"

"Right here, pal," as he pats his breast pocket.

"So, why not just tell me what's on the list and I'll keep mum about it?"

"As I said, because Chennault realizes that you are a bit of a maverick and have likely operated slightly outside the boundaries originally given. So if you come up with stuff that he did not know about, it gets added to the list. I compare the list with what you have to offer and add things he did not know about. Then the new list will get signed by you and the ambassador, with a copy to Chennault and the State Department. All nice and legal and inclusive. I'd talk fast, if I were you, because you're not getting out of here until the list is signed, sealed and delivered, if you know what I mean. You and I are going to be great pals by the time you're out of here."

"Any chance that the food might be improved so that my memory is sharper? I mean, a fellow can hardly be expected to do justice to a great story on an empty stomach without a bit of red wine, now can he?"

"I'll see what I can do. If the police have difficulties with providing you the proper inducements, I can make some adjustments myself, I am sure."

"Oh, and I've been in here three days now and haven't had the opportunity of a good crap. A trip to the john now and then would be nice, if you can arrange it."

"No hay problema, amigo."

"How about now?"

"We'll give it a try. Watch me work. Guard, I need to leave for a minute and return. Open up, please." He whispers to Jim, "See, I said please."

The peephole slides open. Jim is sitting on the pallet and Tony near the door, peering out the hole at Yellow Eye. Lock turns, door opens and Tony winks as he leaves.

About 10 minutes later, by some reckoning, he is back at the door, calling to Jim to come to the door. When the door opens, Tony is dwarfed by Mighty Joe Young with his trusty truncheon at the ready and they parade down the hall to the toilet.

Jim takes his time to experience the ecstasy of elimination over the squat toilet in the foulest facility he has seen since the train to Kunming. He enjoys every minute of it. Running water being a premium, he wipes his hands on his shorts and exits the room. Tony greets him with a smile, Mighty Joe Young with a scowl, and Tony mentions something about the fact that Jim has not bathed for as long as he has held his bowels in check. It might be time for an ablution and a change of clothes. Jim agrees, and Tony confers with Mighty Joe, who is obviously not pleased. Mighty Joe puffs himself up saying that it is not permitted. Tony, ever the diplomat, points out that Tony's boss is essentially Mighty Joe's boss and maybe it would be better if Mighty Joe just agreed now rather than later when Tony has gone all the way back to the embassy, where their boss lives and where Tony will get appropriate authorization. That might just make Mighty Joe look bad. Mighty Joe looks from Tony to Jim, and back to Tony, hits his hand with the truncheon in a tender, menacing fashion and gives in. Mighty Joe is angry but smart enough to back off when he's beat.

The bath, after the dump, is exquisite. Jim is in the middle of luxuriating in it when he hears a truncheon rapping purposefully on the bathroom door.

"Right, I was just getting out. Have the clean clothes that Capt. Arizza sent arrived yet?"

"No clothes, come out! Now!"

"Alright, alright, I'm coming." and Jim wraps the towel around his waist just before opening the door.

"What you hiding under this cloth?"

"Nothing except the family jewels."

"You have valuable stones under this cloth, give to me." "Different jewels. It is just a saying in America. It means your balls. Understand?"

"Let me see these jewels."

"Wait a minute, it is a way of kidding. Not real diamonds or anything."

"You have diamonds? You must give to me. They are illegal in this place. The superintendent will keep them safe for you. Give to me."

"OK, look, no diamonds, see?" and Jim drops the towel."

Whack, the truncheon sounds like a pistol shot as it hits the side of his left shoulder and Jim goes down in a heap.

"What the hell did you do that for?" he squeaks between gritted teeth.

"You think I am a fool. You say things to me that are not true because you think I am stupid."

"What? I was not ridiculing you! I was just using a casual way of talking in America when men talk about their private parts. It was not teasing you. Ugh, I think you broke my arm."

"No, it did not break. You can hear easily when the arm breaks, and it did not break. Get up, put on this cloth and we go to your room. New clothes may come later. Get up now or your feet will feel the side of my stick."

"Right, right, I'm up. See, I'm up."

"Cover yourself and go."

Back in his cell, Jim inspects his arm just below the shoulder and the bruise is quite impressive. He can't lift his hand backwards at his wrist, or seem to be able to straighten his fingers. It feels like there is no strength in his left wrist, and he cannot grip anything. The ache is intense and his arm throbs from shoulder to his finger tips. Sure enough, there are no clean clothes in the cell. The towel is his only garment. After awhile he notices that, aside from his throbbing left arm, he is relatively comfortable in his new garb, and being a utilitarian at heart, he decides to use it as his main clothing for awhile. Even when the new clothes arrive, assuming they do, he'll probably keep the towel as his version of prison uniform, maybe over his shorts to decrease the chafing that has started.

In the late afternoon, Tony arrives, with his change of clothes and marvels at the bruise that is now down to his elbow and seeming to pool there. Jim relates the story of how it got there and Tony is ready to call the superintendent when Jim restrains him, finally convincing him that stirring a mess will most likely just make Jim's stay even more eventful.

Tony says, "Well, we are on the way to getting you sprung from here. I would say that the bureaucratic B.S. should take no longer than three more days. And then you'll be on your way out of the Philippines. I'm ushering the paperwork through the embassy and then through the judicial system. If we let them wander their own way through, it would likely take more than a month. But walking it through, with the ambassador's contacts aiding and abetting the process, the whole thing is much smoother."

"Why?"

"Why what?"

"Why are you and the ambassador taking such an interest in an American nobody who happened to fall into your jurisdiction?"

"Let's just say that certain events in Asia, for which you have particular knowledge, would more likely result in better outcomes if they do not become public any time soon. You realize that all this special treatment comes with a price, right?"

"Of course. When did it ever not? But what makes you think that once out of the Philippines I won't spill the beans to any one of a number of newspaper or magazine publications where I have friends and acquaintances looking for exclusive material relative to the Asian conflict?"

"Because I am certain that you are not so stupid not to realize that the State Department has tentacles everywhere, and the extradition from the US back to the Philippines would be no trouble at all. That bruise on your arm would be nothing to what you could expect, if you ever had to come back involuntarily. Clear?"

"Quite."

"Now, why don't you tell me about training the Chinese to fly?"

"You want to hear about it now?"

"I suspect that if I'm going to hear as much of the story as possible, we better get started. You won't mind if I keep notes, will you?"

"Who will see them?"

"Just me, the ambassador and his secretary who will transcribe them."

"Alright then, let's see, Kunming."

Jim related the story from Hong Kong to Kunming, not really seeing the necessity of going into his flight training and departure from California. First, the freighting of DC- 3's from Russia to China. Then he skimmed over his role as flying instructor, only going into the difficulties of teaching in a situation requiring constant translation and the students insisting on rote learning. Flying was anything but a rote operation, as was any functional activity. Somehow, the other two teachers seemed to get their points across, even to rote learners, but his charges were hitting the ground hard at regular intervals. Chennault pulled him out of flight school to institute the importation of DC3's into China and to explore the Wujiaba to Chabua route. They got some detail since they were fun, if complicated, and successful.

After confirming the possibility of the route to Assam and mapping his flight to and from, he pulled cargo duty to Peking. Funny how the spelling did not sound like the Chinese pronunciation. Anyway, he began his regular job with three flights a week, flying mostly military cargo to the nationalist army in Peking. They had been battling the Japanese full bore since the July '37 Marco Polo Bridge incident. Some of the supplies coming down from Alma Ata were being ferried to the battle area around Peking.

It was 1,300 miles one way, Kunming to Peking. Landing with an overnight stay and returning with flight students the next day - three times a week - had been a full-time job. The plane needed some modifications to allow additional fuel, since there were few or no refueling stops available and the flight distance was just outside the operating range of the plane. The extra fuel cut down on the amount of cargo it could carry, but getting something there in a timely fashion became more important than how much arrived on each flight. Since there were at least six pilots assigned to the route, more flights could make up for any shortfall in cargo capacity.

He got tired, but wealthier, each month considering $650 a month, plus the hazard pay he had negotiated. The chronic fatigue was offset by the additional hazard pay, which is appropriate since he never knew who would have control of the landing strip when he landed. At take off, the radio could say one thing that by the time he landed was no longer the case. Twice he had to abort the landing and find his own alternate route when he took considerable fire from the ground on final approach. A couple of live rounds landing in a cargo of munitions could put a real dent in his day.

The last flight he took to Peking started out as usual, wind off the western mountains, getting him off the ground with minimal fuel expense. During the long tedious flight over central China he could see areas of intense activity where Chinese factories were being erected after being transferred from vulnerable areas to the east. No airfields were available, though, since these new factory locations were still purposely primitive.

Closer to Peking things heated up a bit, and the tension in the cockpit rose accordingly. Finding regular alternate landing strips was always instructive, but the ingenious codes used to guide the plane to alternate sites usually kept him occupied as well as safe. This evening, as the sun was going down, he was on final approach to the makeshift airfield. The sky lit up with tracers and anti-aircraft fire as he banked to port, dived, then climbed to starboard to escape the onslaught. As the stall indicator light appeared, he leveled to traveling northwest and circled to the west to see the remnants of a DC-3 on the ground below. The tracers were falling harmlessly behind and to the southeast as he escaped.

"Now, what the hell do we do? Harry, code in 'alternative' and we'll see if anyone is listening."

Harry toggled the radio transmit switch like a Morse key and they waited, as the fuel gauge dropped to reserve and they were disappearing into the sunset. Nothing happened and then, five long minutes later, the radio burst into patterned static that repeated twice. Harry was able to get it down and they banked to the south. Suddenly, the evening sky lit up with tracers again, and they started dodging right, left and up until they left the tracers behind. Another burst of patterned static and Harry gave Jim new coordinates that required a shift to the southeast and descent to 5,000 feet. This altitude made Jim very nervous, but within three minutes there were parallel rows of lights on the ground and he circled, just to be sure. Smoke indicated a westerly wind and he lined up at the southeast end of the makeshift runway, settling into his approach. This landing he let Harry handle, especially since Jim's nerves were shot, he was very tired, and still didn't do landings well, even in the best of circumstances. And these circumstances were not the best.

The ground had been scraped, after a fashion, and the first bump of contact was followed by several more, as the plane and its cargo bounced down between quickly shortening rows of kerosene fires. At the end, actually past the end, of the "runway" Harry turned the plane and taxied back to the top end where there was a jubilant reception committee. Neither Jim nor Harry could understand a word of rapidly chattering Chinese, but a tall, lanky fellow with receding hairline broke through the crowd below the cockpit window and motioned the two pilots to join him on the ground.

Opening the waist door, Jim was impressed with the excitement and efficiency of the waiting crowd; he and Harry quickly got out of the way of the unloading crew. Ben Sheffield was the Anglo fellow with the receding hairline, and neither Harry nor Jim had met him before.

"Just arrived, old sod," Ben said. "Interesting operation here, eh?" Without any sort of uniform to identify his allegiance, Ben declared it with his Aussie accent. He towered over both Harry and Jim, at six feet, seven inches, sunburned face, bare arms with rolled up sleeves, and short pants worn as summer uniform by every military person Jim had met from any commonwealth country. Ben showed a ready smile, which had not necessarily accompanied the shorts of other military types.

Ben was instantly likeable, and the three exit the pandemonium of the loading of four trucks Ben had brought. The back of Ben's personal truck is half bunkhouse and half radio equipment.

"Gotta keep moving, fellas. The Nips have some mean radio signal location gear, so moving the transmit site keeps me out of their hands, a bit longer anyway. How about a short snort?" and he pulls out a bottle of Glen Nevis from behind the driver's seat.

"Where the hell did you get that?" Jim asked, eyes as wide as the summer sky.

"Brought it with me. Only have half a dozen left, so must ration, mates. But this is an occasion, eh?"

"Sure as hell is." said Jim and Harry with one voice.

They saunter off to sit in the dark under a nearby mimosa tree and enjoy a bit of Scotland. The bottle was three quarters full in no time, and Jim gave Harry a quick nod that said let's not ruin our welcome. As they watch, the unloading is finished and the barrels of fuel are still being pumped into the plane. In all, the stop has taken one and a half hours and half a bottle. The volunteers shake hands as the two rows of fires were lit and Jim and Harry climbed back into the plane. Ben backed off as they fired up the engines, gave a wave. They turned to taxi back down to begin their take-off run. As they lift off, tracers lit up the sky just behind them, and they saw the trucks barreling away from the makeshift strip toward the darkness of the countryside. No banking of the plane to change directions here. They left the tracers behind as they got beyond range, then banked to port for a southwest bearing toward Kunming.

The flight "home" was uneventful, but Jim and Harry were constantly changing duty at the yoke. They were both beat, fatigued from being awake and under stress for 22 hours straight. Finally the mountains rose in front of them in the noonday light, and the airfield was in sight. They concentrated intensely to make sure they did not do something stupid this close to safety. Harry set the plane down, they climbed out, and looked at one another with the same thought, "Is this what I really want to be doing right now?"

They were met at the edge of the tarmac by none other than Chennault himself. He invited them to his office for a short conversation, to be recorded by a stenographer. It took at least one and a half hours to tell the whole story. Jim and Harry checked one another for details, and Chennault picked at the story incessantly to pry out as much information as he could to fulfill part of his responsibility to General Chiang. Jim couldn't give a shit about the Captain's responsibility to General Chiang. The adventure was getting out of hand.

Chennault ended his debriefing and R & R was in order with a tumbler of red wine over a chunk of ice. Leaning back in a wooden kitchen chair, Jim relaxed. Harry asked, "So where are you now, 'cause you sure as hell ain't around here?"

"Nowhere, mate, nowhere in particular, anyway. Just gone from here. I think it's time for a change."

"Not me, fella. Money's too good."

"Can't buy a new ass, Harry, and we came preciously close to losing ours yesterday. I can only see things getting hotter. What happens when Chiang starts bombing runs out of here? You think the Japs are going to sit still for that? Next year this place will be smoking."

"So we leave next year and suck on this tit as long as it's givin' milk."

"That milk we were dodging last night didn't have much human kindness in it. Nah, you stay as long as you like. I think I'll move on soon. Just don't know where yet. It'll come to me. Wine's making me sleepy, that and going strong 24 hours straight. Gotta start thinking more clearly. Can't do it now, and pay day is tomorrow."

He put the glass down unfinished, moved to his cot, removed his flight boots and rolled to the wall. Less than a minute later, Jim was asleep and Harry left.

The blast on the loud speaker outside his window caused the anticipated roar, "Goddamned son of a slimy whore!" Rubbing his eyes as he looks through the window, Jim was surprised that it was still sunny out. Understanding came slowly when he examined his military time watch and saw it was only 07:30.

Further evidence from his senses told him he actually slept the whole night through. Mouth like the bottom of a bird cage, aches in places he had forgotten, and an overwhelming urge to pee. No heading to the john down the hall. He opened the louvered french doors on the other side of the room, walked out onto the little catwalk balcony and let fly over the railing. For once, no one was below at the back of the building. He was spared having to sit (or stand) through another Chennault personal hygiene lecture.

"Gotta do something about the taste in my mouth." He drained the remains of yesterday's tumbler into his mouth, swishes it around, gargles a bit and spits over the railing into the backyard. Grimacing, Jim said, "Bad idea. Should have looked for flies in it before putting it in my mouth."

After dumping yesterday's clothes into the middle of the floor, he found his relatively clean ones in the box under the writing table, dressed and headed toward the dining hall for a cup of coffee, or two. Black coffee in the mug, large inhalation of the delicious dark aroma, and he was almost well. Just as the cup reached his lips, a shout came from across the room. "Tuck! Upstairs, chop chop!" Jim jerked and spilt the coffee on his pant leg, none of it reaching his mouth.

It's Anderson, Chennault's aide. A growl from below his belly button made Jim yell back, "Coffee first!"

"Now, jerk off. It's payday, remember, and tardiness gets docked by the minute."

"Madre mia! May you rot in the pits of hell!" Jim started walking across the hall, cup in hand.

"Leave the cup, asshole. You're seeing Chennault, himself!"

"If your mother had any children who lived, they would know that if his lordship wants to see me promptly at this hour, he'll see me with my coffee. Got a cigarette? I'm out."

"He's not going to like it."

"I don't care. Give me a cigarette and a light."

"You know you can't smoke up there."

"Give me the goddamned cigarette, you witless slug, and let me worry about where I smoke it."

Anderson fished a pack out of his shirt pocket and Jim lifted the whole pack neatly from Anderson's hand as he took a sip of his coffee. "Now the matches. Pay you back later. Come on! Don't keep me waiting!"

Cigarettes and matches in one hand, coffee in the other, he trudges along the wooden floored hallway, looking out the windows onto the airfield. A lot of activity around his plane, Harry doing the flight walk counterclockwise around the aircraft. "What the hell's going on out there?" Jim said to himself. "We're not scheduled into the rotation for two more days." His trudge becomes a lope, crossing from barracks to the control tower building, spilling coffee with nearly every step. Rising two steps at a time, he arrives at Chennault's office, swigs the last gulp of tepid coffee and pockets the cigarettes and matches.

At the first rap on the door, Chennault's distinctive voice calls, "Come," and Jim enters the room.

"Here's your pay envelope for last month. There's a bit of a bonus in there for your good work the past few days, and for the fact that I need you to fly out of your rotation. Blain's DC-3 is disabled for at least two more days, Christiansen broke his ankle last night when he broke his co-pilot's jaw, and I received a coded dispatch from Shanghai at 5 a.m. requesting an emergency shipment of small caliber ammunition. That means you and Harry are it."

Taking the envelope, Jim looks up at Chennault to respond, "I saw Harry walking the preflight and had a pretty bad feeling. Where in Shanghai?"

"Loudian directly, or Suzhou on the Nanjing Road. The ammunition is needed at Loudian, but it may be too hot there to get it directly in. Ben Sheffield flew into Suzhou last night to coordinate logistics with us and confirmed the situation is slightly past desperate. So this lot has to get through today."

A slow, determined look came over Jim's face while he began to outline the situation as he saw it. "Well, if the situation is that desperate, then I suspect the delivery is just that much more dangerous. Correct?"

"Correct, to a point. The comparison is, of course, not exact, and you'll agree that…"

Jim interrupting, "To a point my ass, which is highly likely to get shot off delivering this stuff!"

Chennault, forcefully, "Please! Mr. Tuck, can we keep this discussion as objective as possible?"

"I'm going to objectify myself a railway ticket as far away from here as possible, and now. Suicide has never been my strong suit."

"Now, calm down a minute! Mr. Sheffield is a highly competent logician and tactician and assures me there is an acceptable corridor for entry and exit of the alternate delivery areas, that indeed there remain areas of Shanghai under nationalist control - thus the need for delivery to ensure a successful counterattack."

"I agree that Ben is good at his job. I also realize he's got the balls of a dinosaur, so perhaps his definition of acceptable might differ from mine. OK, listen. Chiang's predicament in Shanghai is really not my problem is it?"

"Well, ummm…"

"Exactly my sentiments. But, I have signed on, contractually, month to month, to provide you, which means Chiang, flight services." Waving the pay packet, "I've successfully completed last month's contract, acquiring a few more holes in my aircraft during the process. This little altercation between Japan and China, as far as I am concerned, is getting out of hand. So, here's the deal:

"I take Harry and a load of ammunition, on a two-day contract – not one month – two days, to Shanghai.

"I bring Harry back and he continues on his merry way flying in and out of hell, while I go mine.

"As my payment for this two-day contract, I'll take that clapped out DC-3 repaired, of course, with all attendant certification, registration and ownership papers transferred to me, and a full load of fuel.

"All the above prepared for my departure the day following my return from Shanghai. "What do you say?"

"Outrageous! Unheard of! Blackmail of the most egregious sort. You're mad!"

"I tend to agree with that last assessment, for even considering making this run to Shanghai. As far as the rest of it, matter of perspective, old boy. Have we an agreement?"

"Absolutely not!"

"As you like, g'bye." And Jim heads for the door. As his hand grasps the knob, Chennault sputters, "You're an insufferable, aggrandizing bastard! Alright! Agreed."

"Well, I'm familiar with my father, but the remainder of the assessment is probably accurate. I recognize your integrity, so expect you'll keep your end of the bargain while I'm gone. Agreed it is. I will be departing China day after tomorrow, assuming I make it back tomorrow from Shanghai. Now, excuse me while Harry and I complete our preparations. If you could get us the flight data

ASAP, we'll be out of here. Back tomorrow, probably in the afternoon."

By the time he arrived at the plane, Harry had finished the preflight walk, which made no difference to Jim. It was his life and he would walk it himself. Harry busied himself with monitoring the stowing of cargo, assuring its stability and balanced position in the hold. The ground crew completed fueling the plane as the flight plan arrived. Jim and Harry looked it over together, noting that they were to fly directly into one of two designated areas, the selection of which would not be made until they were less than half an hour out. The landing spot would be radioed to them using the toggle switch system of coded Morse transmission. As the distance to Shanghai was a fair amount shorter than to Peking, there would be no refueling at the unloading site, to save time. The refueling would take place near Anqing on the Yangtze River, which was far enough from the Japanese to allow a safe landing and enough time to accomplish a full load of fuel. The only problem there was Ben would be near Shanghai and not be able to coordinate the fueling. Cho Han would be the contact person. Since he was educated at Stanford - returning to help fight the Japanese - his English would be good enough to assist the landing and take off.

"Kunming to Shanghai looks to be roughly 1,100 miles, if we fly it directly. But since the Japs are likely aware we are coming, we'll not give them a straight bead on our destination," Jim said. "So a few tacks to port and starboard will be in order during the trip, resulting in squeezing a five- and-a-half hour trip into seven. That will leave us that much less fuel remaining for the getaway. Do we have any current information about Japanese troop locations inland?"

"No."

"Shit. Thought so. We get about as much good information as we do good nights sleep. OK, we'll make it up as we go. Par for the course."

General flight plan in place, rendezvous points located reasonably closely, firmly strapped into their nylon webbed seats with their lunches packed in between them, Harry started the engines and Jim contacted the tower to coordinate take off. Nothing was scheduled for landing until tomorrow, but China and schedules rarely mixed, so everyone relied on the two spotters with binoculars to assure clear runways. The clear skies today made the work of the spotters much easier, and they reported the air clear of traffic, as did the radio operator. Chocks were pulled from the wheels, engines revved, and they rolled toward the downwind end of the runway. Even at max throttle, the go signal could be heard over their headsets, and Harry released the brakes. They were on their way: Harry happy as a clam to be moving again, Jim happy to be on his last daredevil mission, and the Shanghai garrison anxiously awaiting the plane. The Japanese, of course, knew the plane was coming, just not where it would touch down. Everything was ready for Jim and Harry to have a really exciting time, which was exactly why Jim was getting out.

Climbing into the northeast sky, Harry toggled the OK signal after which the frequencies were changed and the transmitter shut down, just for safety's sake.

It wasn't four hours when the excitement started. Maybe three and a bit; suddenly the afternoon got very active. They had just received the toggled confirmation of crossing the Yangtze and the blinking light to the starboard for course correction and all hell broke loose. Tracer bullets fore and aft, starboard and port seemingly had them bracketed. Evasive action was immediate and frantic. The last zig had taken them north, which was the plan, but now they veered even further north, rose to 15,000 with their oxygen masks on. Immediately the next turn was to starboard and a drop to 5,000. The gas was getting used up at a furious rate as they saw the shining strip of Yangtze pass first on the port side then the starboard side, which caused an immediate correction to port and the bullets were behind, way behind.

Oxygen masks came off and sweat poured down over their eyes. "What the fuck?" said Jim as they each examined the instruments and verified that the machine was still intact as far as they could tell. "Are we back on track, or close to it?"

Harry nodded without a word, then squealed out "Next landmark is Hefei to starboard, 20 minutes by my reckoning, then Nanking to port, in another 30, with the delta opening up under us. Gotta stay north of the delta, remember. Not nearly so many Japanese north of the delta, swing out to sea and in over the northern edge of Shanghai. That's when we toggle for directions."

"Shit and Buddha be praised. This is going to be a hairy one if it starts an hour away. How do the bastards know who they are shooting at unless they are getting information early? I want to find the prick who is sending it if they are."

Harry grunts, "Just fly the friggin' plane. That shit can wait, for sure. We get out of here, then we can think about revenge. God, I gotta pee!"

"Use the jar, just don't forget to put the lid on tightly."

BAM!

A huge explosion off to starboard sent metal rain peppering the fuselage and then more further back. One hit in front and they are climbing fast, jig to the left and level at 8,000 feet. Several more explosions can be heard in the distance behind as they turn back onto course, beginning to wonder if they will be able to find Shanghai after all these emergency corrections. "Somebody besides Chiang knows we are coming," growls Tuck.

Nanking finally shows on the starboard side with the river to its north, but significantly further away than dead reckoning put it. They slide a bit south to correct and take a more southerly correction and return to avoid some deadly fireflies coming up in front of them 20 minutes later. Finally Nanking shows on the port side with the widening delta off to the front and starboard. Correcting to the east, they flash out over the coast and start their long curving turn to flank the northern edge of the city. Sure enough the toggle starts up. No voices, just dots and dashes as they cruise along at 200 knots. A slight starboard correction with toggle confirmation and suddenly there is a small runway with three blinking lights dead ahead. Two toggles back on the transmitter from Harry and eight automobiles, four on each side, turn on their lights, illuminating the landing strip in the rapidly dimming evening light. No extra passes, wind in their faces they set it down and come to a stop as the plane is swarmed by small sweating men in loincloths and sandals. The doors rip open and the unloading begins before the engines are fully shut down.

As Jim is sliding out of the restraining harness, he spots Ben Sheffield sauntering through the headlights, a bottle in each hand, grinning ear to ear. Jim and Harry push through the local calamity in the back and get to Ben before he reaches the plane. "Gotta kill some folks soon, Ben. They knew we were coming, from where, and what destination. Gotta check the hull for holes. Come on, since you've got the bottles."

"Ah, Jim. You're not going to deny those little yellow fellas their fun are ya? They're just down there sweating in the paddies by the river, day after day, and need some entertainment from time to time. Besides, the buggers still have difficulty hitting the Hindenburg, let alone this little sport plane. Here's to their nearsighted inability!" Off comes the lid and Jim takes a long pull, handing the bottle to Harry. "Cheers, mate, and thanks for the medicinal bottle," Jim says.

"That was one of the more exciting runs so far. They were waiting for us before Nanking! How the hell are we supposed to get back? Got any ideas? Shit, look at that hole. Must have been the first flak explosion. It was close, or felt like it. Imagine it hitting the load, and five tons of ammunition goes up at once. Harry, check the tail will ya?" The grimace from Harry would stop a clock, so Jim reassuringly says, "Don't worry, we'll save you some. Oh heck, Ben, give him the other bottle. Now check it. We'll be sitting right here."

"You look a bit feverish, Jimbo."

"Glad it's only a bit, Ben. That was more interesting than I want to experience again. This is my last run. I'm outta here once I get back, assuming…"

"What a shame, and we were just getting a good start. I had big plans for us as a team. With your good looks and flying ticket and my logistics and access to fine goods, we had a chance to set ourselves up for an easy life after this little altercation is taken care of. I can see it now, back on the Murray with a few sheilas around to keep it interesting and some mates dropping by for a bit of hunting or fishing. Off to the highlands when it gets too hot, some sheep and several good horses for herding them as well as a couple of racing stock. Get the picture, you little bugger? I got it all planned, and the goods for exchange all lined up. What do you say?"

"Ben, you ever hear the saying about counting chickens before they've hatched? Son, we don't even have eggs and you're counting. This unpleasantness we've gotten ourselves into is going to get bigger before it gets better. This is just the beginning. How long can we last in this area as the only white faces around? Word is going to be out, IS out. Our asses are grass unless we can get quickly gone."

Harry slumps up, sits and is looking a bit bleary. He has made a serious dent in the bottle and Jim takes it gently from his hand. "We gotta get home, boy, tonight. At least part way home. I need your steady hand in that right seat, one more time, OK?"

Ben pipes up, "Are you with this plan of chucking in the towel this early in the fun?"

Harry looks up, and says, "Well, when we left Kunming, I was dead certain I was here for at least awhile longer, but those holes in the fuselage and the welcoming committee we have dodged on the way here are having an effect on this volunteer. Oh, tail's fine by the way."

"Well, I have some ideas that I think you should consider before any hasty decisions, OK? I'll be in contact with you blokes from my hidey hole day after tomorrow, so no rash actions in the meantime. Got it? It's important! We need to stick together. The future is bright!"

Jim looks past the struts they are leaning on and sees the retreating line of workers and the trucks pulling away in different directions. "Looks like they're done. Gotta go now! Hope we have the fuel to get to Hangkow."

"Oh, forgot to tell ya, Hangkow just fell to the Japs. They took the railroad line there. Your refueling is just north of Nanking, about 25 miles. There will be a toggle this side of Nanking, swing north, and look for the light blinking code. They'll light you up to come in just as we did. No one speaks English over there, but they are good and you can spend the night, leaving the next night. No getting to Kunming tonight and they want this plane back in relatively good nick."

"Fuck. Nanking was no fun on the way over," Jim mutters.

"All the more reason to use it. No one will think of you using a strip there, no Japs anyway. Oh, word is you glide into the landing, engines off, from three miles out. Should be fun!"

"What? Someone has completely lost their nut! This thing is no kite. It's a lump of lead and glides like it. Whose idea was that? And why?"

"Chennault wants you to give it a go as a stealth technique for getting into and out of tight places undetected. Good, eh? Should counteract the effects of the whiskey, I'd say. Think of the stories you'll have for your grandkids."

With that, Ben is off to his truck and the transmitter. Jim and Harry sit for a minute looking at one another, take a deep breath and clamber out from under the plane.

Once back in their seats, they start the powering up sequence, the props start turning and they get the toggle from Ben in their headsets. With a confirmation blip, they do a 180 and taxi to the end of the strip, turning 180 again. The lights come on and off they go, building speed faster with less weight, and they are in the air. As they reverse the turn to head west, they look out the port window to see explosion after explosion at the landing site. Then the pressure waves bounce the plane around, and there is one huge explosion that momentarily lights up a huge area. Ben's truck is gone; where it sat is a huge hole. Jim and Harry salute and settle into the next hour's excitement, anticipating more of the same.

It's about time to see some lights of Nanking, and Jim and Harry are both searching diligently to starboard, straining their eyes to pick any source of light. Harry shouts, "There, one o'clock!"

Jim looks and sure enough there seems to be a faint glow at one o'clock. He starts drifting that direction, checks the fuel gauge again to verify that a half hour max is left, and WHUMP, there is a huge explosion to starboard. The sky lights up all around them with light beams traversing back and forth searching them out. Another WHUMP, this time to port, and tracers start rising up from below all around them. It seems they have invaded firefly heaven, but the noise and shear amount of weaponry is terrifying. Another WHUMP, closer this time and slightly above to starboard makes Jim dive to lower altitude, veer to port with engines screaming, then back to starboard. He tries to evade the explosions, tracers and lights that are slowly, seemingly inexorably getting closer. He has the yoke hard right when the radio starts to toggle.

"Harry, right that down or get it somehow. We gotta get out of here.

"It has to be the local contact Ben told us about!" Harry reports, "XYTL."

"What?"

"Over and over again, XYTL".

"Shit, what the fuck is he doing? Ben said English is a second language. But this makes no sense at all." Jim is fighting the yoke to bring the plane back to port, rise to 8,000 feet and the lights blind him as they hit the cockpit windows. WHUMP, WHUMP, all around them as the light follows and he dives to port then switches to starboard passing 5,000 then rising. The fuel gauge is dropping like a stone. "XYTL. XYTL! What is he doing?"

Back at 12,000 feet, Jim stops jerking the yoke around long enough to say, "OK, we have to assume this guy is on our side and is trying to get us down safely. XYTL, it's gotta be his attempt at a code with Japs all around. What does it mean?"

"Fuck if I know, tracers to starboard!!"

After a veer to port, Jim says, "Cross Yangtze, turn left. Cross Yangtze, turn left. That's it!"

Harry is hysterical but squeaks out, "How do you know that?"

"Because that's what we're going to do, because I have no other ideas, and we are out of gas. Where's the Yangtze, do ya see it?"

"No, can't see shit with all this ordnance going off. Wait, there it is! Three o'clock."

Jim immediately swings the plane to starboard, passing the western edge of Nanking and the radio starts rapidly toggling.

"Get it, Harry. We gotta get down in a hurry!"

"Left, left! OK. Now straight five minutes."

"Doubt we have five minutes in the tanks, but we'll see." "It's saying descend to 5,000, look for blinking lights."

"Descending and looking. See anything?" Cough, sputter starboard engine.

"Shit, shit and mother of God here we come."

"LIGHT, LIGHT! DEAD AHEAD!" Harry is screaming his head off. Starboard engine cuts out and the plane immediately yaws to port, but Jim fights it back around. They are at 2,000 feet and descending when six lights in three pairs show up directly ahead, and the port engine stalls. All is quiet except for the rush of air past the windscreen. The plane glides like the rock Jim described earlier; they get the chance to land quietly, as if the plane suddenly disappeared from the sky as far as the Japanese are concerned.

Down, down, still 200 knots. Jim pulls back on the yoke like he's lifting weights and gets some response since there is still enough wind speed to provide a bit of control. The first bounce of wheels on grass is just before the first pair of lights. The second bounce is after the last pair, and the third settles so the tail wheel comes down; and Jim stands on the brakes with the plane sliding and shimmying. He manages to stay aligned and skids to a stop. Jim looks out from the cockpit window and sees nothing but space. Rising in his seat he looks down and there is nothing there, probably at least a 1,000 foot drop. He sits down and pees his pants, finally.

A set of lights comes racing up to port; there is banging on the port cargo door. Harry opens to see a bespectacled face, beaming at him and yelling at the top of his lungs, "WAHOO!"

"Wahoo, what the hell kind of Chinese is that?" says Harry.

"It's the kind you learn at a Stanford University pep rally! Welcome to Nanking West! I'm Cho Han, your host and guide for the evening. Care for a little scotch and some fuel? In that order?"

By then Jim is at the door, crotch soaking, shaking a bit and gazing at the figure in the doorway. "You got it right, scotch first, then gas. But someone is going to have to get us back from the edge of eternity out there since we have no fuel left to maneuver and there isn't room anyway."

"They are hooking up to your tail strut as we speak, and will be pulling you back shortly. Care to join me? We are safe for at least two hours. I have lookouts placed strategically to warn us of visitors. Come on!" Jim and Harry climb down, Jim asking for a fresh pair of trousers, which magically appear. The waist is fine, the legs about four inches too short. It's not a beauty contest.

As Jim is changing, Cho is driving back to the far end of the field where there are several fuel drums and a hand pumping mechanism. The plane is being unceremoniously dragged back from the edge, slowly and carefully, to avoid damaging the tail's strut. It arrives just as Jim is handing out his tin cup for a second dose of nerve medicine. It's not Scottish, but perfectly acceptable. The plane is stopped about 20 yards in front of where Jim and Harry are being entertained by their Stanford alumnus host, who is peppering them with a thousand questions in between providing a thumbnail sketch of his resume'. He was at Stanford studying mathematics when Japan invaded China. He endured the ordeal of very little information coming out of the conflict while trying to maintain his studies. Finally he doubled up on his course load, graduated a year early with a Master's of Science and came home to Nanking. His parents had fled to the west, but he agreed to help the logistics of Chiang Kai-shek's republican army and so was in place for tonight's adventure. He is still obviously flying high, buzzing like the free end of a live wire.

Jim is truly impressed, for once, and gives well-deserved praise to Cho for his code and efforts at assisting a safe landing. Although he and Harry have no gifts to leave in appreciation, they say they will be sure to mention his efforts, explicitly, to Chennault who will assuredly pass them on to Chiang. Cho is beaming as Jim and Harry climb back into the plane and prime the engines before trying to start them. After much coughing and sputtering, first port starts, then starboard and Jim wastes no time warming up before he is pushing the throttles far forward, picking up speed, and heading for the drop at the end of the runway. Luckily the wind had come up and there was sufficient lift about 100 yards before the precipice. The tail comes up and the wheels come off the ground just as there is no more ground. Jim and Harry look at one another, shrug and head west. When the river can't be seen any more, they change course to the southwest with full tanks and a snootful of fine Chinese liquor, just enough to stop the shakes. Soon, the adrenalin is gone, Jim's head begins to nod and he calls Harry to take the wheel for awhile. "Harry! Take the wheel, asshole. I gotta get some rest!" Harry is sound asleep, with his head resting on the side window, mouth half open, drooling down his chin. Comatose.

"Shit!" Grind it out, grind it out. Push up against the straps, sing (a voice that would keep anyone awake), pinch his arm, cheek, inside his thigh. He's going to look like he was in a fight. Finally, he can't take it anymore and whacks Harry on the left shoulder, knocking his head harder into the window. Harry jerks awake. "What, what? Enemy fire? What!"

"Won't need enemy fire to take us down if I don't get some sleep.

"Can't take it anymore. Your turn. Take the controls, NOW!"

Jim lets go, turns his head toward the window and is gone. Harry has control into the airfield, another four hours. When he lands, Jim does not move, make a sound, or otherwise acknowledge he is alive. Harry has to shake him awake, which causes a jerk and Jim's head bangs the window and generates a marvelous string of vulgarity, one that Harry has not experienced before. "We're home, bud. Get your ass out."

Jim rubs his eyes and his head where the knot is rising, and unbuckles his harness. They both slowly exit the cockpit to the port cargo door, open it to blazing sunlight. The heat is stifling and the ground welcome. A dust cloud announces Chennault's dash from the tower to the plane. "Well done, chaps. Well done indeed. Now for the debrief. In my office in 10 minutes, if you please."

"We'll be there sometime after 10 a.m. tomorrow," Jim said. "Have the structure checked for holes and the struts for damage. Drain and refill the tanks since there might be material fouling the fuel from the last refill. Landing silently works, sort of. That's it for now." And Jim, pulling on Harry's shoulder, leads them toward the barracks, Chennault sputtering something about lack of dismissal and insubordination that Jim does not hear, nor care about.

———— ✦ ————

"So, that's when you got your DC-3 and skipped town, eh?" Tony is incredulously focused on Jim's face, a look that says something like, "This is total B.S."

"Couple of days later. I eventually had to debrief, but Chennault could pound sand awhile, as far as I was concerned, when I fell out of that plane. He got his Shanghai job done, I am sure Chiang got the credit, and I was exhausted. Gave the debrief about 10 p.m.

that night. Let him know that in extreme cases the no-power landing works, but it is nuttier than my mom's fruit cake to try it. A few good men out there in the wilderness, one less after that trip since Ben got his ticket punched.

"But, yes, I did hold him to his agreement, and he kept it. The plane I got was not what you might call among the best in the stable, but had some useful hours left in it. DC-3's go forever, sort of like flying Model T's. I figured, with the war heating up, there would be financial opportunities elsewhere in the area that did not require high wire walking to achieve success. Funny that, eh? Irony's a bitch."

"So, how did you get to the Philippines?"

"Wasn't easy. I wanted to go straight to Hanoi and then Manila, the best route it seemed to me, but things were heating up in Vietnam. So I went to Luang Prabang instead. Fuel cost was a whore's redemption there, but I was able to fill up and then dodge my way out of southeast Asia and over the South China Sea to Manila. This town is quite the enterprising Mecca, I'd say. Wasn't long before I found that Micronesia had things to offer the Philippines, including people who wanted to get here, and hard goods sell well there, all with U.S. dollars as the medium of exchange. All it needed was a way to transport the exchanges. Worked well for about eight months. Would have had quite a nest egg built up in another year or so if dirty gas hadn't caught me."

"And a half dozen passengers and your co-pilot, eh?"

There is a long pause then a simple growl, "Yeah."

"You packed?" Tony looks around the cell and realizes he's just made a joke.

Jim sits up quite straight, "Why?"

"We got a boat for your trip outta here. It leaves on the evening tide, heading south."

"Today? That's better than good, it'll get you to heaven, I'm sure. But I got things to do before I get on any boat. Why a boat?"

"Planes are full, and busy with the hullaballoo to the west. Things have heated up in China since you left, and it looks like they will head our way in the near future. So any planes available are being used by MacArthur. A boat will get you where you need to go in a few weeks. You got here on one, what the fuck you worried about? In a hurry?"

"Once it is time to go I want to get gone. But I need to get to town ASAP to the First Commercial Bank if I am leaving today. Can you get me there? Also I need to get to South Manila after the bank. Some last-minute business to take care of there as well."

"Do I look like a taxi service? We can get you to the bank, but wandering around Manila during the day, particularly South Manila, will take us past departure time for the boat, and you do NOT want to miss that boat. I can keep the assholes off your case a little longer, but this deal is not to their liking. No bureaucrat likes getting pushed around and you've just about used up your allotment of luck on this one. A lot of your story sounds like bullshit, to tell you the truth, but something must have happened to have Chennault contacting MacArthur to spring your ass and keep it under wraps. So, benefit of the doubt is in your favour, but cruising overtime in South Manila during high traffic time is not, especially when you've got a boat to catch."

"OK, OK. Keep your pants dry. So I'll give you a small package and an address and you'll get it delivered, right?"

"What's in the package?"

"None of your goddamn business, but I can make it worth your while to get it safely delivered, and it's not illegal."

"Right, I'll do the delivery, and you'll be on your way before 6 p.m. So let me collect these papers. Shit, this is a hell of a story. Ain't goin' nowhere, though."

Jim collects his toothbrush, Tony collects his handwritten notes for later transcription and calls the guard. The observation port slides open and a yellow eye peers in accompanied by a grunt. "We are ready to leave, open the door," Tony says.

The port slides shut and footsteps start receding down the hallway. "What the fuck! Hey, asshole! You just got yourself a short tour in the basement if this door is not open in exactly five seconds; five, four, three, two..." Scratch, the handle descends and the door opens in. Mighty Joe is standing there, truncheon and all, twice as tall as Tony and weighing three times as much. The glare would freeze a boiling pot.

"Get the fuck outta my way, low life. You are definitely messing with the wrong soldier. With me, to my left, march, now! Jim, fall in behind!"

The little armada wends its way to the front of the building where a sergeant is just climbing up onto a stool behind the reception counter. Tony marches in, erect and face flushed bright red. "Sergeant!

The sergeant looks toward Tony, grins and looks away.

"Get your sorry ass off that stool, before I bust you to PLO, permanent latrine orderly!"

The sergeant slides down more insolent than maybe he intended and Tony mentions the name of the officer of the day, takes the phone and dials 110, listens for a minute and says, "Arizza," puts down the phone and faces the sergeant. "Get this piece of shit up against that wall now," indicating Mighty Joe.

The sergeant looks at Mighty Joe, looks at Tony and smiles, "You gotta be kidding."

Tony smiles, and whispers, "No, I am not."

The sergeant is about to suggest to Mighty Joe that he move to the wall, when a major enters the room with three military police officers, each the size of Mighty Joe, or larger.

"Captain Arizza, nice to see you. How can I help?"

"I suspect, even in penal institutions operated under auspices of the U.S. military, insubordination is still rarely tolerated, am I correct?"

"Of course. Is there a problem here?"

"Your sergeant seems to think orders are recommendations, and this employee seems to think that cooperation is optional, that corporal punishment is the order of the day. This gentleman has been held at the pleasure of General MacArthur while arrangements for his repatriation to the States were being made. Examine his left arm please."

The bruise is nicely green now, from just above his elbow to the wrist. "Truncheons are necessary equipment for guards, but to be used sparingly. And when the guard outweighs the guest by at least 150 pounds, probably not all that necessary, wouldn't you agree?"

"Hmmm…"

"In addition, Sergeant Alexander here seems to feel that military discipline is a requirement for others, not himself. Sitting in the presence of an officer, refusing an order and slovenly demeanor are all outside my experience in the U.S. Army, and I would think that perhaps a short refresher course in the necessities of command structure might be in order. However, I am certainly not here to run your shop, but when the general arrives tomorrow for inspection of the premises, I think it would be to your benefit if the sergeant were elsewhere and your miscreant warder somewhere below street level. Good day, Major. Off to the embassy for a bit of business."

Tony and Jim exit as the major is saying, "Inspection? What inspection?! Smith, take over the desk. Taylor and Bliss, escort our new guests below and make them uncomfortable."

Mighty Joe does not look happy as his truncheon is removed, and the sergeant is ashen as the two are marched down the hall to the basement.

"Guess that takes care of a couple of hanging threads, don't you think, Jim? Now to get your paperwork in order and you to the bank. We'll have to hustle a bit since the bank will be closed for siesta in an hour and we definitely need the embassy first."

Tony's military green painted car is sweltering in the tropical heat, but Jim could care less as they hit 50 mph straight out of the prison grounds, onto the causeway and into the center of town. The breeze is wet and glorious on Jim's face. He even leans his head out the passenger window, his hair blowing back from his head, eyes tight shut, smiling ear to ear.

The embassy stay is mercifully short; wheels seem to have been greased ahead of their arrival. A new passport only needs his picture inserted and his signature, exit permit is already typed and signed, as are his boarding papers for the freighter Eastern Star under Captain Julio Vargas, departing six p.m. from Pier 18.

The bank is a bit more tedious, the ceiling fans ineffective, making the sweat soaked paperwork difficult to sign without soaking it. The manager accompanies Jim to a small office where a bundle of U.S. currency notes is stacked on a desk. Jim takes his time counting, verifying, and then asking for a small parcel, large enough to hold $10,000 in $20 notes. The parcel arrives, is packed and Jim addresses it to Juanita Alvarez, 800A Menendez Plaza, South Manila. He then takes an envelope and places 20 $50 notes inside with Tony's name on the front, and leaves the room, soaking wet, but smiling.

Back in the car, Jim hands Tony the parcel. "The address is right there, and no one gets it unless she absolutely identifies herself to you. Picture I.D. is best and she has one, I know." Handing him the envelope,

"This is for you. I know you'll get the parcel to her. Now how about a glass down by the pier and some appropriate travelling clothes along the way?"

"You got it, buddy. I know where we get the clothes."

"And I know where to get the glass of cold whatever - the International Club, just up the street from Pier 18."

The clothes are light, airy and comfortable. Jim actually looks pretty good with his full beard and new togs. He has been thinking about the beard and decided to leave it. It grew by necessity and neglect since he has had such little access to toilet facilities; but now that it is there, except for the itch, he thinks it just might stay.

The International Club is perfect, with open windows everywhere, ceiling fans almost making it comfortable in the humid heat. And the ice machines work great. First, a toast to life outside of prison facilities using Johnny Walker Black Label, then onto more serious discussions, having liberated a bottle of locally produced red wine. The table is a substantial size, right near the door facing the wharf. The sea breeze drifts in with its mixture of diesel fuel, salt mist, dead fish and the distant raucous clamor of dock workers tending the ships.

The Eastern Star is three ships down the pier with only her mast showing behind the two in front of her. Jim has already quickly checked her out and was pleasantly surprised at the paucity of rust on her superstructure, or even the hull. Maybe the trip won't be that bad after all, but five weeks is five weeks, and even a large ship can feel cramped after awhile. At least it always has to Jim.

Now, sitting and letting the heat slide around him, the sweat trickling down under his arms and off his nose, he is as content as he has been in several years. "What are you thinking?" asks Tony.

"Actually, nothing. Absolutely nothing. It's odd because I have not had that experience for years, come to think about it. The last time I had this mindlessly restful state, it was as hot as here, but dry, very dry, in the high Mexican desert. I was riding a horse, enjoying the heat, rocking away toward a distant peak across nothingness. It was very calming and I had not a thought. Wonder if meditation is active brain relaxation?"

"What will you do back in the States?"

"Probably go find Daryl F. Zanuck and sell him a screenplay."

"You have got to be the weirdest son-of-a-bitch I ever ran across. What makes you think you can write a movie script, or sell it?"

"Look Tony, you have one shot at this bit of time. No others. Why sit around wondering if you can do it, or if it can be done? Just do it! What happens if that effort fails? If it is dangerous, you might die. I just came close, a couple of times, close enough to be ready for NEXT! If you die, you go out doing what you wanted, the way you wanted. Most of the time, all you lose is a little effort, and you always learn something. So, you're smarter than before, did what you wanted, and are ready for NEXT. You never lose giving it a try."

Jim continues his monologue: "Say you bet on the stock market, like the assholes in '29, and lose your shirt. Move to where it is warm! People who allow themselves to get stuck always lose more than anyone else. I don't get stuck. Not yet anyway. Sometimes it takes a little help from your friends. Thanks, mate. But I know for a fact that people are more willing to help out someone who is trying and putting it on the line than someone who lays back and waits for it to happen to him. I've seen it, many times.

"So, first stop, once I hit the beach, it's Zanuck's office, probably with a first draft in hand. Lots of down time riding a boat for five weeks. I'll let you know what happens if you're around. Poste restante in L.A. will get to me. So if you're gone from here, send me your new contact information to the L.A. post office. I'll use the embassy to update you. They'll forward, won't they, if you're already gone?"

"Yeah, they usually do. There are rumblings of needing more pilots soon and I may have to go active service again before long. That makes it trickier to find me, as you can imagine, but still possible. So, you saying you think keeping in touch is something you want to do?"

"Look, you pulled my ass out of the fire this time. Without you, I'd have been in there at least a week longer," Wide grin. "Anyway, shared trials cement friendships. We are both flyers, we seem to understand one another easily, and everyone can use a friend now and then. So, stay in touch, and so will I."

"Five-thirty, so better make it down the pier, right?" Tony starts to pay the bill, but Jim puts his hand over Tony's and puts a $20 bill on the bar.

"Keep the change, pilgrim." The barman looks at the bill, and at the back of Jim's head as he and Tony make their way out the wide open door in front of where they had been sitting. The barman smiles as he opens the till and makes the change.

Boarding the boat is uneventful, with one small canvas bag with the few clothes he purchased during the day. He waves over the rail to Tony and then is shown his bunk, seriously smaller than the prison cell he just left. At least he can leave when he wants. He is a guest, but shows his new seaman's book to the captain. In the midst of the bustle of getting under way, the captain says he might be able to use him from time to time to cover a shift for some of the crew, particularly in a storm.

Departing Manila is like dodging cars at sea, but the tugs make it possible to avoid collisions and the trip south is under way. It turns out it is a milk run, stopping at every port big enough to handle the draft of the ship. So Jim gets to see the whole of the Philippines' west coast; days blend into one another as ports slip behind, the coast rarely out of site to port. Jim assists with unloading at a couple stops, but is mostly adrift around the boat, or sitting in the crew mess with pencil and paper sketching ideas, themes, partial plots for stories that might show up on a screen. As he starts another idea, the boat's horn blasts two quick reports and he realizes Zamboanga must be coming into view.

On deck he leans on the port rail and examines the green shrouded mountains that seem to dive directly into the sea, the native fishing boats with their own individual colorful sails, shifting back and forth between the ship and the shore. He peers around to the starboard side of the masthead and, sure enough, there are scores more, like butterflies skimming the sea. Tugs are making their way from the port, which is still out of sight, pushing bow waves that rock the fishing boats. As they join the Eastern Star, each hoots once, with a return from the ship and all three boats begin the slow turn to port. As they come around a headland, the low-lying city, smoke and all, hovers into view. The breeze keeps the sweat at an acceptable level, but really caused havoc whenever he tried to write on deck. Slowly, the ship makes its way directly into the port, the wharf parallel to the shore. Jim is fascinated with the scene, probably the most impressive he has had all the way down the coast. The boat is eased into the berth, the lines off to shore and the gangway lowered to the pier. Jim is standing at the head of the gangway, looking toward the pier, and his eyes follow the line from the end of the gangway down the causeway connecting the pier to the shore and continuing as a street right into the center of the city. The whole land side picture is hazy from smoke and dust, but the composite is really stunning.

"You will be here when I return from harbor control, I am sure. The look in your eye I have seen many times, particularly here. It is beautiful, is it not?" Captain Vargas gives Jim a friendly stern expression with the comment, leaving no doubt that he means it. His instructions are clear in the paperwork accompanying the passenger; no departure from the ship until California.

Jim gives his most ingratiating smile and reassures the captain that his intentions are pure, and "When is departure from Zamboanga?"

"Tomorrow morning, 9:30."

"I'll be here, but it is a bit like Tantalus, you know. Dangling this luscious bunch of sweet grapes under my nose and forbidding me eating."

"That is the reason for the reminder. I see the desire. It is right there on your bearded face, but the papers leave no room for interpretation. We go, you stay on board."

"Aye, aye, Captain," Jim says with a bit of a lefthanded salute, and the captain descends the gangway and is gone.

It is really hot. He is in the shade of the mast and stack, but it blocks some of the breeze and he sweats just standing there. His beard is starting to itch, which starts him thinking. He moves aft and gives the crew a hand with some of the cargo off loading, and when that is finished, the crew disappears below to change and go ashore. He returns to his viewing station by the mast, which is now in full sun and causes him to shift closer to the stack where there is even less breeze. By now he is soaked in sweat and decides he really should at least rinse off and try for a cooler location, perhaps a net hammock further aft, with a book.

The splash of water from the bucket, while not cold, is cool enough to be rewarding. A second bucketful and he towel dries, putting on dry clothes: shorts, sleeveless shirt, canvas deck shoes. His hair is tousled and uncombed, but there is no one to criticize, and he likely would tell them to kiss off anyway. He methodically collects a few items, sharp scissors, straight razor and strop, shaving cup, soap and brush, and puts them in his room, with a full bucket of water. Finally, he takes up his book and heads aft to the hammock he has placed in as much breeze as there is and in shade that will not leave as the day progresses. Lying curved on his back with elbows outside the edges of the hammock, small pillow under his head, he is as comfortable as he has been in years. Sweat still trickles down from his armpits and off his elbows when they are down. The perspiration tends to run down into his eyes, except when the small hand towel tied around his head catches most of it. As he is reading Hemingway, one of his least favourite authors, he is concentrating little on the prose, and much more on his plans. Tomorrow is to be a big day.

Evening meal finished, washing up completed, Jim makes his excuses to the crew that is around and retires to his cabin and bunk. After locking the door, he strips and begins the arduous task of getting rid of the beard, scissors first, then razor, stropping almost between strokes since the beard is so coarse. He hums out of tune and finally finishes, collecting all the hair in paper bags and ditching the bags out the portal. Now that he feels bald as a cue ball, he extracts clothes from his wardrobe that he has yet to wear on the ship, an off-white shirt with matching twill trousers and a ball cap, laying them on the back of the metal chair along the opposite wall and goes to bed in his single bunk, no clothes, no sheets, no noise.

Dozing, he does not react to the door opening quietly and a head peeking around the corner. The head gives a slight nod and retreats. Even in the twilight zone, Jim realizes the captain is checking up on him. It makes the adventure a little more intriguing.

CHAPTER 3

Hello Zamboanga

Next morning, Jim is uncustomarily lazy, lies in bed until 7:30 a.m., missing the crew's breakfast. Lying there, he hears the preparations for departure and gets up when he is fairly sure the final scramble for last-minute items from shore is under way. His canvas bag is packed and on the floor, he is into his clothes, dons the cap and is out the door, bag and all. The exit from the forecabins to the deck is 10 feet down the walkway, and he is out the hatch with the cap on and his canvas bag on his right shoulder. The gangway is directly ahead and he makes his way to the rail, down the gangway and keeps walking straight down the pier toward the wall at the edge of the port. As he reaches the gateway, the marine horn on the boat sounds, but he does not flinch, turn or acknowledge it in any way, just keeps walking at a moderate but steady pace.

Just after the gateway, the pier becomes Calle Voluntario; Zamboanga at least is still using the Spanish street names. A block later the customs house is on his left, where he delivers his passport. Holding his breath, in case Manila has put a hold on it, he looks around at the colonial décor, an interesting combination of Spanish architecture and American signage.

Bam! The stamp comes down on his passport, the clerk smiles broadly and salutes him, saying, "Welcome to Zamboanga," and Jim is out to door. Staring at him across the street is a monumental building, the provincial building, with the provincial offices on the second floor and the first floor entrance shaded by sidewalk café umbrellas. Looks inviting enough to coax him there, even though he is still a stone's throw from the boat. A glance to his right confirms the lines are now being cast off the shore, the boat slowly eases away from the pier, and the tugs place themselves to escort the Eastern Star to the open sea. The first smile of the day spreads across Jim's face, knowing that Vargas won't turn himself around to come back and collect the miscreant. Question is whether he will do anything to cause the forfeiture of the fare he received to take Jim to California. Since it was found money for the captain, Jim is guessing he is safe.

Across the street, up the stairs leading to the provincial building, he claims an outside table, bag onto the ground under the table and waits for the wait staff to notice him. It is 9:45, hot, he is sweating in the trousers, and happier than he has been in a long time. He watches the traffic. Mostly military vehicles with a smattering of other motorized traffic, and lots of animal-drawn carts, plus bicycles and motorcycles in front of his table and along the corner across street.

The young Filipino man who shuffles up to the table looks carefully at Jim while Jim glances at him. The white outfit he is wearing is destined to be much dirtier soon, given the dust in the air from unpaved streets and the dense traffic. "Can I help you?" asks the young fellow.

"I need to eat breakfast. Can you tell me what you have?" Jim's gaze is now completely on the waiter, making him nervously shuffle his feet in front of him. He hands Jim a tattered menu with breakfast on one side and lunch on the other. "Three eggs cooked any way you can cook them, bread, coffee and juice, if you have it."

"Juice?" responds the waiter.

Jim makes a calculated guess, "Jugo".

"Ah, si senor," and he leaves.

Looking at the entrance to the building, Jim realizes he desperately needs the toilet, and leaves his bag under the table to go find it. Luckily the loo is immediately to the right as he enters, and the smile expands on his face. Returning to the entrance he notices a bulletin board with public notices. One stands out, from the municipal administrator's office, with a thin black border around it.

Wanted immediately, manager for the Mindanao Herald, Southern Philippine's leading chronicle. Apply at the reception. Fluency in English required, experience with writing for public consumption an advantage.

Rubbing his naked chin, Jim turns away from the notice board and starts for the outdoor cafe'. The waiter sees him coming toward the door and excitedly approaches him saying, "Sir, sir, your bag."

Jim notices the young man holding his canvas bag out to him and the worried look on his face. Taking the bag, Jim replies, "Is there something wrong?"

"I see you leave this bag under the table, and that is dangerous, for many here would take it. I take it and keep it for you until you come back."

"Thank you for your help," says Jim with a large grin. "What's your name?"

"I am Antonio Amad Fali, but most call me Tony."

"Well, Antonio Amad Fali, what sort of family name is that you have?"

"My father is Hussein Fali. My mother is Catholic and my father Muslim. I am given one name from each."

"That makes you different, doesn't it?"

"Very different. I have no friends. My father and mother do not have many friends. Our family has no friends. Maybe that is why we stay close together."

"If you have no friends, and your parents have no friends, how did you get this job?"

"I ask the boss to try me, and I work for no money for one month, and then the next month. I work every day very hard and now I get paid for working. Most of the other workers do not like to talk to me, but my boss does not let them hit me anymore because I work too hard and the customers like me." A crooked smile crosses his face as he finishes his small speech. He looks up to see the cook waving frantically in his direction. Tony hurries away just as Jim is about to ask another question.

Jim has his breakfast and sits and ponders the conversation awhile, then walks to the counter and pays his tab. The boss, with his somewhat white apron wrapped around his considerable midsection smiles as he takes his U.S. currency and gives Jim U.S. coins as change. Just as Jim starts to leave, he stops and turns back to the counter saying, "I really enjoyed my time at your table, largely because you have such a good waiter. I will be back if Tony is still here. Thank you."

The rotund fellow behind the counter waves and responds with a broad smile, saying, "Adios." Jim responds likewise, realizing that it seems Spanish is more prominent here than in Manila, or at least their version of Spanish. There are still many phrases he cannot understand, but he is getting more than he is missing. He likes the familiar feeling.

As he is making his way toward the street, he stops then reverses direction, entering the building from the veranda where he had eaten. Half a dozen steps further into the building is the reception desk referred to in the notice, with no one present. A silver call bell, the kind you tap with your palm, sits on the counter and Jim hits it firmly once, loudly ringing. Nothing happens, no one appears, people pass behind him with a glance his way, but no one from behind the counter. Bing! He hits it again, harder. Nothing. A fellow in one of the formal barong Tagalog shirts comes up to him and says that the hour is too close to noon for anyone to answer the bell. Someone will likely answer it around 2p.m. Jim gives one of his deepest growls, with a half smile, and thanks the grey- haired, stately man. "Do you know where the office of the Mindanao Herald might be?"

"Why, of course, it is at the top of these stairs, to the right," the gentleman says. "The office is small, but I know someone is there now because I just left there."

"Do you work for the paper, by chance?"

"No, dear me. My business advertises regularly in the paper and I had discussions with the editor. Poor fellow. I am afraid he is a bit over his head with trying to run the entire operation nearly by himself. I am not so sure the paper will survive if there is not someone who will take the reins of management."

"Well, that is actually why I was using the bell. I want to apply for the manager job, and the notice states to apply here at the reception desk, but it is difficult if no one is here. I'll just go up and apply there at the office."

"Be cautious, young man, as the editor serves at the discretion of the governor and the governor is in love with his rules and regulations. I admit that the paper is important to our community here in Zamboanga, and I think the governor has the central government send money to help the paper with a subsidy, keeping a portion for himself, of course. But he does not take so much money that it will make too much difference to him if the paper folds. The editor serves only with the permission of the governor."

"Thanks for the background information. Not sure if it can help me, but we'll see. My name is Jim, Jim Tuck, by the way." He reaches forward and receives a handshake for his effort.

"Julio Matunkup. I have a bit of a farm north of here, northwest of the barracks, Pettit Barracks. I believe many of your compatriots stay there. You are American, are you not?"

"Yes, as a matter of fact, but have not been in the States for awhile. I was on my way back to California when my boat stopped here, and I must admit this is the loveliest port I have seen on my way south from Manila. So, I thought perhaps I might stay awhile. There will be other boats, I am sure. Say, do you know if Zamboanga has an airfield?"

"Why, most certainly it has an airfield. We are not totally without modern amenities in this remote area. As a matter of fact, the only three ways of departing our fair city are by airplane, boat or on foot. The roads, of which you see a few outside, do not extend past the headlands, where the mountains enter the sea, perhaps 30 miles on the east side of the peninsula and 15 miles on the west side. No roads pass the mountains in the interior, so we are a bit on our own here. The airfield is a very valuable part of our existence, as you see."

"Thanks again. Perhaps we will meet again."

"In Zamboanga, it would be most likely. Good luck in your application, but I am not quite certain of your success." Julio turns and walks out the main entrance without a glance backward, white hair reflecting the sun, as does his Barong Tagalog.

With another glance toward the reception desk, confirming its vacancy, Jim casually walks to the notice board and takes down the yellowed newspaper management notice and heads to the stairs. One flight, and a landing then a turn to the left for the next flight, he arrives at the next floor. He turns back to look down at the lobby/reception area with the indoor restaurant tables; he notices the vacant desk, the open main entrance, and feels the warm breeze as the air flows past him into the hallway behind. It feels good, even if warm.

Turning on the tile floor, he immediately notes the open door with the following logo printed on it: Mindanao Herald/ Augustus Merryweather, Editor. Walking through the door, Jim sees the usual reception counter - vacant - a swinging gate to the rear of the office and a hall from behind the counter into an office area.

Putting his bag on the floor, Jim taps the call bell, same as the one downstairs, hoping for a different result. Just as he is about to raise his voice and call, a slender, as in practically wasted, man of indeterminate age comes from the rear, slowly advancing into the reception area. His emaciated look is enhanced by clothes that are at least one size too large, his tousled sandy grey hair dangling messily into his eyes. His eyes peek out from behind large horn-rimmed glasses that are in danger of falling off his nose. His slightly stooped tall-man's gait makes his arms swing slightly side to side as he approaches the counter. There, he gazes down at Jim and places his huge hands on the counter, fingers splayed. He stares without blinking into Jim's face. A very deep rumble comes from his chest as his question emerges: "Help you in some way?"

Jim stands a bit straighter, trying to make up a bit of the six- inch difference in their heights and offers the notice. "You're Merryweather, I presume. You won't need this downstairs anymore. I'm the one taking the job. Just arrived, saw the notice and realized immediately this is our lucky day. Jim Tuck is the name, by the way. Wrote for the L.A. Times, a bit for The New York Times, and think Zamboanga is the place for me, for awhile anyway. Advertising and promotion are my strong suits so you won't need to worry about satisfying the customers anymore, I'll take care of it. With a monopoly on the publishing scene here in Zamboanga, no reason you shouldn't make a mint off this enterprise, especially with me pulling in the advertising. When do I start? Got a place I could stay a day or two while I'm settling down? Quick man, let's not waste too much time sorting details."

"I'm sorry, my young fellow, what did you say your name was?"

"Jim, short for James Tuck, recently of Manila, China for a short while, then L.A. before that. Bit of a vagabond right now, but this place looks like it has good potential and might be a good place to sit a bit."

"Well, Mr. Tuck, this enterprise has been publishing in Zamboanga for 40 years. I am the second editor, the first dying with his boots on, so to speak. I've been here for 10 years now, and I can assure you there are no fortunes to be made in the Zamboanga newspaper business. I can also assure you that there is a protocol to obtaining a position with the paper, a protocol that does not allow for instantaneous acceptance of the first, second or twelfth applicant. Your application will be considered in the order with which it has been received."

"That's fine, how many are ahead of me?"

"That is, of course, a matter for management to care for and not for public consumption. But I can tell you that you might hear within a week, 10 days at the most, whether your application has met with success."

"Not good enough, fella. Look, this notice is as yellow as a drunkard's eyes, been hanging down there for an age. You actually need me more than I need you, but I fancy the idea of using my writing and imaginative talents. So we have a match. The likelihood that someone better qualified will walk in here in the next year or two is somewhere between slim and none. How much are you paying?"

"I do not think we are quite at the salary negotiation stage yet, do you?"

"Tell you what, don't pay me a dime. Take me on commission only. I get 20 percent of the value of every ad placed with the paper from this day forward. Give me a place to stay and the 20 percent and it's a deal."

Augustus' eyebrows go up, he straightens a bit, and furrows his brow as he begins his calculations. "Come in the back."

Jim picks up his bag and pushes through the gate to follow the measured progress Augustus makes toward the last office on the right. The door is open and they walk into a room with a view of the scene in front of the building. His office overlooks the terrace with the café, the street, and the ocean and port to the left. It is a beautiful view, but the clutter covering the desk, furniture and floor suggests Augustus does not have much opportunity to enjoy it. Shoving some of the stacks of paper off the only chair in his office, Augustus has Jim sit down. He passes him some paper, a pencil and the information Julio Matunkup left behind for advertising. "This was just left for inclusion in the next paper. Write it up, one-column width, five-inch length. Give it to me when you're done."

Jim takes the two sheets of paper and scans the details of the farm products. Sensing that export is a large part of Matunkup property business, he launches into extolling the enterprise, the quality products and benefits to Zamboanga society of the Matunkup farms.

Looking again, he realizes the Matunkup farm business is a major player in the business life of Zamboanga, tinkers with a few phrases and gives the final product to Augustus just as he walks back in the door. "What? Is the assignment too much for you?" asks Augustus.

"Not quite. Piece of cake. Done."

Augustus takes the handwritten paper, checks the word count, then the content, sits and smiles. Then he projects his hand and says, "Actually, the name is Gus. Not too many people use it, but it will be good for us, I think. Be here 6:30 a.m. tomorrow. We start early since thinking in the heat gets difficult. I accept your conditions, and will even start you with a list of contacts. Your first appointment will be with Mr. Matunkup to confirm the copy for his ad. It is different to what he is used to from this paper, so it would be good to make sure it is acceptable to him. As you might guess, he is a major contributor to the paper's finances, so we keep him as happy as possible. Transportation will be provided to the Matunkup place. See the tailor at this address and get a proper baro to wear for tomorrow. I'll pay for that one."

"Thanks. I go by Jim. I'll be here at 6:30. What is a baro?"

"Barong Tagalog. It is traditional Philippine formal wear, nontucked shirt with no lapels and light, to compensate for the weather. We are only six degrees north of the equator, you realize. Tell Wang Chi the tailor I sent you. Until tomorrow," and he shakes Jim's hand at the counter.

"Oh," Jim says while holding Gus's hand, "Do you know an inexpensive place to stay while I am getting settled in?"

"Talk to Wang. If anyone knows, he will. See you in the morning."

"OK. Where's Wang's place"

"Villa Lobos, about three blocks from here. Out the front door, turn right to the corner, right again two blocks and left on Villa Lobos. It's on your left with scissors hanging over the door. He is open late, not to worry."

"6:30 then, and thanks. Oh, you should consider getting a copy boy. Additional personnel would lighten your load considerably, make it actually pleasant to be here all day."

Gus looks askance at Jim with a wry smile, then says, "Jim, that's a great idea for a place that actually makes money. This paper, as you can guess by now, doesn't."

"But it will, it will, and best to be ready when the work hits the fan. And I just happen to have a name for you to consider. Since you are not paying me out of the till, just commission, why not put some of the savings toward the copy boy, and Tony Fali, downstairs, is just the go-getter you need for the job. Go get a cup of coffee and see if I'm not right. Ask specifically for Tony, ok?" Gus just stands there, bemused, then nods his head and Jim is out the door.

Time to sweat a bit. Midday is no time to be moving around in this tropical paradise, but business is business. "Gotta get a decent hat. I'll die in this if I don't." Sure enough, right around the corner of the building is a cart with hats, lots of hats: camposinos, fedoras, skimmers, all straw. He picks one with a nice wide brim, pays the smiling woman in her colorful wrapped skirt and vest top and is off to Wang's. It is still hot, but he is no longer squinting, his forehead is not tight. It just feels better, even though he is soaking wet from the inside out.

Some of the buildings are more than five stories, most are two or three; everything is densely packed. The city is squeezed between mountains and the sea. Villa Lobos is a street populated mostly with artisan shops and commercial suppliers. The walkway on either side is about five feet wide, many of the shops have a roof over the walkway, and there is a bit of a curb separating the sidewalk from the dirt street. The air is reasonably thick with dust, smoke and mosquitoes. If they are out this much in the daytime, what are they like at night? The flies are almost friendly.

Up ahead he spots the scissors hanging over an open double door, the right side shut. "Wonder what color this place was when the paint was new?" The boards are mostly bare, the putty around the windows is either cracked or gone. It looks like a good wind would blow the panes right out of the frames. Stepping onto the bare wood floor causes the glass in the front window to rattle ever so gently. The room is small, with material in neat stacks behind a bare counter that extends wall to wall. Windows in each wall as well as the front. Lots of windows. "How does this guy keep from getting burgled daily?" Jim walks to the counter and spots the ever-present silver call bell, gives it a tap and slouches in the expectation that there is likely no one coming. Siesta time, remember?

Immediately, the skinniest man he has ever encountered emerges through the curtained doorway and Jim straightens again. "What?" is the entire sentence from the thin apparition.

"I am working at the newspaper. Gus told me to come here and get a Barong Tagalog made by you and that you might know where I can find a place to stay while I get settled here in Zamboanga."

"What!"

Hmmm, this may not be as easy as I thought. "Do you speak English?"

"Engrish, yes, yes, yes. What?!"

"Gus?"

A huge smile, then flapping hands waving him to a seat by the right wall at a small table. "Gus! Yes, yes, yes. Sit. Tea!"

Off he goes just as Jim is trying to say he does not need hot tea with the temperature near 100, but Wang is long gone before anything comes out of Jim's mouth. He sits by an open window in the shade of the room, a bit of breeze ruffling the brim of his hat.

How the tea arrives so quickly is still a mystery, but there it is with Wang hovering over Jim as he samples his cup. The tea is actually delicious, very mild, the color of weak horse piss. Jim smiles, Wang smiles, Jim smacks his lips appreciatively, which nearly sends Wang over the moon. Then Jim puts his cup down and points to his soggy shirt saying "Baro, want baro."

Wang gives a small joyful skip and jump. Jim says, "Gus pays."

Wang gives two jumps and pulls Jim out of the chair. "God, this guy is strong!"

He leads Jim through the open portion of the counter top to a stack of material of varying colors - linen and cotton it appears. He raises his eyebrows while running his hand down the stack. "Pick," is the implied question. Jim chooses a light blue, which brings an even larger smile from Wang, who extracts the bolt of cloth from the pile and pulls a tape measure from the hook on the wall. With three swift movements Wang has taken Jim's measurements and unwound the bolt of fabric three times, and the cloth is cut. It is doubled so twice the area is available once it is unfolded. It is quite soft and smooth to touch when Jim reaches to caress it. Wang gives Jim a smiling thumbs-up signal. Jim decides to ask the accommodation question, but he's not quite sure how.

So, a pantomime begins with Jim pointing to himself, placing his palms together and resting his head on his hand, signaling sleep. Wang is instantly onto it. With Jim in tow, he leads him through a beaded curtain into the back of the shop where there are three treadle sewing machines, two women looking at him. Both are from the local Moro tribe apparently. Jim smiles faintly at them as he is hustled up the back stairs.

Up two steps at a time and at the top, on the right, is a closed door that Wang ushers Jim through into an extremely neat, but spare room, no larger than 10 feet by 10 feet. There is a thin reed mat on the floor with mosquito net dangling over it suspended from the ceiling, tied in a loose knot. There is a small chest along the wall under the window, and a row of wooden hooks on the wall above the mat. The walls are painted a faint yellow, the glass in the window is well puttied with the trim around the window painted white and each frame of the window delicately painted, no stray paint on the glass. Very precise. It is about as different from the entrance as you can imagine. Jim looks at Wang, smiles and nods, then raises his eyebrows and pantomimes washing his face. Wang does another small leap with a turn and they exit the room to continue along the narrow hall to a smaller door at the end. Wang opens the door and there is more porcelain than Jim has seen in two years. There is a small cistern with a few fish of various colors swimming in it, a squat toilet, and an ablution area with a drain. The walls are varnished natural wood, the porcelain is white, gleaming white, actually; it is all spotless. There is a wooden bucket, lovely finished and bound like half a wooden barrel, with a ceramic handle. Wang takes the bucket and dips it in the cistern and pours it down the squat toilet. Wang then turns to demonstrate how the shower works. Jim smiles and shakes his hand saying, "Good."

Wang is nearly beside himself. They descend to the shop through the back where the women have stopped again. Wang forcefully says something that gets them moving again, and then he and Jim are out front behind the counter. Jim points to the cloth, to his chest then his wristwatch and raises his eyebrows with his hands up and out from either side of his head, i.e., "When?"

Wang does not hesitate, but points up, slowly bringing his arm down toward the horizontal, and just below clicks his fingers. That afternoon? Jim is wondering? Jim makes the sleep mime again and Wang confirms that before he sleeps he will have his baro. Jim raises his eye-brows questioning whether it can be finished that soon, but Wang sets his jaw and Jim says, "OK, OK!" Wang smiles, shakes Jim's hand, and Jim decides to broach the subject of rent. Hmmm, how to do this one?

Jim points up toward the stairs in back, then rubs his thumb against his first two finger tips, the international sign for money. Wang is pensive, looks at Jim then writes a two on the counter top with his finger. Jim raises his eyebrows and then looks for a calendar. There is one on the wall behind the last stack of cloth. He pulls it off the wall and brings it over to Wang, points to today's date, and then writes two with his index finger and asks the question with his eyes. Wang points to the same day the next week, holds up seven fingers, and it is settled: two dollars a week. Jim is going to like it here. The smile on his face tells the whole story, and Wang is smiling back as they shake hands and Jim hands Wang his first week's rent.

Jim takes his bag upstairs, smiling to the ladies on the way. They shyly smile back, curiosity getting the better of their fear. He leaves the bag in the corner of the room, comes back down and motions that he has to go out for awhile. Wang smiles and waves goodbye as Jim heads back to the newspaper office to see Gus. He just wants to make sure this whole setup is not too good to be true, which is his usual experience. If it looks too good to be true, then it is.

Gus is just about to lock the doors when Jim tops the staircase. He looks up to see Jim advancing on him, a curious look in Jim's eyes. "What?" is all Gus says. Jim bursts out laughing, they both do, and Jim offers to buy Gus a drink downstairs.

In the café Jim describes the scene at the tailor's and Gus is appropriately amused. "Too good to be true, eh?" Just then Tony comes over to the table to take their orders, smiling ear to ear. "Il Alhamdulillah. Gracias, amigo!" he blurts out and takes Jim's hand, trying to wrest it from the arm. The pumping action is vigorous.

"De nada, amigo. What was that first thing you said?"

"Thanks be to God. Allah must have sent you. Now I can have two jobs, yes?"

Gus says, "I guess you two have met, eh?"

Gus smiles, Tony is beaming and he and Jim both nod the affirmative. The order is given and Gus says

Tony starts next week, working six days at half pay until he proves his worth. Jim responds with the tale about Tony working the first month at the café for free and Gus just sits and thinks for awhile.

Jim looks at Gus, with a serious appreciation and then responds, "Yeah. So, now with regards to Wang, when does the other shoe fall?"

"As far as I can tell, it won't. Wang is the real article. There is not a merchant in Zamboanga more honest than he, better organized than he, or better connected. His business runs on word of mouth advertising, so I have never been able to sell him an ad. But he makes all my clothes, I send all my friends and acquaintances to him, and I got him a discount on his protection costs."

"What protection costs?" As soon as Jim said it, he realized he was being stupid. "Oh!"

Gus just nods his head. "There is nowhere in Asia you can go and operate a business without paying local taxes. The tax system is a bit different than what we know in the States. It is a private enterprise tax system. In the States they call it graft. Here they don't call it anything, just bong. The city is divided into sectors. Each sector belongs to a certain sheik. Ours is Tamil, who lives on the way toward Julio Matunkup actually. Tamil and his family make sure no one in this sector is molested in any way. If something untoward happens, Tamil himself comes to investigate, and God help the poor bastard who was foolish enough to perpetrate. Disputes of all types go to Tamil: land, water, traffic, everything. Electricity and road maintenance and a few other services are still municipal responsibilities, but nearly everything else goes to Tamil and he gets paid for it. Not a lot, mind you, on the normal scale of taxation we are used to in the States, but it still can bite sometimes. So I was able to work a deal with Tamil that gave Wang a discount, and Wang has been appreciative ever since. It works here so I participate, and not even grudgingly."

"Believe me, I have no problem with it. I just wanted to get some idea what was going on and what to expect. You are right, I have not experienced a too-good-to-be-true situation that wasn't. Truth be told, I am still skeptical, but seems I can't lose on this one, at least not so far.

"Will Wang get hassled for renting to a white face? They may shake him down for more money."

Gus sits and thinks a moment then, "No. Tamil is serious about his protection business. No one gets past him without paying, or going out of business; interestingly, he is an honorable man. I've never heard of him changing the details of a deal without negotiation, certainly not on a whim. That's why this sector has no empty buildings. People want to live and work here, mainly because Tamil is good to work with. Not all the overlords are as amenable. Hmmm, not nearly so." And Gus looks away for a minute, lost in a memory.

"With you being in a municipal building, do you have to pay protection as well? I'd think the local police would take care of their own space."

Now Gus smiles and just slowly shakes his head. "Jim, we are going to get along just fine. I am a natural born teacher and you have a lot to learn, especially about life in the Philippines. Yes, we all pay Tamil, everyone in this sector. The businesses in this building actually pay a little more since it is a complex site to monitor, but it is worth every penny. The mayor's office does not pay cash, of course. It arranges a steep discount on Tamil's property taxes. The other sheiks do not receive the discount, which rankles, of course. In some ways it puts Tamil at the top of the heap, even though he is not the wealthiest sheik, nor does he have the largest estate. But he has a special arrangement with the city government, which is essentially the provincial government, that brings prestige. And he rides that prestige to the everlasting envy of the other sheiks. The sheiks have a loose organization that functions to prevent competition spilling over into outright hostilities. The local police are mostly toothless, but only a bit. The mayor has access to Pettit Barracks, if needed. That has not happened in my term here, but it is a nice ace in the hole for the local government. While the government has resources, the sheiks have a lot more collectively. However any single sheik would be no match for the government forces. That's also why they stick together as much as they do. Make no mistake, if there is a threat to any one of the six, the other five will come in support. But during ordinary times they are all jockeying for position and more revenue. They are businessmen, make no mistake. Scrupulous to their customers, much of the time, never to one another. Can't say they hate each other, but you sure won't find them attending each other's weddings, if you know what I mean. Interesting balancing act, and Tamil does have a bit better balance than the others because of his special status with the government."

Jim sits for a few minutes, sips from his orange juice mulling the data. Pretty steep learning curve here. But, what the heck, that makes it interesting, and he has a job and a place to stay. "So we have a deal concerning my salary, yes?" Gus nods, with his eyebrows up. "Does that include the Matunkup revenue I am working with tomorrow?"

"Now that would not be quite kosher, would it? Mr. Matunkup came to me, I made the deal. Why pay you for that ad revenue?"

"OK, fair enough. So what does he usually pay for an ad? He has been doing this for awhile now, so there is some track record."

"Typically, it is $150 for a four-week run."

"OK, how about I get my 20 percent for anything over that?"

"Done."

"How do I get out there? I don't even know where his place is."

"I'll have Manolo pick you up at Wang's 6:30 in the morning, bring you here so we can talk first, then take you to Julio's."

"Who is Manolo? Does he work for you?"

"No, he has his own taxi business and I contract with him for services. Taxis around here usually don't make much, simply because there are such short driving distances. So he appreciates the contract and gives me a good deal."

"Fine, Manolo at 6:30 at Wang's, er, my place. But I prefer to get myself around when I need to travel, so soon I will need some sort of independent transport. What do you suggest?"

"The best way to get around is motorbike. It is the cheapest, most convenient, but the scariest. Traffic is chaotic, so you drive with eyes in the back of your head. Might makes right is the primary rule of the road here."

"Fine. I'll work on getting a motorbike this weekend. I suppose, given what you've told me, Wang would be a good one to help negotiate that one."

"Perceptive, Jim, very perceptive. Now I must leave. See you here in the morning." As they stand, Tony comes racing up, taking first Jim's hand then Gus,' shaking each slightly more vigorously than the other, back and forth. Then the two men are able to extract themselves and go their separate ways.

There is still plenty of daylight left in the day so, to fight his fatigue, Jim leaves the municipal building and walks away from the pier into the city to explore. Walking is easier without his pack, which he left at Wang's, but he still has his stash in the money belt under his shirt tight against his belly. It is soaked, but safe. The U.S. dollars won't melt, but they are taking a beating being constantly wet. He will have to find a safe place to store the bulk of his cash. But for now he has it with him in large $100 notes and the small money in his pockets. The Philippine pesos are all coins and clanking around in his left pocket while the one dollar bills are in the right pocket. He has enough money to hire a taxi but the sense of the city is fairly lost riding in a car, or even in a motorized rickshaw. He strolls along Calle Voluntario past the Rizal Monument on his right. He doesn't stop to read the dedication, which is in English, and continues on past the commercial buildings on the left and a small plaza on the right. He is brought up short as he views a dusty monument on the other side of the street in a small triangular park. He dodges the traffic, crosses the street to examine a bronze statue of a military rider on horseback. It is John Pershing himself. "What's he doing here?" The dusty street has managed to cover the statue in a thick coat, but the inscription is still legible.

After a few minutes contemplation, he walks on until he reaches Calle Pilar at a complex intersection. Ahead it looks more like a maze than organization, but to the right there are still streets in a grid. So right he goes, ambling and taking in the sights, smells and ambience. Sure enough, after two very long blocks, the next intersection is labeled Calle Via Lobos, home street. He turns right and examines the crush of single, two- and three-story buildings, most wooden-sided, with a few brick buildings interspersed. There are cafes and hardware stores as well as two car repair shops, a furniture store and more variety than he can sort in his head. Each building has residential facilities above and shabby fronts below. Some windows are boarded up, some doors are sagging on worn hinges, and gaps show around window sashes. The street is dilapidated, but he remembers Wang's scissor-adorned shop. Jim files his questions away for Gus in the morning.

The sun is quickly descending when he arrives at Wang's, the left side of the door open and the sound of treadle sewing machines whirring away in back. As he enters, Wang scuttles through the curtain and, on seeing Jim, his whole face lights up in greeting. "What, what!?"

Jim laughs, remembering the exchange with Gus, and simply says, "Hello, Wang."

Wang purses his fingers on the right and brings them to his mouth, the eating gesture, with a questioning look on his face. Jim says, "Yes, very hungry!"

Wang rushes back through the curtain clapping his hands and jabbering a mile a minute. The machine sounds stop and, a moment later, the two women come through the curtain, stopping abruptly when they see Jim. They drop their eyes and slump their shoulders as they sidle as far from him as they can as they exit the room. Once on the street, they turn left, glance back and then start giggling, tugging at one another's sleeves and jabbering away as they disappear with one more glance over their shoulders. Jim is amused and perplexed about their behavior, but Wang interrupts his thoughts with an abrupt "Go!" and holds the door for Jim to exit the room.

Outside the shop, Wang locks the door and then takes Jim by the arm to walk him right one block, then left and they are in a neighborhood that looks more residential but obviously poorer in structures.

The smoke from cooking fires is becoming thick and aromatic. Two blocks along, Wang makes a left, pulling Jim along until they arrive at a fairly dingy-fronted shop with a solid door, no windows and a pull chain by the knob. Wang pulls the chain and a small window clicks open immediately in the upper middle of the door. Jim can hardly control his shivers at the yellow eye peeking out through the small window, recalling Mighty Joe and his truncheon. Wang looks oddly at Jim, quivering beside him. Wang addresses the eye in Mandarin.

The door opens immediately and they enter a red and gold emporium, lush carpet on the floor, magnificent stairway directly ahead with a passage either side. No one is in sight. Wang leads Jim to the right of the stairs into a lush dining room with a ceiling fan and several full-length windows that open onto a courtyard with a fountain and dense foliage accented by a tall shade tree, barely visible in the developing gloom. The soothing fountain is obvious because the light from the room spills onto the courtyard.

Wang waves toward the nearest open window and moves smoothly down the hall to a door that opens silently as he approaches. Jim watches attentively until Wang is out of sight, then moves to the window and steps out into the night. The breeze is barely palpable; the temperature is absolutely neutral, the water splashing from the fountain tepid to touch. Around the fountain is a square flagstone walkway with the irregularly shaped stones set into crushed quartz gravel that contrasts with the grey flagstone. Three vine-covered brick walls enclose the far side of the courtyard. Jim walks closer to the far wall and notices small white flowers scattered like stars through the dark green. His nose tells him he is surrounded by jasmine. What a scene of tranquility.

The courtyard has three backless bench seats of highly polished wood, one on each side of the courtyard. Just as he sits on the nearest one, he hears, "What?"

Looking up, he sees Wang, backlit by the lights in the dining room. Wang has obviously changed clothes. Standing, Jim walks closer to gather the sight. In place of a skinny, agitated man now is a perfectly composed Wang standing in a bright red, full-length silk robe, huge sleeves dangling to his sides, his hair coiffed into a bun at the back of his head. Wang stands very erect in the window frame, just like the picture of a Chinese mandarin.

Jim has seen many pictures of Chinese warlords and chieftains, and Wang certainly looks the part. The smile on Wang's face complements the fact that Jim's mouth is hanging wide open in amazement. Wang laughs and Jim laughs louder. Wang indicates that they should sit at the low table in the center of the room. There are no chairs, just cushions on each side of the highly polished table. Nothing is on the table.

Sitting opposite Wang, Jim tries to compose an intelligent question that can be mimed. As Jim begins making elegant facial expressions and waving his right hand, Wang says, "I hope you will pardon the small charade I have perpetrated today. But I have certain obligations to meet and need to know that the people I am dealing with are worthy of my trust. Your time in Manila was painful, I am sure. Perhaps it was as painful as your time in China was exciting. However, you are now in Zamboanga, and I should be happy if we could reach some working arrangement that might be beneficial to us both."

Jim's right hand is still in the air, having frozen there at the start of Wang's small soliloquy. He slowly lowers it, but says nothing for a long two minutes. Then he leans back and laughs and laughs. Then he rubs his hands together, suggesting this might be a fruitful arrangement for both of them. Wang is silent through the hilarity, then he goes on, "You see, I have many resources at my disposal. Your history is unique among the white faces I have encountered - here in Zamboanga, in Manila, in China, even in the United States where I lived for several years. I suspect you bring certain skills to Zamboanga that I will find helpful to my businesses, and I am certain that I have resources you can put to good use as well. I suggest we cooperate."

"I suggest we eat, I am starved," replies Jim.

Wang smiles, raises his left hand off the table top and two liveried young men enter, one with a tray of food and the other with a tray of tea. Each tray is set in the center of the table. The plates are placed in front of Jim and Wang with chopsticks leaning on small ceramic ridges next to the plates. The waiters silently back out of the room.

"I can certify that none of the staff speak English. I have been very careful about this over the years. They speak Tagalog and Mandarin. The chef also speaks Spanish of necessity for purchasing the food for the kitchen."

"So this place is yours?" asks Jim.

"Yes, of course. It is a rather exclusive club, you see. Membership is by invitation only. The main members are the six sheiks of Zamboanga, and each sheik has nominated two additional members. I have installed three members myself and I bring guests from time to time. You are my guest. You will not be a member. Members are permanent residents of Zamboanga, and you will not be permanent to our fair city. But, as my guest, you will have the opportunity to meet and socialize with each of the other members, assuming that interests you."

"Of course it interests me. Being near the center of any organization has always been interesting to me. Knowing what is going on is even more interesting, and I suspect this establishment plays a large part in developing what is going on in Zamboanga. Tell me, what part did Gus play in setting up this meeting tonight?"

"None, other than providing advanced notice of your arrival at my shop. Once I had the chance to meet you in person, I was able to contact a few acquaintances in Manila who were able to provide the rest of the information I required, for a fee, of course. You are welcome here in Zamboanga for as long as you might need to stay. You have an appointment with Matunkup for tomorrow I understand. Now, I suggest we eat as, even in this weather, the food is likely to become cold."

Jim just shakes his head, picks up his chopsticks and digs in. The rice is perfect and each small bowl of sauce and condiment is exquisite. After half an hour, Jim lays his chopsticks parallel to one another, leaning on his plate, facing away from himself, indicating he is finished. Wang raises his left hand slightly, Jim's plate is removed and a fresh pot of tea is set in the center of the table. Wang fills two cups without handles, offering one to Jim, takes the other and says, "Salute."

Jim returns the favour, and Wang raises from the floor in one fluid motion. Jim slides back from the table and stands, offering his hand to Wang. Wang looks for a moment, then takes the offering into both of his thin, strong hands, nods his head slightly and asks Jim to wait one moment. Wang turns and flows through the door, back down the hall to the opening door and disappears. Moments later, he reappears as the familiar Wang, hair unkempt, shorts, T-shirt and sandals, still skinny as a rail, smiling ear to ear.

As they open the door to leave, the two waiters appear, one on each side of the door. A large fellow with distinctly yellow eyes steps from behind the stairwell. Then, from down the hall, comes a fellow dressed in a stained white apron. Wang greets his chef, speaking in Mandarin, to which the fellow bows at the waist with a serious smile on his face. Wang turns to each man in turn, smiles with a nod and even yellow eyes gives a half smile in return. Then Jim and Wang are out the door, walking down the block. "Don't you live there at the club?" Jim asks.

"Oh, no. That would not be appropriate. You see, I have several businesses to operate and I need to be available at all of them during the day. The tailor shop is probably the most important, for the contacts and information it provides, but the others need supervision as well. The taxi is likely the next most important. I must be out and about all during the day, as well as making useful clothes for important people. So staying here would not project the proper image of a local businessman. Of course, many people know who is the owner of the club, but those also know how to maintain silence. They, and you, are the only ones who realize who has influence there. Gus must know, since he assists with much that I accomplish here. But Gus maintains the illusion of white superiority that provides part of the veil of my life here. I suppose you understand that Gus provided me with assistance from Tamil. Correct?" Jim nods. "Good, so the illusion is maintained. Your support for Tony Fali is admirable, and I suspect will be fortuitous." That brings a broad smile on Jim's face, eyes up, mouth wide and his head swinging to and fro.

Wang continues, "So that makes nine people in Zamboanga, outside of the club, who are aware who controls the activities of the club. That is the best way. That is the way it will remain." Wang provides a fixed stare into the amused and confident face of Jim.

After a moment, they set off toward the shop, walking in silence until Jim asks, "OK, so your involvement with the exclusive club is a closely held secret, right?" Wang just nods. "Since it seems highly important that you remain anonymous, why let me in on it?" Jim says. "I work for the newspaper, for God's sake! Why share the information with a reporter and a stranger to boot?"

Wang walks silently for another block, then stops. Checking all directions for listeners and finding none, Wang starts his history and economics lesson, one that Jim could probably do without. "You have certain skills that are highly valued here in Zamboanga. In fact, you arrive with more skills than first estimated. So your value to our rather small and exclusive community is unique. First, you have firsthand experience with the Japanese efforts at empire building. You must realize that Japan's efforts will not stop with China, Korea even, but will extend to all of Asia and the Pacific. It must, to protect its empire and to acquire the raw materials for nation building that are lacking in Japan itself. So Japan is coming to the Philippines, most certainly. Their arrival will bring many hardships to our islands, particularly to those of us who have been economically successful. We will lose much during Japan's occupancy. Japan will lose, of course, and must withdraw, but we will still lose our entire livelihood as a result; our family inheritance built over many years, even centuries will be lost. My contacts in Asia are significant and wide, but limited in the U.S.A. In the future I expect that several of my colleagues and I will require your assistance securing assets in the U.S.A. that we must protect while Japan controls our country. Our contacts in Manila are a bit distant and you are here. That makes your assistance more desirable should the need arise. Do you understand?" Jim nods slowly.

"Good. Tomorrow you will visit my good friend Mr. Matunkup at his estate. You will confirm his advertisement with your paper and attempt to obtain even more revenue from him in order to increase your personal salary from Gus." Jim's eyes betray his amazement even though the rest of his face tries to remain calm. "Yes, I have information. It is the only way to successfully function here in Zamboanga."

"What makes you think I would just do your bidding? What makes you think I want to participate in your enterprise here in Zamboanga at all? I could just take the assets and run."

"Just as I have information that is useful to me and my associates, I have information that is useful to you, usefully kept quiet, I believe. Authorities in Manila assume you are on a five-week boat trip to the U.S.A., do they not? The radio contact between Zamboanga and Manila is fast and effective, and I am sure you have no interest in returning there. With the Japanese controlling just about everything to the north and west, that leaves the south and east as your options, and you already know that there is nothing there. Besides, the Japanese will soon control those directions as well, even if it is for a short time. No, your best option, for as long as I am here, is also to be here. I said I have limited assets available in the U.S.A., but I did not say I have no assets there. I believe you would agree that cooperation is preferable to a life of wondering if you were found out, eh?" A small, sly smile flickers at the corners of Wang's lips. "Come see me after you have had your talk with Gus and reported your success with Mr. Matunkup. It will be successful, I assure you."

With that, the walk resumes, Jim deep in thought, not watching where he is going until they turn right onto Villa Lobos and walk right into a group of five ruffians. More than a little drunk, they are looking for a good time out on the town. The largest one walks right up to Jim, standing a head taller with a bandana covering his hair, muscle shirt exposing his physique, and a swagger exposing his inebriation. He says something in local Spanish-Tagalog dialect that Jim does not understand at all, which obviously heightens the tension. Wang says, "He is wondering what such a white face is doing out on his street at night."

Jim looks back at the fellow and politely smiles. He tries to step to the right to get around the hulk, but is restrained with a hard grip on his left shoulder. "How do you say 'let go?'"

Wang tells him, which he repeats, and the drunkard turns and takes a huge swing back and forth at Jim's head.

Of course Jim sees it coming before it starts. Boxing his way across Mexico taught him a lot, particularly about clumsy fighting style. His response is quick, sure and seemingly effortless. The big guy winds up flat on his back, immobile. The other four start circling Jim until Wang softly speaks. Their advance stops, they look at one another, regroup, then pick up the hulk by his arms and legs, dragging him off around the corner Jim and Wang had just emerged.

"What did you say?" asks Jim.

"I just reminded them whose sector this is. They will each receive a visit tomorrow and will not be attempting such barbarism again, I assure you."

"Do you know who they are?

"Not all, just the big fellow, and his brother who was closest to you after you dispatched him. Good work, by the way. It seems I have a few holes in my information. It is nice to see them being filled."

At that moment they arrive at the shop. Wang unlocks the door and closes and locks the door. Jim asks, "If you have such good protection in your neighborhood, why bother locking the door?"

"Two reasons. First, it is just a habit. Second, it helps avoid unnecessary inconvenience that might occur should an ignorant person decide to steal from me. I have to have the person found, hopefully with the stolen goods, or more likely replace the stolen items in order to fulfill the orders of the shop. It makes life easier to prevent theft in the first place, and I am protecting the karma of the potential thieves. They will not have to bear the burden of their thieving if it does not happen. Here is you baro, by the way. Try it on. You will need it in the morning, for your visit."

It is, of course, a perfect fit, and feels wonderful on his skin.

"Thank you for getting it ready so quickly."

"I was certain that it will help with your negotiations tomorrow. And your happiness and contentment will assist our mutual needs, I am sure. Good night."

"Good night." And Jim is upstairs, undressed and on the mat under the mosquito net in no time at all. Five minutes later, he is sound asleep. Wang's light is still on for another hour as he writes notes to Tamil, Matunkup and his older brother who lives in the hills at the end of Tumaga Road. Finally, with the messengers having departed with their written messages, he lies down to the sleep of the righteous.

CHAPTER 4

Zamboanga Business

F ive a.m. arrives as usual before anyone is ready, but arrive it does. The women arrive at 5:30 to start work, the treadle machines humming by 5:45. The smell of coffee is rising up the stairs and welcomes Jim to the world of the living. Sliding out from under the net, he rises in his undershorts and heads to the bathroom at the end of the hall. Emerging from the room 10 minutes later, drying himself with a towel, he returns to his room and dresses, donning his new baro, with a clean pair of shorts and sandals. By 6:10 he is downstairs drinking his coffee to a smiling Wang, who is in his work attire of shorts, T-shirt and barefoot. "Are you hungry, Jim?"

"Yes, but I plan to get something at the café downstairs from the newspaper office. There is someone there I want to see."

"Tony usually arrives at seven a.m. so you have time for your meeting with Gus. Then you can have breakfast and still make your appointment. The taxi will be waiting out front of the municipal building."

Jim's eyes and mouth betray him this time. "So there really is nothing I can do here that will not be anticipated, is that what you are saying?

"No, I am sure that a man with your talents will find many ways to surprise us, my friends and me. But for now I would say we are truly working simultaneously."

"Simultaneously. Good word. OK, so given my itinerary for today, when do you anticipate my return?"

"I would say you will likely be back here at six p.m., after your tour of the estates, lunch and negotiations with Mr. Matunkup and discussion with Gus. Yes, six p.m. is most likely."

"Thanks for that." It comes out with a bit more sarcasm than Jim intended, but seems to pass unnoticed right by Wang. Seems since Wang rerouted the taxi for the morning, Jim walks the four or five blocks to the municipal building, arriving at 6:35, just as Gus is extracting his keys from the door. "Come in, come in. Punctuality is appreciated. What a beautiful baro! Wang certainly knows his business, eh?" There is more than a bit of a smirk on Gus's face as he turns toward his office hallway door. "Let's have a short conversation before you are off to Matunkup, OK?

"Sure, although from what I have seen so far, it seems my trip is superfluous in the extreme. Everyone knows what is happening already except me, of course. So why all the intrigue?"

"Not intrigue, old sod. Just a bit of care and security. Besides, there are aspects of this visit for which the outcome is anything but determined."

"Not, apparently, for Wang," Jim responds. It is interesting, and a bit unnerving, but Jim has never enjoyed the feeling of being a pawn in someone else's game. Control of his destiny is important, and right now he feels that he has less than at any time, other than his jail time in Manila.

Gus is examining the changing moods coming over Jim's face and then offers, "Oh, by the way, there is a police report of five young men of uncertain occupation who all turned up at the hospital this morning with various broken and distorted limbs. It was very curious how they all seemed to be in the same motor accident, but their stories are all the same. So the authorities have not pursued it. I got the word by phone this morning before coming to work. The motor accident was reported to have occurred east of town on the way to the headlands. What those young tough guys were doing way out there, where there is no work other than subsistence farming, baffles the authorities. Maybe when you get back you could ask around downstairs. Looks like there might be a story in there somewhere." With that, Gus's eyebrows lift, a slight smile sneaks into the corners of his mouth as he turns to his file folder labeled Matunkup.

"Now for your trip today. I have arranged your transport through Wang. Perhaps he mentioned something. Your safe transport in Zamboanga is assured, so there will be no need for you to obtain a motorbike. OK? Now for your information: Matunkup's estate is out San Jose Road, several miles actually. You will see the fields running down to the sea on your left, as well as various planted fields on the right of the road, about as far as you can see heading up into the hills. At the end of an unmarked road you will come to the hacienda among the trees. It can't be seen until you reach it, but it is impressive. The road, or drive as it were, ends there at the house. It is well- maintained in order for Matunkup to get his various products to market and to the docks for export. His primary exports are rubber, sugar and copra, while most of his coffee, rice and pineapples are for domestic consumption. If he has a bumper crop he will export these as well. What land is not cultivated is used for cattle and he has a fair amount of stock. His total acreage is unknown, even by the provincial government. But somehow he keeps track of it and seems to continue adding to it over time. He is one of the 12 wealthiest men in the province, and among the top 100 in the country. Somehow he maintains his civility as he is among the most magnanimous of the local patrician class of ancient times. There are a few who carry their altruistic ideals into their commerce, very few, and he seems to be one. I will be interested in your view as an unbiased outsider with no prior experience of him or his family or history. I will also be interested in his maintaining a sizeable account with this paper, increased if possible. He certainly can afford it. Whether he needs it or not is another question. Work whatever magic you have, and I'll see you back here this afternoon."

With that he hands Jim the folder containing the draft of the advertisement, examples of previous ads and blank contract forms to use in case an agreement can be reached on the spot. A short history of previous advertising revenue from Matunkup is also included with the notation that it is to be kept strictly confidential.

Folder in hand, it is ten past seven a.m. when Jim emerges from the office and heads downstairs for breakfast. He locates the table he had yesterday, only yesterday for heaven's sake, and sits, weighting the folder down with the sugar dispenser to keep it from blowing away. As he looks up, he sees Tony hustling Jim's way, order pad in hand, pencil at the ready and a huge smile on his face.

"Hello, Tony. You must be excited about starting at the newspaper next week."

"Very good morning to you again. Yes, very excited, and Mr. Gus will pay me the same I now make here at the café. What a swell surprise! Look at your beautiful new clothes. You look like Zamboanguenos, for sure."

Jim smiles in return, accepting the compliment and says, "It looks like I will be here for awhile now. I also have a job at the newspaper and am staying upstairs at the tailor's shop on Via Lobos Street. I am very hungry and must eat soon because I have to go to work and visit Mr. Matunkup. Do you know him?"

Tony's eyes grow impossibly wide as he nods his head vigorously. "Of course, everyone knows Mr. Matunkup. He is very rich and has a beautiful house in the hills. You will go to his house?"

"That's the idea. But I need to eat first. So I will have three eggs with bread and a sliced tomato and sliced papaya and two cups of black coffee. Can you get that soon?"

"The soonest for you, Mr. Jim."

"Actually it is just Jim?"

"Certainly, Mr. Jim. I will be right back." And he is gone before Jim can make the correction again.

The temperature is going up. Jim appreciates the umbrella over the table as it allows the breeze to feel cool. He looks down the street toward the sea and watches as a freighter is shifted by tugs onto the pier at the end of the causeway. It is at least a quarter mile away and the perpetually open gate in the wall separates the dock area from the city. But the sight is still impressive, maybe because of how hard he has to work to appreciate it. Just as the freighter touches the pier and the ropes are tossed from the ship Tony arrives with his breakfast. The smell is divine and he is starving. The eggs and toast disappear first so the papaya can be savored with the second cup of coffee. He is satisfied when he finishes. As he walks to the counter to pay his bill, he passes Tony, who is already serving another table, and slips him two 50 peso coins. Startled, Tony looks in his hand, then smiles ear to ear. A whole day's wages right there. Tony is talking with the new customer when Jim passes behind him, pats him on the shoulder and gives him a thumbs-up signal. Tony almost misses the man's order, but refocuses in time to record it and hustle off to the kitchen.

The ride to Matunkup's starts by negotiating the maze of downtown Zamboanga. A sign indicating San Jose Road appears on a corner and the driver turns left. Block after block of commercial buildings and hotels, as well as shops and multistoried buildings slide by on both sides of the street. After stop-and-go traffic for about 15 or 20 minutes, the buildings become more spread apart and a bit of a view of the hills to the north emerges. The sea is too far away to see since they are driving on the coastal plain, but Jim can smell it for sure. Low tide smells about the same everywhere. The taxi's pace picks up with fewer stops and the car begins to cruise at speed, maybe 40 miles an hour. Not fast but certainly not stop and go. The area opens up as a residential area encroaches on the road, slowing heavy traffic: a few cars, half a dozen trucks, motor bikes, bicycles, horses, mules, donkeys and every sort of conveyance. And dust. Again the path opens with fewer buildings; the traffic thins and the taxi speeds up. There are more pedestrians than cars. How they can breathe is amazing with all the clouds of dust the cars raise. Closing the window to keep the dust out just makes it that much hotter; his sweat quickly turns to mud. So Jim opens the window, preferring brushing off the dust to rinsing off mud. At an intersection he can see road signs indicating they are still on San Jose Road. Passing an obvious air strip on the right, they cross a small waterway and angle left. The road becomes a bit more narrow and they are now in mostly rural scenery for about 10 minutes when the scene opens to a view of the sea to the left. Light glistens on segmented fields as the sea intersperses with very dark green fields of tall plants, like some sort of reeds swaying in the sea breeze.

These fields come nearly to the road where workers hoe the fields or guide water buffalos over the soil. Jim sits up straight to look ahead toward the sea where there are five or six people in one of the segmented fields holding what look like long fishing poles. Just as he questions his eyes, one of the women holding a long pole jerks it up and a wriggling fish dangles on the end of the line. It is not huge, by any means, not a prize winner in a fishing contest back home; but it obviously delights the woman as she takes the fish off the hook and deposits it in a covered basket beside her. The car turns right as the fish flops into the basket, causing Jim to lose sight of the rustic scene.

He is lost in thought, almost missing that they are in the midst of a vast coconut orchard. The road becomes more narrow and rutted. They are obviously off the main road - no traffic, only pedestrians carrying farm implements, either heading toward the sea or the same direction as the car. The car slows down on its winding path up the hill.

As they climb the hill they start to leave the coconut orchard behind and enter another vast area of dark-leaved trees. At a rise in the road the hilltops are lined with row upon row of low-growing spiky plants. The fields Jim observes are vast, larger than anything he has ever seen, even the fertile agricultural centers of California.

The car descends into a small valley again, reentering the forest of trees with hanging containers. As the car rises again, it enters yet another vegetation area. This time he passes through shrubs or low bushes with what looks like berries within their canopies. The berries are small and red; the low shrubs are over a vast area, farther than Jim can see. He does not notice they are arriving at a more open area ahead; he then spots the hacienda buildings as the trail makes a bend to the right and comes to a stop. The three houses are in a small triangular arrangement: the main house is in the center with the smaller ones on either side at 45-degree angles to the main house. All three are single-story buildings with large verandas surrounding each, wood siding and large windows. The main house has a double-door entrance in the center.

The houses are painted, the center one white, with the smaller ones light yellow; all three have brown trim around the windows and doors. The windows open on hinges that allow them to swing outwards onto the veranda; the glass is in two parts separated by the horizontal frame painted the color of the house. All the windows are open with thin white curtains blowing out, making each house look like it is fluttering in the breeze.

Thick supporting pillars line the veranda roofs of each house.

Three wide steps with no rail lead to the center of the main house porch and Jim climbs them, appreciating the breathtaking scenery. Colors contrast with one another, the reflections from the far-off sea and the overhanging shade trees all join to create an idyllic atmosphere. A half dozen wicker rockers are lined up across the veranda, three on each side of the open double door, all facing the sea. As he reaches the top step, he uses the file folder to dust himself off. The screen door opens and Julio warmly greets him to Hacienda Matunkup. "It is good of you to come all this way. I am happy to welcome you into my home. Please, please, come in and you can freshen up a bit before we talk. Come, come!" With that he takes Jim by the right arm and leads him through the door into a high-ceilinged entryway that divides into a large sitting room on the left and a dining area on the right. There are wooden pegs on both sides of the entryway where hats and rain gear hang. Straight ahead Jim can see an open back door with sun streaming in through a screen door. Julio motions for Jim to follow him through the kitchen to a bathroom featuring a gleaming white porcelain sink. Jim closes the door and is surrounded by a large, cedar-walled room with a sink, tub and toilet as well as a dressing area and small sofa. He rinses off a significant amount of dust from his face and hands and combs his unruly hair. He emerges to find a smiling Julio Matunkup bearing a large sweating pitcher and two glasses.

"Come, we can sit in the back where the breeze is stronger and the shade can cool you from your long ride."

They exit through the rear double doors onto a shady, U-shaped veranda. Straight ahead, down three steps is a garden of stones, a fountain and many, many flowers blooming among the stones. The cooling breeze blows in from the hills above, so strong that it shuts the screen door behind them. On the other side of a small arching bridge is a gazebo, raised and surrounded by the garden, holding a modest wooden table and six wicker chairs. They cross the bridge and step up onto the floor of the gazebo. The scent of the garden blossoms wafts through the air as they sit down at the table. Julio places the pitcher and glasses down as Jim, mindful of the breeze, places his folder on the table under one of the glasses.

"This is my favourite place to do business. The negotiations usually end in my favour in this atmosphere. Not entirely fair, I am sure, but there you are." A sly smile arises at the corners of Julio's mouth.

"I can see why you have the advantage. Being my first visit, I am sure you can imagine the impression I have.

Your place is truly amazing, first rate I must say. Have you been here long?"

"Only 25 years. I saw the opportunity when land was selling very inexpensively during the Moro altercations. So I purchased from Manila and then came once General Pershing brought some stability to the area. I have slowly gained some respect and cooperation from the local sheiks, who continue to wield considerable influence with the Zamboanga population. With the profits from my estate that I am able to provide, I suspect that their cooperation is assured for the near future.

"Each sheik is represented in the management staff for the various sections of the farm, and nearly all the workers are relatives of one sort or another. So the amount of money moving directly from the estate profits into the hands of the local aristocracy is significant. It is certainly more than goes directly to the provincial or municipal governments. I even contribute to the welfare of the soldiers at Pettit Barracks with the annual Christmas party. All the food for the party comes from here, as well as the preparation. It is the only time of the year that the kitchen staff at the barracks does not need to prepare a meal, and they certainly appreciate it. Of all the thank-you responses and cards I receive at that time of year, two-thirds come from the kitchen staff at the barracks. It is fun to provide a bit of cheer, is it not?"

"I suppose so. Can you tell me a bit about the fields I saw on the way here? I am not much of a farmer, so could not really tell what I was seeing, just that there was a lot of it."

"Certainly. The main road enters the estate from the south and carries on right through. Toward the sea there are rice and sugar cane fields. I love the contrast of colors between them, don't you?" A nod from Jim as he remembers the tall dark and short lighter greens on the way. "At a certain point the road turns right off the provincial road and the land begin to change, so that as you climb the hills and the road curves through the valleys and ridges, you are able to see agriculture for two of the main exports of the Philippines: coconuts and rubber trees.

"I suppose you remember the small containers attached to the rubber trees with dark leaves?" Again, a nod from Jim. "They were gathering the liquid latex, which is the natural base for rubber manufacture. You then passed through the coffee area, which has always been my pride and joy. I do love good coffee and the plants are beautiful. Unfortunately we are experiencing some sort of disease in the orchard that may prove disastrous. Most of the coffee harvested here is sent directly to Manila for processing and is sold within the Philippines.

"But many farms are experiencing the same difficulties with this disease and I am not sure how long the Philippines will have its own coffee supply. I am hopeful for a solution, but I do not know now." For once, Julio's face does not have its usual luster, the eyes are downcast and he is quiet for a minute or more, what seems like an eternity in a conversation. Then he looks up, and asks, "Did you see the fields of pineapple?" Jim looks unsure, and Julio continues, "Surely you saw fields of low-growing plants that have spiky tops?" Jim suddenly nods vigorously. "Those will be the salvation of my estate. I am hoping we can save the coffee trees, but, if not, the pineapples will make the difference. Everyone loves pineapples, here in the Philippines, everywhere."

A gust of breeze flutters Jim's folder, bringing him back to his task. Holding the papers down, he lifts his glass and sips the cool, tart lemonade. "This place is truly amazing. I am not sure that Zamboanga appreciates what the hacienda does to support the whole community. How many people are employed here?"

"I actually do not know at the moment, maybe 300 or 350."

"Wow! See what I mean? This place has significant value to the area over and above the exports it sells and the cash it puts in the hands of the elite."

"It is an interesting observation, one that I have made from time to time," Julio says, "but you know how it is when you must concentrate on daily details. Thank you for your generous thoughts." Julio has a wide smile, obviously taken with the energetic praise of this young fellow. Then he shifts his smile to a slightly more sly look. "I don't think you came here to be the tourist, no? We have some business to attend to, do we not? And, if I am not mistaken, you have something else on your mind."

Jim appears hurt at Julio's directness. He puts down his glass. "Sure, I have brought the draft of your advertisement for the paper for you to review and hopefully approve. We can make any changes you think will help. But, I have to say, I truly meant what I was saying about the hacienda's importance to Zamboanga. I believe the community needs to recognize its contribution."

"Let us finish first things first, eh? Then we can perhaps discuss adding to the fame and acclaim of Hacienda Matunkup, which I suspect might also add to the income of a local paper. Am I not correct?"

Jim realizes that he has probably met his match and decides to play it straight. "Good, let's look at the ad copy. Then maybe we can discuss ways to promote the public image of the hacienda that will also benefit the paper - and me."

Julio's eyebrows raise ever so slightly, a half smile raises his left lip and he extends his hand for the folder. Jim hands it over, sips his lemonade, and watches Julio read. Julio's head is nodding slightly. He stops and rereads a phrase, puts the folder down and asks, "Who wrote this?"

"I did, why? Is there a problem?"

"Not at all, quite the contrary. It is not the usual advertisement, so I was not sure how Gus could have written it. It is actually quite good. I like it quite a bit. Here, I suggest placing the date of completion of the sale, but that is my only suggestion. Congratulations on your good work."

Jim says, "I believe it is all accurate, is it not? Nothing oversold?"

"It is accurate."

"One thing you may not have noticed is that it is also shorter than the usual advertisement you have, so it is less expensive."

"Is it really?" Then Julio begins counting words, and when he finishes he looks up smiling even more widely. "You are correct. It is 12 words less than usual. But it is also clearer. That is truly well done, Jim." That is the first time he has used Jim's first name in their negotiations. Jim suspects it means something and presses on.

"I like what I do, and have done it before in the U.S.A., where advertisers can be very picky, as well as tight fisted. Now, can we talk a bit about how to promote the hacienda in the Zamboanga community and the Philippines, as well as Southeast Asia?"

"Oh my! You seem to have a rather grand idea of what my little farm actually is."

"Julio, this place is perfect for the region and for a large part of the world. I have been around, seen quite a lot of the world, and I can tell you that you have a serious slice of paradise right here. And very few know of it, it seems."

"I am not entirely sure that I want much notoriety, actually."

"I understand completely. This place is great because it is so peaceful and beautiful. But that peace and beauty can also be used as an asset in promoting your product. It adds to the value of what you sell. It can also bring more revenue to your company, which might be useful in times when the produce has trouble, like now with the coffee crop. If you had another income source that the weather gods cannot stop, it would be good, yes?"

Julio sits and thinks, quiet for awhile. Then he looks up at Jim and says, "You are, of course, correct. What ideas do you have?"

That simple question starts a collaboration between two men who have mutual respect for one another's talents and skills. This relationship will introduce Jim to the elite of the Zamboanga community and provides him with a steady income from commissions that he will earn from Julio and his associates.

And so, in four short months, Matunkup's hecienda bustles with new life. International visitors come to sightsee, additional crops are established, coffee is exchanged for vanilla plants, and the hacienda's extra houses become a secluded getaway for upper level diplomats of the Spanish embassy. All the while, the newspaper promotes various sectors of the business community, making the sheiks wealthier than ever.

In the midst of this explosion of enterprise, Jim receives an invitation to the official unveiling of the 1938 vintage of the Zamboanga Winery to be held in two weeks. The irony of a winery in a Muslim neighborhood does not escape Jim's notice, nor does the nicety of neighborly tolerance. The annual vintage opening is an event that receives great attention from local folks, even though a large proportion are Muslims and do not drink alcohol. Invitations are coveted throughout the province and Jim has one in hand. He thinks he knows how he came by it: Julio, his "El Patron," as Jim has come to think of him.

Gus is quick to recommend various angles for a feature article on the opening; he suggests Jim talk to Wang about getting some formal wear for the evening festivities. "Wang? Why talk to Wang? What does he know about wine celebrations?"

"Just talk to him, OK? The sooner you get over your prejudices, the better you will perform here in Zamboanga."

Prejudices? When has Jim ever been prejudiced about anything or anyone? He is a bit angry over that suggestion until he remembers his first interaction with Wang. So. that afternoon when he returns to the shop he finds Wang in the back simultaneously instructing the two women on their projects and laying out a suit: pinning, cutting and jabbering, lamenting. His hands wave overhead from time to time - just being Wang.

"Wang, do you have a moment to talk?"

The look Jim receives suggests Jim might have lost track of his senses. With a huge sigh, Wang carefully places his fabric on the table top and motions to the door in the back. They walk through the beaded doorway, beads rattling back together behind them, and Wang opens the icebox to extract two cold bottles of Coca Cola. He sits on a low stool under the open window. Jim takes the chilled bottle and sits on the low stool opposite with his back to the wall. After long draws on the bottles, each lets out the small burp that accompanies carbonated drinks. "I have an invitation to the wine vintage opening," Jim says. "Gus thinks I may need more appropriate clothes for the event. He wants me to write a feature article about it. That means I probably will need to be able to talk to as many of the important guests as possible to get a sense of the activity. So, I suppose he is right that I need to look good. Do you have any suggestions about what I should wear?"

Wang sits quietly awhile, looking Jim over. Then he closes his eyes. Jim is beginning to wonder if he has fallen asleep when Wang suddenly stands up and pulls a large folder from the shelf over Jim's head. Placing it on the counter by the sink, he opens it to an inner page and motions Jim to come look. Jim leans over and examines the page. Wang grins, obviously very pleased with himself. "You expect me to wear something like that?" Jim says.

"Since you will be accompanying me to the opening, it is entirely appropriate. You will be part of my entourage and should look the part."

"What entourage? You say you are going as well? Why didn't you tell me? When did you get an invitation? You never said anything about it before." Jim's whole demeanor shows he is more than a little bit agitated.

"Do you want me to start at the beginning, eh? The vineyard belongs to a consortium and I own the majority value of the business. So essentially the invitation for you came at my instruction. I make the invitation list each year and pass it on to my colleagues, who in this case agreed since the second largest shareholder is Mr. Matunkup, who agreed instantly. It seems you and he are quite chummy.

"You are to be commended, Jim," Wang continues. "Gus is correct. You will need some decent clothing to wear to the opening. I have not mentioned it before simply because I have been too busy creating some of the other costumes for the event. I do not make all the clothing, just most of it. I have been busy and was expecting you to come soon. Gus did well to send you now. We still have time to make something special."

Jim is again way out of his depth and reluctant to show it. He asks anyway, "The invitation came from you and not Matunkup?" Wang gives a silent nod. Jim goes on, "Why an oriental outfit like the one you wore at your club? I have never worn such a thing, wouldn't even know how to put it on. I'm afraid that I would look quite stupid in it."

Wang sits and takes another long pull on his bottle. He motions to the agitated Jim to take a seat. "We all venture into the unknown and sometimes uncomfortable territory from time to time. Have you ever challenged yourself with a task that you felt was beyond your capabilities?"

Now Jim blushes and his discomfort falls away instantly. "Of course I have. I suspect I would not be here if I had not."

"Of course you have. Try these clothes. I think you might be pleasantly surprised."

Having Jim's measurements already, Wang simply transfers them to the design of the silk robe and sash, royal blue with dark red piping and accents. The robe has a high collar, wide sleeves, and no pockets where they can be seen. The design is common in Wang's shop so the women start quickly cutting and sewing; by the next evening they are ready to try it on Jim. The silk is smooth, cool to the touch and breathes easily, much better than his cotton twill. He actually feels cooler with the long robe than in his cotton shorts, long socks and short-sleeved shirt. As he turns, and peeks in the mirror, he does not really recognize his image, even though he can tell it is him who is moving and looking back.

It is a bit like Alice-Through-the-Looking-Glass. The feeling is splendid; the robe's neck is a bit tight, as are the shoulders. So the ladies remove the robe to make the adjustments and Wang stands smiling in the doorway. "Alright, you were right, and I was wrong, OK?

It feels marvelous. If I am standing next to you, I suppose I won't feel a fool."

"Why would you feel a fool anyway? Are these clothes so outrageous?"

"No, no, no! It is just that they are foreign to me, and, even though they feel great, I will still feel self conscious in public, unless I have company to share the spectacle. Do you understand?"

"Of course. Now, let us retire for the evening. I have more to discuss with you in the morning, perhaps some of which can appear in your newspaper, eh?"

Breakfast is at six a.m. Wang is bright and lively as Jim sits at the table for coffee, fruit, and bread and jam. The coffee is good, great as a matter of fact, and his spirits rise as Wang starts a short recitation.

"I came to Zamboanga in 1903, as a laborer in the coconut plantations. The work was hard, the money was not regularly paid and the Chinese were not welcome by the Spanish population, the Moro population, the Malay population, any ethnic group. We stayed by ourselves, as often happens with Chinese immigrant populations. We had our own social groups, our own banking, an entire separate society. When we were successful, we were careful to keep our successes to ourselves. Successful immigrants are not liked. Therefore, as you might guess, my financial situation is not exactly as it appears, and will remain hidden from public view. Very few people are aware of the extent of my holdings, and that is exactly what I want. Am I making myself completely clear?"

"Exactly, understood. So, if your financial standing is to be held so secretly, why have you invited me, a reporter, into your shop and into your various pursuits? How can you keep so much activity confidential when you are friends with Gus and me?"

"Gus is a gentleman and almost wholly ignorant of the extent of my enterprise. Those two factors make him a valued colleague, plus the fact that he is able to share much information about the life in and out of Zamboanga. His counsel is highly valued, as is his ignorance and discretion. He is aware that there is more to the tailor shop than making clothes, but his awareness is quite limited. His contacts are valuable and they have become more valuable since you arrived. As for your access to my shop and life, I have confirmed my original assessment of your skills over the past few months. Those skills and abilities are proving very important to my businesses and to the future of Zamboanga. My future depends on the future of this city and province, and beyond.

"Your stories of the conflict in China are troubling because my family and ancestors are directly affected. But the possibilities that the Japanese barbarians will expand their conflict to other areas in Asia makes immediate access to international information critical. You have that information, as does Gus, but you also have skills, which you have demonstrated with your promotion of Mr. Matunkup's enterprise. These skills will benefit my businesses. We will be able to work very well together because your greatest efforts are in support of your own success. And you have confidence in your ability to succeed. It is evident from the contract you negotiated with Gus that you will leave Zamboanga a wealthy man, assuming our arrangements remain undisclosed, as do the details of my financial and business situation. Understood?"

"Completely."

"To be clear, you are probably aware that you would not be able to successfully depart Zamboanga if any part of our agreement is violated. Correct?"

Jim is now feeling the heat of the morning; something is increasing the sweat in his armpits and on his upper lip. But, examining the faint smile on Wang's face, he relaxes his shoulder blades and exhales slightly. "No need to be more explicit. I get your point. Why do you think I will leave Zamboanga a wealthy man? I am certainly not starting out great! I've been here for four months already and am still barely breaking even, even with the low rent you provide and many free meals thrown in."

"Your future will become more clear in two weeks at the opening. In the meantime you can prepare by visiting more of the local business owners. Perhaps Gus is interested in the upcoming Philippine Medical Society meeting in Zamboanga at the end of this month. I imagine there will be many business owners interested in advertising in one of your special editions during the convention. This advertising will provide you a decent income for this month. I will refer you to several colleagues, who can then refer you to others who might have other references for you. Your 20 percent will take care of your needs until after the vintage opening."

"One question: how did you know about the medical convention?"

"My nephew lives in Manila and works for a doctor who is on the planning committee for the convention. He knows I have many business interests in Zamboanga and thought I would be interested. So he sent me a letter that arrived yesterday. The convention is scheduled for April 23, so you have at least two weeks to organize the advertising for the paper."

"Does Gus already know about the convention? He has not said anything to me."

"He found out this morning, so I am sure he will be mentioning it to you when you get back to the office."

Jim checks his watch, which he rarely has done in the past month or two, springs up from the table with a quick thank you, and vaults out the door. The opportunities are beginning to pile up and he does not want to spoil any by being late. The conversation with Wang replays in his mind over and over as he is taken by rickshaw to the front of the municipal building.

Gus meets him at the door. He already has a ready list of prospects for the special edition. He first takes Jim into the back office for a quick overview of each potential client, including the types of businesses and strategies to approach.

The coffee is stale and lukewarm. Jim leaves it in his cup, not wanting to spoil the memory of Wang's excellent drink. He gives Gus the lead talking about the upcoming convention. Gus is excited, and Jim wisely lets him talk as if Jim hasn't a clue.

Briefing over, Gus waves Jim off down the stairs into the bright hot sunshine, and returns to his backroom, rubbing his hands in anticipation. Sending Jim out with a list of prospects, especially given his success with clients to date, is nearly money in the bank.

Jim hails another rickshaw and heads straight back to Wang's, where he shows Wang the list Gus has given him. Wang studies the list, takes a pencil and marks through a few names with a shake of his head, then adds five more names with addresses at the bottom of the page. Finished, he looks at Jim saying, "Don't bother with the ones I struck off. They pay little, do not usually advertise much, and are not my friends. I substituted names to replace them, names of people who will appreciate a visit from you and from whom you can expect some serious advertising. Go out the back and find Filipe. He has one of the cabs ready to take you on your rounds. By this evening Gus should be a very happy man, which will make you happy and me as well." Wang returns to the cutting room to join the women. Jim turns left and out the back door.

The day is hot, sticky as usual, and passes quickly and profitably. Four-thirty comes around soon, and Jim finds he has completed two-thirds of the contacts that Gus and Wang have provided. Taking the taxi back to the municipal building, Jim files the advertising orders, releases Filipe for the day and arranges for an early start the next day. Two days and he will have made more from advertising than he made in two months. The walk back to his room above Wang's is slow, and he stops at Popeye's Pub on the way.

It has been several days since he'd visited the pub; he could use a nice, cold beer, or at least a tepid one, after the long day on the road. Sitting on the veranda under the palms and the jasmine arbor, he reviews the day's events, particularly the conversation with Wang this morning. Clearly Wang is a force to be reckoned with and he must be cautious how deeply involved he becomes with him. But it is also true that the influence Wang wields in Zamboanga, and possibly further, is serious and possibly could be the answer to many of his problems. His income would not be such a problem from here on out, allowing Jim to avoid dipping into the stash he came with. Wang most likely has contacts if Jim needs to move on. Life is a bit rough upstairs at Wang's, but it is certainly better than what he had in Manila. Right now things here in Zamboanga are slightly dangerous, but good - just the way he likes it.

The two weeks before the medical convention are frantic. The ads get published and the hoopla Jim has been able to generate gets a crowd onto the pier for the arrival of the doctors eager to spend money. The fledgling brass band is in uniform, sweating profusely but playing in partial tune. Dignitaries, from the mayor to prominent businessmen, suddenly raise a cheer as the boat rounds the point entering the harbor. The band is magnificent in its efforts to play together, hats are waving when Tony finds Jim to hand him a regular newspaper telegraph from Manila. He thanks Tony, looks at the telegraph and loses his tan instantly. Right there is the news that the medical committee has changed its mind and decided not to bring the convention to Zamboanga after all. They opted for Manila instead. Just as Jim finishes reading, the crowd gets quiet. Then the murmuring turns to grumbling and Jim sees what they have already noticed: the boat is empty of passengers. No doctors on the decks ready to grace the boulevards of Zamboanga buying from all the shops that have advertised in this week's paper. As he slowly slides to the periphery of the crowd, Jim hears the murmurs become more vociferous. Jim spots Gus at the back, mouthing one word: "Refunds." There goes his income for these two weeks, and perhaps for some time to come. Ugh! He will have to face many of these same people at the vintage opening tonight. Off to Wang's for safety and solutions.

The taxi drops him at the back door of Wang's shop. As he reaches for the door handle, the door swings into the room and there is a grim-faced Wang. "Did you not recheck the medical society plans before starting that ad campaign? What were you thinking?"

Jim takes a step back and stands outside the door for a moment, collecting his thoughts. "So, you've heard."

"Of course. Did you think I would not?"

"I understand your network is wide, but I did not realize it was this fast. Look, I sent telegrams late last week, early this week and only received the response as the boat was pulling into the dock. It does not make the paper look good, for sure, but I am afraid that it does not make you look good either. I think we should both work on this problem using everything we have at our disposal and make the result as good as we can. What do you think?"

Wang stands inside the door. The sounds of treadle sewing machines continue, rapidly making many garments for this evening's vintage opening. Jim stands outside the door sweating in the sun. Suddenly, Wang's face splits into the biggest smile. "Of course! Gus must also participate in this solution. He will make it happen."

Jim comes in, closes the door behind him and retrieves two cold Coca Colas from the ice box. Then Wang unravels one of the most elegant problem solutions Jim has ever heard. Jim takes notes as Wang elaborates. Then he springs out the back door to the taxi that is still there, and is off to the municipal building where Gus is waiting.

Gus is standing just inside the office door, more morose than ever, certain that the Mindanao Herald is no more. The office phone has been ringing nonstop with irate shop owners. Jim rushes past, takes Gus by the elbow on the way to Gus's office. "Look, we don't have time to spend with our jaws on the floor. We have to get this situation under control NOW! Here are a few ideas."

Jim quickly sketches the suggestions, which have actually taken the shape of a full-blown plan. Refunds are essential, but rewards are even more important. Laying the blame for the problem directly where it belongs, on poor communication from Manila, would also establish the advertising prowess of the paper at the same time. Jim and Gus quickly design a flyer to go to all the advertisers of the special edition and a separate one to go to every business in Zamboanga. The Mindanao Herald would initiate a contest for free full-page advertising space, and each of the disappointed advertisers will receive his own ¾-page free of charge and a banner headline in the paper next day. The paper will run a story explaining the poor communications with Manila and some of the recent consequences. The winner of the contest receives a year's worth of ½-page ads. The latest issue of the paper was already laid out but Gus and Jim were finalizing contest rules, designing a flyer, and revamping the front page of tomorrow's paper. The first order of business is to reset the paper and print and distribute the flyers. The typesetters will be busy all night.

By the time Jim leaves the next morning, the flyers to the current advertisers are set and delivery boys have gathered to distribute them to the shops before the close of business. The recovery is well on its way. While Jim is at the newspaper office, Wang has been sending his runners around Zamboanga alerting his colleagues, and many others, that they will be receiving interesting news shortly. By the time Wang's last runner has returned, the flyers are starting to arrive at shops and smiles are starting to return to the faces of many shop owners. Some continue to gripe with their neighbors, but most are thrilled for the opportunity to get such large ads in the paper. Even their sense of humor begins to return. Wang quietly arranges for the first edition of the paper to be hand delivered to the homes of the shop owners most affected by the no-show medical convention. Catastrophe averted, Wang and Jim begin to prepare themselves for the vintage opening.

"What a day!" Jim is upstairs in his room, sprawled on his pallet with a huge tumbler of red wine and lots of ice in it, trying to calm himself and recover. He just about dozes off when there is soft tapping on his door. Outside in the hall is the younger of the two seamstresses with his robe and his matching silk shoes. Thanking her with a slight bow, he closes the door. Holding the robe to the fading light at the window, he is impressed again with its sheen and colors. After a quick wash, he dons the robe, buttoning it to the throat. It no longer collects his shoulders tightly, the sleeves fall quite comfortably from his shoulders and slightly cover his hands. He slips on the shoes, which are much more like bedroom slippers and they fit perfectly, of course. Compared to his boots, they have no weight at all. He feels light on his feet, actually twirling to spread the robe and feel his feet contact the floor. He barely recognizes himself in the mirror. He is deep in thought when he hears a loud tap on his door. He opens it to find Wang in his splendor, wearing a black flat hat and waiting for him in the hall. He steps back half a step, as if to get a better view of Jim, then smiles very gently, gesturing toward the hall and stairs. Wordlessly, they both descend to the taxi that will take them to the opening.

When they arrive at a ballroom in central Zamboanga, they have a chance to observe the other arrivals as they step out of autos and horse-drawn carriages. Many are wearing exotic native dress from their countries of origin. It looks like a gathering for a formal dress ball. Finally it is Wang and Jim's turn. The liveried doorman opens the taxi doors as many crowd around to see Wang arrive. When they see both Jim and Wang, a murmur ripples through the crowd. As they begin their slow entrance into the ballroom, applause ripples through the crowd. The applause builds to the point that neither Jim nor Wang can hear what anyone is saying to them. Jim attempts to keep a straight face, while Wang's expression becomes even more opaque. They make their way through the crowd, with Chinese guests bowing and others offering congratulatory handshakes. A few are holding tomorrow's paper in their hands, as well as the flyers Gus has distributed; and everyone congratulates Jim on his excellent work. Those in the know quietly nod to Wang, giving their recognition for another coup he has accomplished. Wang may raise an eyebrow but that is all, while Jim tries to answer two or three questions, obviously enjoying the attention.

If the evening were to finish there, Jim would be delighted, but he actually stumbles on information that may solidify his place in Zamboanga business society. As he attempts to glide with grace from group to group, almost succeeding in matching Wang's smoothness, he finds that in talking to one vintner after another, a recurring theme is their desire to expand production, diversify their products, and maximize their harvests.

Some years, when the weather is bad, they have barely enough production to fill their standing wine orders in the Philippines and east Asia. But in other years, like this one, their production is so immense they have so many grapes that they don't know what to do with the excess crop. Walking and listening to the same concerns from group to group, Jim finally spots his boss Gus, pulls him aside, and asks, "Where does provincial wine go to be sold?"

"Well, the vast majority must be shipped out. There is a small market here in southern Mindanao, but most is sold outside the province."

"Why?"

"Jim, you must have noticed by now that most of the people attending this event are not drinking wine. They are Muslim, and don't drink alcohol, just like the rest of the province." Looking around the room, Jim sees that Gus is correct. Relatively few people are holding wine glasses. The rest are drinking coffee, water, or a Coke or Fanta. As he takes another look around the room, he overhears the conversations from small groups of well-dressed local aristocrats. The sheiks tend to spread out so they do not impose on one another's territories; their wives are not in attendance, but they are surrounded by sons and members of their respective communities. Wang has talked with each small group in order of importance over the course of the evening. Jim has watched him circulate out of the corner of his eye. After the vintners' speeches, and the official opening of the vintage by the governor, the crowd begins to disband and Jim listens to the last wisps of conversations as people depart.

This event reminds guests of their pride in their heritage - and especially of their province - just as the Philippine world is changing. There is a sense of isolation for them, but also one of being unique. Jim's mind is mulling over this and soon a sliver of an idea starts to form. He is certain Wang will be able to help him develop this idea. Just then there is a slight tug on his left sleeve and Wang slants his head toward the door. They glide away together, Jim thinking deeply, tired to the bone. Wang is as fresh as when they arrived, a slight hint of a smile in place.

CHAPTER 5

Things Are
Heating Up

As they sit in the back seat of the taxi, Jim stretches his legs and feet in relief. His visions for the future of Zamboanga dance in his head. Wang says nothing while they are in the drive of the ballroom. Then he murmurs, "Well done," once they are on the road and the noise of the tires covers his voice. Jim's face brightens and he starts to tell Wang about his concerns when Wang gently raises his hand off his lap as if to say, "In a moment."

When they reach town the taxi drops them in the rear of Wang's shop. Entering the back of the silent shop, Wang lights two candles rather than start the generator for electric lights. It is after 10 p.m. and municipal electricity is off. "Now, my friend, what have you brought away from the opening?"

"The growing of grapes in Zamboanga province relies solely on the province's ability to export wine or grapes. Making a profit depends a lot on other businesses, particularly transportation and import/export. Local wine growers would be more secure if there was more of a market in Zamboanga and nearby populations."

Wang sits and examines Jim with a distant stare. Minutes pass while Jim wonders if Wang has fallen sleep or is in a trance. Suddenly Wang leaps to his feet and dances a small dance, just a few quick steps. Then he faces Jim with a large smile on his face. "For some reason I was certain it was a good idea to heed Gus's request and offer you support during your stay in Zamboanga. I decided based on no information, just my instinct and Gus's word, something I never do. That decision is likely to be the best one I have ever made, best for my business and best for Zamboanga. I will discuss with Gus the possibility of a major advertising program, I think you call it marketing, and you must be the person in charge. Of course, I will be very closely involved as I have the best information about Zamboanga. But your ideas will be the first ones to consider at all times. The program must bring stability to the grape growers of Zamboanga and increase their profits by selling grapes to local processors instead of foreign wine producers. In two years I want to see more grapes produced in Zamboanga province than in all of the rest of the Philippines or overseas. Can you do that?"

"Sure."

Wang steps back and looks at Jim with a severe expression, looks again, dips his head slightly, then breaks into a smile and claps Jim on the shoulder hard enough to knock him off balance. When Jim catches his balance on the back of a chair, Wang grips each of Jim's shoulders in his small hands, and says, "I believe you, and that is why you are here now. Tomorrow you start." With that, he releases Jim, turns and disappears into his own small apartment at the back of the shop. Jim stands for a moment, then walks upstairs to his room. He disrobes and sits sweating on his pallet until sleep overtakes him. In what seems like an instant, he is awakened by a cock's crow and banging on his door. In the dim light of dawn streaming through his window he can just see the door shaking from the heavy knocking. "Yeah!" he bellows.

"It is getting late, Mr. Wang is saying, and the day needs your attention."

"Ugh! Please tell Mr. Wang that I will be down soon."

"I am instructed to bring you with me downstairs, Mr. Jim. Please come now or I will have great trouble."

Jim rolls to his side, sits up and rubs his face vigorously, suddenly realizing that the voice in the hall is a familiar one. The growl has barely left his mouth before he opens the door and there stands Tony Fali.

Jim's jaw drops, the growl disappears and Tony says, "You seem surprised. Don't be. Mr. Wang has called me to be your personal assistant for the next few days. Mr. Gus agrees. Can we go down?"

"If you are my assistant what the hell are you doing disturbing me now!? Get away from me!"

"Mr. Wang suggested you might answer like this and suggested I offer you this in response." With that Tony presents a small tray with a large mug of coffee and a hot, fresh pastry that makes Jim's mouth water. He gives Tony a look, takes the tray and says, "I'll be down in five minutes."

"Thank you."

"Argh! Get out of my face!!" Slam goes the door and Jim takes a large gulp of the coffee, which eases his weariness considerably. The pastry is magnificent. He has never tasted better, or similar, and he finally starts to wake up and dress in his usual uniform: shirt, shorts, boots, and high socks. Then he takes it all off and puts on the robe he wore last night, realizing at once that he is amazingly more comfortable. Wearing the robe, carrying the mug and brushing the last of the crumbs from his mouth, he descends the stairs to the shop, where Wang waits for him in the front room.

"Well, you certainly know how to prevent messengers from being killed in the early morning. What's going on anyway? The sun is not yet up and you have me standing in your front room."

"I see some of the lessons learned last night have remained and you have selected appropriate clothing. I hope other lessons remain as well and we can continue our conversation from last night."

"Yes, I remember the entire thing. But why are we up before the sun?"

"Because this is a most auspicious day and we must not waste any of it. Gus will be here in half an hour to discuss the advertising campaign and its funding. I wanted you to be completely clear before he arrives. The three of us have much to do, and you have the most. Please begin by writing down the main points we discussed last night. Paper and pens are there on the table. There is plenty of light now coming through the window, even though the sun is yet to appear. Please have the document ready for Gus when he arrives. It is always easier to work from a written document than just from spoken words. When you have finished writing, Tony will copy it using carbon paper so we each have a copy. There will be no other copies. Only the four of us will have any of this information. Your help and your cooperation is most appreciated."

With that Wang turns, walks through the beaded door and disappears. Jim walks to the table and slowly takes pen to paper and begins to write. In 15 minutes he finishes the highlights of his conversation with Wang. Instantly Tony is at his side. "Is it finished?"

"Yes. There are more details, but these are the basics."

"Thank you very much." And with a wide smile, Tony takes the two pages and retreats. Jim stands and stretches, unlocks the front door and goes out onto the walkway that fronts the shop. He sits at a small table and chair on the porch in the early morning, watching people on their way to the market and shops in the town center. Most people are walking, many pushing carts, some lead animals, each steadily flowing down the street. Sheep bleat at those tugging their ropes, men and women grunt as they push their heavy carts, a few open- air vendors shout out their wares, whether sharpening knives or repairing pots. It is very peaceful in its own way and Jim settles into its meditative rhythm. A slight breeze draws him back as Wang slides into view from behind his right shoulder. "Could you come in for a moment?"

Jim reluctantly rises and re-enters the front room where Tony is standing with papers in his hand. Wang lifts two pages from the counter and hands Jim two as well. "This is accurate and to the point. Your memory is very good. Please look at the copy you have to be sure it is what you wrote."

It has been no more than 10 minutes since Jim finished the original, but here are the two pages in fine script on carbon paper copies. Looking through them, Jim is satisfied with their accuracy and nods to Wang. He smiles at Tony, who beams back. "Good, now we are ready for our discussion with Gus," Wang says. "He will be here shortly. We have done well so far this morning. I am sure today will be very successful."

Just then, Gus opens the front door and Wang greets him as Tony retreats to the back. "Can we get you some coffee to help start your day, Gus?"

Gus looks at Wang, nods, then looks at Jim. "I saw you in that get-up last night and was not sure what I was seeing. What's going on?"

Jim glances at Wang, then looks at Gus with a wry smile, "Just getting up to speed with local customs and sartorial wisdom, old boy."

"Sartorial wisdom? You look like a Mandarin freak! Wang, is this garb acceptable to you? Don't you agree that he looks like a clown in a sideshow?"

"It seems you are not pleased with Jim's appearance."

"Pleased? I think he has lost his mind. Who would believe he has anything respectable to offer a newspaper dressed like that?"

"Hold it, old son. These clothes are the most comfortable I have had since I got here! So just get your tit out of the wringer!"

"I think our conversation is best held in my small office with additional coffee and perhaps some bit of food, no?" With that, Wang pulls aside the beaded curtain and Gus stomps through, followed by Jim whose temper is simmering. Wang, letting the beads fall back in place, follows closely and places a small hand on Jim's shoulder, giving the gentlest of squeezes to reassure Jim that Wang is in charge of the conversation.

Entering the office, Gus crosses and sits in his customary seat. Wang moves behind the desk and Jim takes the stool beside the door. Wang rings the small bell and Tony Fali appears. Wang says, "Gus, I believe you are quite familiar with Tony and his work, are you not?" With a brief scowl, Gus nods, and Tony shyly gives a small wave. Wang requests more coffee, cut fruit and pastries. With that order, Tony disappears.

"You were absolutely right about Tony's skills. He is obviously an energetic young man, eager to rise quickly. I agree he deserves this opportunity. So now he works for me a bit after finishing with you during the day. Today, as you suggested, I asked him to join us." Wang reaches onto his desk and retrieves the two papers containing the basics of Jim and Wang's idea. He passes them to

Gus. "This is the topic of discussion for us this morning. I hope you will be able to appreciate the delicacy of this information and that our discussion will be fruitful for us all." With that, Tony is back in the doorway with a large tray holding three mugs of steaming coffee, cream and sugar containers, a bowl of cut-up fruit and three skewers, plus several warm pastries on a plate. The tray is beautifully set with snowy white linen on the center of the desk. "That will be all for now, Tony," Wang says, and Tony silently slips out the door.

"This looks very good, Wang. Almost makes it worthwhile for me to get up this early. And you are right. I think Tony is better utilized here than at the paper, considering what you have outlined. Let me have one of those pastries. If it is what I think it is, it definitely will be worth it."

One bite and Gus sits back with a bit of a smile on his face. The coffee seems to perk him up and he puts the mug down to re-examine the paper. After five minutes, he looks up, brushes the crumbs from his face, and then looks first at Wang, then Jim. "This analysis is right on, I would say. I would guess that anyone with significant interest in the commercial grape harvest would be interested in the proposal. Of course, the paper has a serious interest in these ideas since the paper would play a central role in marketing, of course."

"You are astute as usual, Gus. That is why I wanted you here this morning. If I am correct, then today is the most auspicious of days, since it is the day after this year's vintage opening. Many wine growers are examining their prospects for the coming year and will be making certain calculations to enhance their profits. I know, as you are aware, what the prospects for the crops are this year, and they are very good indeed. So good that I expect that, without some other outlet for the grape harvest, much will be tossed into the sea. That would be a tragedy of great proportion. Thus we have the opportunity to strike with a marketing program while everyone's attention is at its peak. That means if we are to take advantage of this year's large harvest, we must start this morning. Do you agree?"

Gus smiles, looks at Wang, then leans back into the chair, looking hard at Jim. "So we have an opportunity now that we have not had in the past. Is that what you are saying, Wang?"

Wang simply nods, Jim smiles, and Gus smiles, saying, "Sorry about the sartorial crack."

"No offense taken," Jim says.

"May I suggest that we form an informal partnership, and include Mr. Matunkup, who has a significant interest in this program, even though he does not yet know of its existence. I will be able to present it to him in a fashion that I believe he will recognize the importance of immediate action. I also suggest that Jim start out this morning with specific plans to develop the program so that the implementation begins tonight. Does anyone object?"

"This evening? That's nuts! How in the world can I get a program together today when I don't even know the business?"

"Your contribution is the ideas, ours is the specifics and overcoming any obstacles. You must not let details of the business slow you down or interfere with designing the best combination of ideas to make Zamboanga the capital of grape production. You may work wherever you want and have all the support you need. Tony will be at your disposal, of course. Now I must call the hacienda in 10 minutes to inform Matunkup I am coming. Where do you want to work, Jim?"

Instantly Jim knows where he wants to work and a vision of what he wants to accomplish flashes before him. Closing his eyes, he opens them to Wang's gaze and says, "I'm coming with you. Tony can come too. I'll be at Matunkup's, in his garden by the gazebo. His land is away from the city, but he has everything, including a telephone if we need to communicate."

"Fine. Gus, you begin organizing the information infrastructure, including the municipal government, for us to make use of available large public advertisement space. We should have a program outline tonight and start the first part of the campaign tomorrow in a special edition of the paper. Yes, I do know there was one just last week that was a disaster. But this one will be no disaster, I assure you. Correct, Jim?"

"Correct. And, besides, you saw the reception at the vintage opening last night, right, Gus? It turned out alright, didn't it?"

"Ugh! Just. It was bloody difficult, but you are correct, the advertisers seemed to be happy by the outcome."

"And this special edition will make them even happier, believe me," says Jim. "We can tie it all together with one bow - the full-page advertisements, refunds, this new enterprise. It all works. Wow, I see the whole thing now! It is coming together. Let's get going."

"Gus, this is between us only now. Do you understand? Your arrangements with the municipal authorities are general in nature, for this weekend or next week, but without details. Correct?"

"I understand, Wang. How many people are in on this?"

"Five: You, me, Jim, Tony and Matunkup."

"OK. When do we meet again?"

Wang looks at Jim, who scowls slightly, and says, "8 p.m."

"Fine, where?"

Wang looks at Jim, then says, "At Matunkup's."

Gus stands, slugs down the last of his coffee, and smiles. "See you there."

Jim and Tony's ride to the hacienda is short this early in the morning, and Julio is waiting for them at the door with coffee. Jim takes a cup of coffee while Tony stands by with his writing materials: a thin folder, a small bag of pencils, a fountain pen, and a sheaf of paper. Wending their way through the center of the house, the three are silent and somber. Once through the back door, they ascend the steps to the gazebo. Jim takes his supplies from Tony, sets them down on the table and again sips his finely brewed cup of coffee. Letting out a long sigh, Jim proceeds to fill in the details, such as they are, that Wang did not convey over the phone. Julio nods from time to time, smiling at the obvious that no one until today has been able to discern. Then as Jim is wrapping up, Julio stands, nods and, with a sweep of his arm, declares, "Mi casa, su casa. What else do you need now?"

"Nothing I can think of. Could you show Tony through the kitchen so he can help with coffee and perhaps additional writing materials? I want to get started now. You are the best, Julio, a man among men."

"No hay problema, amigo. Tony, would you care to come with me?"

The sun is warm. The shade of the gazebo and the breeze off the mountain cools Jim off as he works. Garden stones litter the table top, holding papers in place from the breeze. Jim's mind jumps from outline, to specifics, to paragraphs, to notes, to next year, this year, next week, to vineyards and venues. He sits back and envisions the crowds at the annual vintage opening, the various ethnic groups, glasses and cups clinking to toast another successful growing year. He recalls the exquisitely dressed women accompanying men with slow eyes scanning the room, smiles hiding their secrets. That brings another burst of energy, more outlines, paragraphs and a call to Tony.

"Yes, do you need more drink, are you hungry?" Tony asks.

"Paper! I've run out!"

"One moment" and Tony scurries off as Jim yells after him.

Less than 30 seconds later, Tony returns with a large sheaf of paper, and a tall lemonade, lots of sugar. Jim brusquely takes the paper, pauses, accepts the drink, gulps two swallows and looks up at Tony, almost seeing him for the first time. "This is great! It is perfect, lad. How did you know I needed that?"

"The sun is warm and it has been three hours since you began. I thought perhaps you might like something to drink."

"Three hours? Well, it must be fun because I had no idea. Better bring a small bowl of rice with something in it. I'll probably be hungry soon."

"Right away, Mr. Jim," and Tony rushes back into the house. As he opens the back screen door, Matunkup peers around the corner and raises an eyebrow at Tony as he walks by. slightly bowing and saying, "He is quite busy. He wants some rice and meat."

Matunkup has the cook give Tony a tour of the kitchen and pantry, then goes back to his office and his own paperwork. Out on the gazebo, Jim takes another swig of lemonade, plunks another stone on the growing piles of paper, and starts another outline. Matunkup can see the gazebo from his office; he sits and watches Jim from time to time. He can almost see the steam coming from Jim's ears as his frantic writing consumes him.

Jim hardly notices when Tony substitutes the setting sun for the glow of a kerosene lantern. Twice he stands and paces in the garden, doing backbends, reaching for the gazebo rafters and stretching his arms and shoulders. He swings his torso and arms while pacing, trying to guide circulation back into his hands and fingers. He returns to his work, glancing at the voluminous piles of papers weighted down with grey garden stones. .

Finally, at 7:15 p.m., he stands up, selects five sheets of paper and motions to Tony. "Make three copies of these so they will be ready when Mr. Wang arrives. He will be here in 45 minutes. Can you do that?"

"Certainly. They will be ready in 30 minutes," and Tony disappears into the house as Matunkup reappears with two glasses in hand. He walks deliberately to the gazebo, handing one glass to Jim, who takes it with a smile. There is considerably less energy in his smile than this morning.

"Well, you seem happy with the results of your labors."

Jim is slow to respond, but then looks up over the whiskey glass and says, "Yes, I'm happy. I think the two of you will be as well. Tony will have copies for us all to look at before Wang arrives. We will be able to start the program tomorrow if you agree with the process I have laid out. It is a fairly simple three- part plan aimed at the long term with a quick start."

Julio is quiet then asks, "What should we do with our friends the sheiks? How can we make sure they and their Muslim followers are on board?"

"That is the first part. Let me explain before Wang arrives and perhaps you can help if he needs more convincing. The sheiks are responsible for the stability of each of the political areas of Zamboanga and they receive a percentage of the profits generated in each area. That is how they maintain their power over the province.

The balance of power among them is very important to maintain. Without it, open conflict is possible and that would be to everyone's disadvantage. In order to maintain the balance of power and influence, each sheik must see that he will profit by this plan. That is what I am hoping Wang will be able to help with through the relationships he has built over time. The first section of this plan has to do with developing the local market for grapes, thus their processing and consumption locally. Consuming Zamboanga grapes must be seen as a patriotic act, raising the status and honor of all Zamboanguenos. If you are a real Zamboangueno, you drink Zamboanga grape juice for all meals, and certainly for toasting special Zamboanga occasions. There even needs to be a new local occasion where Zamboanga grape juice is required for making special toasts. No juice for the occasion is tantamount to insulting our heritage."

Jim continues, "Since the manufacture of grape products, the growing of grapes, their transport, their consumption in cafes and restaurants, and the advertising and marketing of the product all take place in different regions, each sheik has a piece of the pie. This leads to the next part of the plan: the elevation of the value of local grapes and grape products. If their value increases in the eyes of the municipal authorities, then that might make local grapes and grape products the prime product of

Zamboanga municipal life. Gus and his contacts in the governor's office, as well as every grower and sheik, take a particular municipal officer as an individual project for special treatment in developing special allowances, official or unofficial, by the municipal and provincial bureaucracy. The list is here. Again, Wang will be influential in making the matches, but so will you with your agricultural contacts and influence. Finally, I will add my personal input with two special projects: the battle of the local chefs, a contest to find the best chefs who can make the most creative meals using grapes or grape products, and the Miss Zamboanga Grape contest to be held as part of next year's vintage opening. Miss Zamboanga Grape will represent the industry, as well as the province, and will most likely belong to one of the prominent families.

"The details are in the sheaf of papers Tony is copying now," Jim concludes. "I can use some suggestions on how to generate the greatest excitement for these contests, while making sure no one's toes get stepped on. The basics of each contest are detailed as well as the time lines and advertising campaigns for products and contests. The whole idea is to have as many blockbusting promotions for this product occur as simultaneously as possible, so there will not be a single Zamboangueno who does not realize that Zamboanga grapes are not only the best in the world, but also the example of patriotism of Zamboanga. To be a Zamboangueno is to enjoy and promote Zamboanga grapes."

Matunkup is very quiet. He is sitting at the gazebo table by now, whiskey glass sweating in his hand with the clink of a piece of ice methodically swirling as he rotates the glass round and round. His brow is furrowed into a mild scowl, then lightens as he raises his hand slightly toward Jim, tips his head and says, "I think today we have seen the last of the old Zamboanga and are looking at the beginning of the new. I suspect Wang will agree, but am not sure. I support your plan." With that he raises his glass toward Jim who touches his to Matunkup's with a graceful clink and each takes a long pull on the smooth, cold Scotch.

Just as the glasses are returning to the table, Tony returns to the gazebo with the copies in hand. He refuses the offer of a celebration toast with Jim and Matunkup and places the copies on the table. "Will you eat dinner here?" he asks Jim.

"Yes, as soon as Wang arrives," Jim replies.

Tony returns to the kitchen to assist Matunkup's staff. Jim and Matunkup return to silent contemplation. Then Matunkup begins to read. Jim rises to walk in the garden, relaxing from the days efforts. As he crosses the bridge in the pond, he hears a car arrive at the front of the house and sees Matunkup put down the papers and leave for the house. Slowly Jim returns to the gazebo, arriving as Wang and Matunkup are coming out the back door to the gazebo. Jim quietly stands at the table as the other two mount the stairs. Jim gives a slight bow of respect to Wang, who returns the gesture ever less deeply to mark their respective rank. This gesture is not lost on Matunkup, nor Jim, who smiles. Wang is in traditional robes, quietly spectacular in their glory.

The three men sit around the table and Matunkup pours scotch into three fresh glasses full of ice that somehow have arrived. "May our labors be rewarded," Wang says, and their crystal glasses gently clink together. They sip their drinks awhile, then Wang takes a moment to review Jim's report before starting their discussion. Matunkup also takes a copy and walks to his office. Wang stays at the gazebo while Jim walks back to the house to go to the bathroom. As he slowly moves through the rest of the house, he peeks into the busy kitchen and sniffs the marvelous smells. He is suddenly ravenous and gets a bowl of cut-up pineapple to snack with his scotch.

As Jim is standing there, Matunkup comes out of his office and walks toward him. They return to the gazebo and find Wang sipping his whiskey. Looking off toward the dark mountains beyond the garden,

Wang says, "This might work, but to change the public perception that Zamboanga thrives on grapes, rather than coconuts, may be the most difficult hurdle. I believe it can be done. Let's start at 6 a.m. with this plan as described here." Wang lifts the papers off the table. "I start with my business colleagues, Matunkup will contact the sheiks he has influence with, Jim goes straight to Gus who will talk with the municipal authorities tomorrow and will publish the first of the articles listed. He must publish the article in this week's paper. We must not hesitate one day. When do you think we should announce the chef contest and the Miss Zamboanga Grape contest?"

"The chef contest must take place six months before the next vintage opening," Jim responds. "We will announce the Miss Zamboanga contest at the chef competition's awards ceremony where we will have the largest audience of influential people. But we have to be sure to make the Miss Zamboanga contest a popular one, not limit the interest to the elite. I suspect the participants will be from the elite, but the excitement and enthusiasm for Zamboanga grapes must be throughout the community. Everyone must realize that grapes are the essence of Zamboanga."

Matunkup nods and says, "Of course. Everyone has a stake in this major undertaking."

"Do you agree with the expansion of grape production that I listed in the plan?"

Matunkup and Wang both nod agreement. More plantings mean more workers. Shopkeepers will benefit from additional workers. And in two years' time, the growers will see a return on their investment, not to mention the influence that sheiks will gain sending clan members from the mountains into town to profit from a booming economy. Additional investments will immediately benefit Wang's associates, as well as Matunkup's and the municipal authorities. The one group not directly mentioned in the conversation is the military, but Jim has even included Pettit Barracks in his notes and intends to visit them in order to bring their influence into the mix. It is in the notes, but since neither Matunkup nor Wang have much contact with the Americans, Jim has taken that role for himself with no complaints from the other two. "I believe we are finished here this evening, are we not?" says Wang. Jim and Matunkup nod and Tony appears as if summoned. "Dinner is served in the house, if you care to come now," says Tony. The three men gather their papers and their glasses, and troop single file away from the sanctuary of the gazebo toward the house. The pecking order remains intact, but relationships are developing. Each is deep in thought throughout the meal and they hardly speak when it is time to leave. As they solemnly shake hands, they remind each other of their next meeting two days hence, again here at Matunkup's. They want to make sure to maintain the momentum of their ambitious project.

Next day Wang and Matunkup are traveling most of the day, making personal calls to their contacts, while Jim starts the day early with Gus as he reviews a copy of last night's program outline. Having read it twice, Gus sits back and lets out a low whistle. "Never saw these fellas in such concerted action before. How did you do it?"

"I didn't. I just wrote down what I thought was a complete marketing program for what they both said they wanted. I can see each of them collecting big time if the project is successful, and, honestly, I see this as a chance to have some fun and for me to make enough cash for a new start back in the States. I think this can work. It covers all the bases as far as people needing to profit, even you, Gus."

Gus looks back down at the outline, puts it aside and leans back in his chair. "I'd say this program relies quite a bit on the influence of the paper, wouldn't you?"

Jim takes his time, stands slowly, and walks to the front window that looks out onto the newspaper office's entry hall. Then he slowly turns, leans on the door jam, somewhat nonchalantly, and takes out a cigar. He prepares it, lights it and walks back to his chair. Jim looks him in the eye and says, "Gus, you have a chance to make a killing in advertising on this project. Are you going to fuck it up?"

Gus drops his feet to the floor and suddenly leans forward, furious. "What do you mean fuck it up? Where do you get off talking to me that way? You just got here, buddy, and your trial period isn't even over yet. I set you up with Wang, I put in a good word with Matunkup. You want to rephrase your question, or you want to walk?"

"Gus, you'd better calm down or you are definitely going to lose on this one. I am not saying you didn't smooth my entry into Zamboanga commercial society. You did. All I am saying is that now that I am in, I am a player, just like you, and closely involved in one of the biggest commercial ventures Zamboanga has ever seen. I have a job to do, Wang has given me the job, and part of my job is to ensure that you and the paper are on board. The advantages for you and the paper are obvious, I think. You are going to be at the center of a huge undertaking, and you are going to have huge influence with other major players. That is assuming you can control your greed and keep your head on straight.

"I wrote up this program, Wang and Matunkup are the major players, the ones with the chutzpah. Not me, not you. They tell me what to do and I do it. Are you in or out? If you are in, do your job and don't fuck it up with your ego. If you don't want in, Wang will come and pick up the keys to the newspaper office this evening and there will be a new owner tomorrow. How do you want to play it?"

The deflation is complete. Gus is bombastic but not stupid. He leans back, puts his feet up on his desk drawer and says, "Got another one of those cigars?"

Jim steps forward and reaches into his chest pocket, retrieving one and handing it over. Gus clips the end, mouths it end to end, lights it and says, "What do you need me to do?" And they are off. Jim goes over the section of the plan involving the municipal leaders with Gus attending in detail. Then they discuss the next issue of the paper, details of full page announcements, what p.r. pieces will reinforce those announcements, and plans for the next 10 weeks of issues leading up to the announcement of the chefs' contest. They finish with story ideas to develop investment news and how to respond to the expected interest from Manila investors.

After an hour, Gus leaves to start his rounds within the municipal offices and Jim leaves for Pettit Barracks, a place he has yet to encounter. The name Pershing is certainly familiar, but only vaguely. Jim was never a military buff, but Pershing's name is certainly known all over the Philippines, even in downtown Zamboanga at the square named after him. The general has been gone nearly 20 years now, but there are still bitter memories, particularly in the Moro community, so conversation with the sheiks, if it ever happens, goes any direction but there. Pettit Barracks and the remaining U.S. Army contingent are still there, and retain some influence in the province. The Americans certainly have a larger per capita monetary impact on the area than any other single group. If they can be brought into the project it will give its chances a serious positive boost.

Now, the sheiks do have long memories which include the unpleasantness suffered by the Moro people at the hands of the U.S. Army and General Pershing. But they have even deeper pockets that, when full, help dull those memories. If the barracks can help fill those pockets, perhaps the past - and a few current difficulties in Mindanao province, the home to Zamboanga - can be overlooked. The barracks commander will understand that. If the barracks are a ready market for a significant portion of the grape harvest, and can underwrite some of the program itself, the effect will help smooth several ruffled feathers in the Moro community. That is the tack he intends to take on his visit. Matunkup has successfully greased this introduction, according to his telephone call to the paper this morning. The taxi from

Wang is at the curb and Jim is off to the northern part of town where the Pettit Barracks are.

The ride was not long and he is in the central command offices within 45 minutes after leaving the municipal building - a much easier trip than the journey to Matunkup's estate. Climbing out of the cab, he takes in the view, which is a tidy two-story building with wide verandas surrounding both floors and flanked by tall palms on all sides. The tile roof blazes red in the sun and he can see curtains billowing in the upstairs windows and shutters on the downstairs windows that dim the light in the rooms, making them cooler. As he climbs the stairs to the double door entrance, a tall American in an army officer's uniform comes out of the door, extending his hand with a smile. "Arthur Connolly. Been commander here about six months." His accent is slightly southern, Missouri or Maryland, Jim thinks.

"Jim Tuck, recently of China and Manila and also about four or five months in Zamboanga. Good to meet you and I hope we can be of use to one another."

"Come upstairs to my office. I moved up there as soon as I arrived. Breeze is better, just have to hold the papers down." They enter the dark wood walls of the hallway and ascend the stairs. Along the stairway there is a window on the side wall that looks out over the parade ground where three uniformed soldiers are marching single file along a white square outlined on the ground, seemingly going nowhere fast. "Fellows needing a little exercise and drying out after a bit of a drunken dust-up last night," Connolly says. "This seems to work as well as anything."

"I don't see any supervision for them. My experience is that punishment details don't work that well without it."

"True, generally, but the alternative here is obnoxious enough that the marching is gladly carried out independently. Everyone can see the grounds anyway, and, if they decide to goof off, the word is out pretty quickly. Then they have the opportunity to work the sugar cane fields."

"You mean the fields at Matunkup's?"

"Those, or one of the other select groups of farms that we have arrangements with. The work is worse than onerous and avoided at all costs. The farmers enjoy the free labor, provide detailed reports on the cooperative nature of the offenders in their care, and it helps make local allies. Been going like this at least a couple of years. Commander just before me instituted it and the barracks seems to have developed a bit of appreciation from the community as a result. Gotta watch for the odd criminal conviction perpetrated for profit, if you know what I mean, but in general it has been foolproof so far."

Reaching the entrance to the commander's office, they enter and an enlisted man stands at attention. Connolly orders him at ease and Jim and the commander enter his office, a bright, spacious room with a desk to the far side facing the door, a sofa to the right facing the full length windows and three interior walls covered with mementos of this and previous commanders. A framed portrait of a man in full uniform with riding crop behind his right knee and left leg slightly forward hangs prominently on the wall behind his desk. Jim is studying the picture when Connolly says, "Pershing."

"I saw that name previously but have to admit my military history is lacking. So I have to plead ignorance except for the fact he must have been here at some time."

"Yep. Military commander and provincial governor until 1913. Hell of a guy. Seems his heart was in the right place but not someone you ever wanted to cross. Had his whole family here for four years."

"You like him?"

"Not a bad sort, I guess. He certainly had his trials trying to govern this area. Glad I just have this job, which is enough, believe me. Now, how can I help?"

"I am helping initiate a program to assist economic development in this area, particularly Zamboanga and the surrounding agricultural areas. The program has many facets, all of which are strictly confidential for now.

You being a military fellow I expect you can be counted on for your discretion." Jim smiles wryly and Connolly simply nods his head, as if discretion is his middle name.

"There are three aspects of this program that the barracks can assist with. First, an expanded agricultural effort resulting in growing more grapes for local consumption. Since the barracks is a major purchaser of local fresh commodities, we are hoping that alerting you to the increased production ahead of time might help the army get good prices when the harvest comes in next year. Second, we are having a local competition for the best provincial chef, which the barracks might like to participate in. The contestants will be creating and producing new or traditional dishes using grapes in some way. Perhaps the barracks has a particularly clever cook that would participate in the competition, and you could also provide a venue for the event. We plan to make the highlight of the competition a formal dinner dance for all the luminaries in Zamboanga society. So, the barracks would have the opportunity to play host to Zamboanga's finest for an evening. You would meet and network with several influential local businessmen.

"Finally, we will be having a vintage opening. You ever been to a vintage opening?" Connolly shakes his head no. "A vintage opening is an amazing event, also attended by all the elite of Zamboanga. I was there the other night.

Amazing! Anyway, at the next vintage opening, and hopefully for many future openings, we are having a Miss Zamboanga Grape contest. The judging will be held the night of the official opening, making it a spectacular event! We are looking for sponsors of the event for this time next year. As I said, these details are, for now, strictly confidential. Marketing events start soon, so you won't have to keep the confidence long. But I hope you will be willing to have the barracks participate in the chef contest, as well seriously consider using the barracks as the cooking venue, provide some sponsorship for the Miss Zamboanga Grape event, and seriously consider utilizing more grapes and grape products at the barracks. The barrack's participation will go a long way toward convincing the rest of the community to participate as well. And I guarantee you will have a lot of fun, I sure plan to."

Commander Connolly sits awhile, pushing his longish, slightly messy, blond hair back out of his eyes, then swivels his desk chair toward the windows. He stands, walks to the window and looks out for some time, as if the marching trio below holds great interest for him. Suddenly he turns back to Jim with a wide smile and says, "I think this is marvelous! What a hoot! Yes, to the venue. And I'll check with my cooks to see if anyone is interested. How many can I bring to the opening and beauty contest next year?"

"Great! You won't regret it a second. You can bring one couple for each $200 of sponsorship. Shoot, why not let the Army support a whole army table? Dress uniform, of course. Gotta advertise, right?"

"Right. Keep me posted and how about we talk again this time next month?"

"Good. You can reach me through the newspaper office. If I am out just leave a message with the owner, Gus, or my assistant Tony."

"Got it. You can get yourself outta here?"

"Sure. Thanks for your time. Good to talk with another American for a few minutes."

"Same here. See ya in a month." And Jim heads back to the paper. When Jim arrives at the tailor shop, an excited Wang appears through the beaded curtain and hustles Jim upstairs where the sharp ears of the two seamstresses are sheltered from the conversation. "Jim, I think we have a very good program here! Every one of my colleagues has given a strong endorsement to the idea and the specifics, but they are a little suspicious of you. I tried to assure them of your abilities and trustworthiness, but they are naturally suspicious people and insist on meeting you directly. They are used to making their own decisions about whom to trust. We will meet them tonight at the club at 9:30 for dinner and conversation. You will, of course, dress appropriately, as you were at the vintage opening. They, of course, saw you there but are still unsure about your character and will benefit from this meeting. We are on the edge of a very big deal, and events are moving very fast. Be ready to leave at 8:30 p.m.. We will arrive 30 minutes early and make sure all is well prepared. I have told Gus, but he will, of course, not be there."

"Why wouldn't Gus be there. He is as much a part of this as we are?"

"Because his face is too white, and he is too close to the municipal authorities. My colleagues would never be able to have an open conversation in his presence, and that is what we need. Can you understand?"

"Guess so. 8:30 it is. I will be here in the front room then." Wang returns downstairs and Jim retrieves his copy of the marketing plan to review. Once he has reread it, he is off to town and the café downstairs at the municipal building for a very late lunch. Tony is there, racing among tables as usual and smiles when he sees Jim sitting near the front of the outdoor area, nearest the low wall above the walkway.

"What are you doing here? I thought you were working for Gus and Wang now?"

"Oh, I am, certainly, but I could not leave my old boss with no good help, could I? I am here three days during lunch rush, at the paper from 6:30 in the morning until I come down here, and then I go to Mr. Wang every day at 6 p.m."

"When do you eat?"

"Oh, my mother makes a very good breakfast and packs plenty for me to eat during the day. Many times Mr. Wang allows me to eat in the kitchen at the club. It is very good food there, don't you think?"

"Yeah, I think. I am just wondering when you have any fun."

"I have very much fun, every day, almost all day. Do you not have fun also?"

Jim looks for the subtle smile that will let him know he is being taken, but Tony's face is entirely open and expectant. So Jim simply says, "Yeah, I have lots of fun. It's just getting a bit wearisome with so little female companionship."

"You have not found a girlfriend yet? That is very strange, especially in Zamboanga!"

"Why strange? It seems that the women are either locked away or taken or too shy to even speak."

"The females here are shy, many are the daughters of very important people who must protect them so they are suitable when it is time to marry. But there are also many, many females who have a different attitude towards having a boyfriend. Many, believe me, I know."

Jim leans back and takes another look at Tony, who is wide eyed and enthusiastic. Just as Jim is about to speak, a customer from across the café raises his hand and Tony is off. How he can see through the back of his head is another mystery for Jim, but he sits waiting for more information that might help him break his sexual drought.

China and Micronesia offered plenty of opportunities for companionship, but Zamboanga, so far, has been a bust. Jim's pride has not allowed him to "pay for it," feeling he has a reputation to maintain. So he just does without; but if Tony has contacts maybe he can break the drought. All work and no play makes Jim a dull boy, and he has been feeling pretty dull lately.

Tony returns to the table and asks, "Would you like some help finding a girlfriend, Jim?"

Jim blushes for the first time in months and growls, "Tony, just point me in the right direction and turn me loose. I don't need encouragement, son, but a little tutoring in local customs or contacts would be appreciated."

"Well, I will be at the club this evening because there is a big meeting Mr. Wang says he needs my assistance with. Can you be there, too?"

"I will be there, certainly. Wang and I are meeting for the project. So I'll talk to you there."

"I will not have many opportunities to talk, but perhaps there will be some chance, or maybe some time after the meeting. I will do my best to help you. It is not good to not have a girlfriend."

Jim smiles, mostly to himself, but Tony takes it as approval and beams ear to ear.

"Now, can you get me a coffee and two croissants?"

The coffee and croissants are good as usual, and Jim sits and savors them while considering a strategy for this evening's meeting. He develops a few options then adjourns upstairs to report to Gus.

Gus has just returned from the municipal offices, so they each have much to share; it looks good so far, from both their vantage points. The mayor and several local officials who Gus briefed on the plans almost immediately said things like, "Why hasn't anyone done this before? This is so obvious. Zamboanga will likely profit from this immensely," and other similar affirmatives. Jim lets Gus know about his visit to the barracks and Wang's progress with his colleagues. Then he mentions this evening's meeting. Gus ponders a minute, then says, "That bunch at the club is Wang's business. If I try messing in it I'll just screw it up."

Jim is somewhat relieved to hear Gus's spontaneous agreement with Wang's assessment and relaxes a bit. He is still somewhat anxious about the interactions with the club group, but figures Wang will back him up if necessary. Things are moving along quite well, it seems. This is usually when the other shoe falls and things start falling apart. Gloomy thoughts. He better get control over his thinking. So, he smiles, sits up straight, puts his feet back on the floor, and stands to leave. "Well, I'm off. No appointments until the meeting this evening. I'll see you in the morning. We still have some ads to develop to keep the paper ticking to help make this project work. See you in the morning."

When Jim arrives at the tailor shop the sun is setting and the sound of the treadle machines is gone. The place is very quiet as he pushes through the beaded curtain and turns left to head upstairs and start the process of removing a day's worth of sweat and dust turned to mud. One foot on the first step and Wang bursts through the door to his residence off to the right. "Jim! We must talk a minute immediately. I have sent the women home a bit early to assure we are not interrupted. Come, come, here into the kitchen!" With that, he nearly wrenches Jim's left shoulder out of socket and begins dragging Jim down the hall.

"Hold on a minute! Can't it wait until I have cleaned up a bit? I'm a grimy mess!"

"Talk first, clean later. Come!"

They enter the kitchen area and Wang removes a boiling pot from the stove, pours two cups of tea using the bivalve loose teaspoon, and dips alternately into each cup. In moments, the tea is ready and he hands Jim one cup while taking the other into his palms. Jim tries the same holding technique and quickly reverts to using the handle because the bottom of the cup is too damned hot to hold. How the hell does Wang do it? Wang is sitting on the other side of the table and starts, "Sheik Tamil will be there this evening. I did not expect him to come. He is more Matunkup's colleague than mine, but already has a grape farm established. He is very upset about the idea of growing more product since it will decrease his profits if there is too much production. Each year when there is a large crop he says his profits decrease because there is too much produce on the market. I have heard that he is very upset, and Matunkup recommended he come to this meeting this evening. He has many powerful friends among the growers, and within the Muslim community. He is Moro through and through, and does not like Chinese very much. I am not sure what influence I can have over him, and obviously Matunkup did not have good luck with him up to now. If his friend cannot persuade him, I am not certain what we can offer him, particularly since he does not like my company."

"Calm down, calm down! Getting too excited will injure your thinking. OK, let's sort through this one step at a time. First, his main complaint is loss of profit, correct?"

"Correct, plus I am not sure how much he trusts foreigners, particularly Chinese and Americans."

"OK, we start there. Then we need to find out who his friends are. If they support us, he is more likely to, correct?"

Wang has stopped wiggling on the chair he is sitting in and is becoming more thoughtful. "Correct, but I am not sure who his colleagues are."

"No, but Matunkup knows, does he not?"

Wang smiles, stops rocking and looks at Jim, "Yes."

"So we start making a plan with Matunkup. He is no dummy!"

"Right."

A trip to the hacienda is in order, and a clean Tuck will aid the conversation. So Jim hustles through his ablutions; he and Wang are off to Matunkup's in less than half an hour. The meeting at the club is soon and this conversation is not for the telephone, so the taxi ride to the hacienda is hazardous. Both travelers are wound up by the time they arrive and Jim has never seen Wang as animated as he is when he exits the car to the hacienda's front porch. Again, before they reach the door, it is open and Julio is standing there in anticipation. The warning call from Tony has produced a furrowed brow on the patrician face, but he gently ushers the two guests into the foyer then through the house to the gazebo where a sweating pitcher of lemonade and glasses is waiting. Both Jim and Wang plop into the waiting wicker chairs, then Jim leaps up again and begins pacing as he accepts a full glass from Matunkup. Then stops, sips his drink and says, "We may have a serious problem with obtaining Sheik Tamil's cooperation in the project. We need leverage to assist him into the program. Who would be the best contact who might have the most influence with him and at the same time supports the project?"

"Well, that certainly is direct and to the point. Hmm, let's see. First, why do you think he is not in favour of the project?"

Wang chimes in, providing information he has already told and mentioning the emotional distance between himself and Tamil. Julio is nodding slowly, as if he already knew this but was just now realizing its importance.

"And Jim thought coming here to confer with me would help sort the situation?"

Wang smiles, nods and raises his right hand palm up, signaling that adding Jim to their group was a stroke of genius. Matunkup stands, carrying his glass of lemonade, and Jim sits down. After circling the table once, Matunkup stops, takes a sip and says, "We should talk with Ahmad Basher. He has one of the largest holdings of grapes, is one of Tamil's closest colleagues, and ostensibly stands to lose the most if the project is not managed properly or the gamble fails. Tamil realizes that, so if Ahmad Basher agrees and pushes it, I am pretty sure Tamil will come along as well. Wang, you should not be a party to this meeting." Wang nods in agreement. "But I must take Jim with me, and we must leave now in my car. We will come to the shop after the meeting to let you know the outcome. Then we can go to the meeting, but first, Jim will go to this meeting with Ahmad Basher with me."

"Agreed," and Wang rises, not having touched the lemonade, and leaves through the back door. Matunkup takes another sip of lemonade, then says, "We will go to Ahmad Basher's now. I am sure he will be available since today he works at his city office. I will call him myself. Meanwhile, Chuong Song Dao, my house man will take you to my rooms and find suitable clothing for you to wear to this meeting with Basher, which you will also wear to the meeting this evening. As you were more readily accepted at the vintage opening with Wang in his attire, you will find greater acceptance with the people at this evening's meeting in attire familiar to them. Go with my house man and I will make the call to Basher. We have little time for slow moving."

Standing beside Chuong the house man, Jim finds for the first time in his life that he is a full head taller than another man. Even in China there was no one this short. With a motion of his left hand, Chuong indicates Jim to follow him to a closed solid wood door. Choung opens the door with the knob that for him is head height and beckons Jim inside. Jim stands just inside the door, taking in the room's Spartan furnishings and the full-sized painting of a striking woman hanging on the left hand wall, where it can be seen while lying in the four-poster bed to the right. Straight ahead are a set of curtained French doors leading to a private porch and a table and chairs outside. The doors are open with interior screen doors. The view falls over the farm, but the ocean is too far away and is blocked by one too many hills to be seen. Its reflection in the sky, though, enhances the blue atmosphere.

Suddenly Choung is in front of Jim with multihued clothing over his arm, indicating that these are for Jim to change into. Jim takes a look, then gives Choung a quizzical look to which Choung simply pushes the clothing into Jim's hands, turns and leaves through the door, closing it behind him. Jim deposits the clothes on the bed, removes his outer clothing, including his boots, and puts on the native Moro garb. There are two, long, narrow cloths remaining after he finishes donning the rest, and he is not sure what to do with them. He stands there in his stocking feet. A light tap at the door and Jim responds, "Come in." Choung enters, examines the results, and takes up the remaining two cloths of roughly similar length. The first he uses to wrap around Jim's waist three turns, folding the end under the wraps. The second he wraps around Jim's head four times, folding the end neatly under the wrap in the back. Then he enters the large closet and returns with a pair of silk slippers and hands them to Jim, who stands there clearly aghast at his appearance and starts to hand them back. Choung simply smiles, turns and leaves the room as Matunkup enters similarly attired. "Ah, very well done. Put your shoes on and we are off. Quickly, we have little time."

"Wait, wait, wait, old boy. You expect me to go outside in this get-up? I look like I should have a magic lamp!"

"Have you ever heard the phrase, 'When in Rome?' We are going to visit a very powerful gentleman for whom this clothing is not only normal, it is formal, preferred and understood. People relax in familiar surroundings and with people who appear similar to them. Ahmad Basher is critical to our success, and his cooperation depends upon his being able to hear what you have to say. You are the spokesman here. No matter what clothes Wang could put on, he would not be accepted, and he knows that. So he fully cooperates. We expect you to as well. Let's go."

With that, Matunkup turns and is out the door. Jim quickly sits, puts on the silk shoes, and hustles after Matunkup. They climb into the front seat of Matunkup's car, a black Cadillac convertible with the top up, that he is driving himself, and they are off. Julio is a masterful driver and is obviously familiar with the road. The dust plume behind the car is high and the car swerves around the curves of the dirt road as he hurriedly drives down through the farm toward the main road.

Once on the straight toward town, Julio puts his foot down and they reach the outskirts of the city in two-thirds the time of a usual trip. In the chaos of traffic on the outskirts of town, Matunkup slows considerably and uses the horn liberally. Finally, in the eastern section of town, Matunkup pulls up to a tall gate in the wall of a small side street, produces one short blast on the car horn and the gate opens immediately, as if his arrival is expected.

Entering through the gate, the car immediately turns to the right and stops in a designated area among palms surrounding a tinkling fountain that is straight ahead. Jim and Matunkup exit the car as their doors are opened by tall liveried men dressed quite similarly to Jim and Julio. The small gravel of the parking area feels quite painful on Jim's tender soles, but he keeps a slight grin on his face and Matunkup glances back to nod his encouragement.

One of the liveried staff leads Jim and Matunkup up a winding staircase to an elevated living area that is open, airy and splendid. The elegance of the building could not be seen from the road, partly because of the wall and partly the trees that shield it from view. Jim is beginning to appreciate the almost universal tendency Wang has already demonstrated: hiding wealth from public view. People must know, in such a tightly knit community, but still no one wants to flaunt it. It is rather nice, actually, and provides constant surprises.

At the top of the staircase Jim and Matunkup are met by another house servant and led into the shade of the veranda, through a beaded curtain into a large room furnished with nothing but low tables and cushions with hanging tapestries separating the room from adjacent areas. The cushions are dark red, almost maroon, with gold piping. The tables are spaced around the room and of highly polished dark wood. Sitting at a central table is a small dark man with a smiling but serious face, dressed much like Jim and Matunkup. He does not stand, but offers them seats on cushions opposite him. As they sit, a sweating pitcher of juice is placed in front of the host with glasses in front of each of the three men and a bowl for fruit in the center of the table. Small plates are beside each glass with a small elegant silver knife to carve the fresh fruit.

Basher opens the conversation, asking about the ride from the hacienda to town, observing that the trip seemed quicker than usual.

Matunkup replies, "Yes, you are, as usual, quite observant. My colleague is Mr. Jim Tuck, whom I have come to realize has certain skills and perceptions that can be quite important to our well-being here in Zamboanga. Jim, my esteemed colleague, Mr. Ahmad Basher." Jim nods and is greeted with a deep, hearty laugh from Basher.

"My dear, Mr. Tuck. You seem a bit uncomfortable in such clothes. Am I correct?"

For the second time in a week, Jim manages to blush and says, "You have me there. It is the first time I have worn such clothes, but I am wearing them in the hopes that the clothes will assist our conversation and make me more easily heard."

Basher contemplates this for a moment then says, "This conversation must be important for you to put yourself through such a level of discomfort. What has this much importance to you and my dear friend Julio?"

With that opening, Jim begins a succinct presentation of the undertaking. The usual formalities and chit chat that would prolong such a discussion are swept away. The conversation still requires at least an hour to answer Basher's incisive questioning. Jim does most of the talking, answering the sheik's questions with pointed answers, Matunkup contributing very little. The back and forth between Jim and Basher is quick, open and brings out a measure of mutual respect in both men. Matunkup simply leans back on his cushion and relaxes, appreciating this new development. He begins to be optimistic about their endeavor with the future extending forward brightly. He savors this vision as Jim and Ahmad Basher wind down their conversation. The three men stand and Basher signals for the servant who accompanied Jim and Matunkup up the stairs. As the tall servant approaches, Basher speaks quietly to him in Tagolog, and he immediately turns and disappears into an adjoining room. Basher says, "He is making the necessary calls to arrange my meeting with Tamil prior to this evening's gathering. After he finishes those calls, he will see you to your car. Come, let us walk a bit."

The stroll takes them out the side door and around to the rear of the house where there is a spiral staircase to the ground and gardens. Back here the noise of the town is muted among the tall garden plants. There are stands of bamboo, bougainvillea draped over trellises, large-leafed elephant ear plants, and more palms some tall and slender, and some squat and wide. The white gravel path crunches underfoot with each stone seemingly coming through the soles of Jim's silk shoes. His face remains serene while his feet throb in pain. The path crosses a small bridge, much like the one at Matunkup's place, and lands at a gazebo similar to Julio's. Jim stands a moment looking around at the lush surroundings. Finally Matunkup says, "Yes, it is familiar, is it not? Ahmad Basher and I share many similar tastes." Realizing that Matunkup is deliberately not giving anything away about who had the idea first, Jim nods and produces a slight smile of recognition. Basher gives a sweep of his hand and asks, "Is this familiar to you, Mr. Tuck?"

Jim simply nods and says, "Please, I am very comfortable if you call me Jim and, yes, I did some work in a gazebo much like this one, very recently." With that Jim glances knowingly at Julio.

Basher smiles with a glance at Matunkup and says, "As Julio has obviously been generous with his accommodations, you can also rely upon me for assistance whenever you might need, Mr. Tuck." The "Mr. Tuck" is delivered with such force that Jim recognizes that friendships do not form immediately in Zamboanga. Jim must be patient, but it is not easy.

Before the conversation continues, the tall house servant arrives with a whispered message for Ahmad Basher. Basher rises and gestures Matunkup and Jim back toward the house. "I am to meet with Tamil in half an hour. So, if you will excuse me, I must prepare myself for the visit. Tamil is a friend," he glances at Jim, "but he is also rather strict in his expectations. I commend your choice of clothing, Mr. Tuck. It will help this evening if you choose to wear the same or similar clothing. I also commend your fortitude. The gravel on my path is not easy on unfamiliar feet. Good day, gentlemen." With that, he disappears to the right while Jim and Julio continue to follow the servant to the front of the house and their car.

As the car drives out the gate, Julio says, "I think we did well this afternoon, Jim. I will leave you at the shop to prepare for this evening. Wang has other clothes similar to these if you feel you need to change. As you can see, my colleagues, many of them, are quite competent and perceptive people. It would be a mistake to underestimate them. Basher will ease the way for our meeting this evening, but he cannot impose acceptance on any of our colleagues. They will each make their determination according to their own requirements. The short biographies of each that Tony will have at the shop by now will help provide you sufficient background information to manage this evening's events to a successful conclusion."

"Me manage? I thought this was Wang's meeting and I was coming along for the ride!?"

"Be calm, my friend. Yes, Wang is the instigator of this meeting, and those attending look to him for reassurance and occasionally direction. But do not think for a minute that they are there for any other reason than to see who you are and whether you can be trusted. They all know that you wrote this plan, and want to see if you have substance or are only American hot air. They will not fill their balloons with the latter. They may cooperate with the former. I will see you at the club this evening." As they arrive at the shop's front door, Jim exits the car, which immediately pulls into evening traffic between two donkey carts and three bicycles before it can escape.

Jim enters the shop where Wang is sitting behind the counter, arching his brows in a question. Jim says, "It is good. Ahmad Basher is on his way to see Tamil now and Matunkup thinks he will be effective in promoting the cause. I am tired and need a nap. Matunkup says you may have more of these duds here in the shop. If so, I think I better change since this outfit is pretty well sweated up. Oh, did Tony come by with paperwork for me?"

Wang simply nods, reaches behind the counter and raises his hand with several sheets of paper. He silently offers them to Jim, who strolls up and accepts them with a half smile. He is tired, but has a bit of work to do before napping. "Julio seems to think that I will be the main course for this evening's meeting. True?"

Another nod from Wang. "Cat got your tongue?" Jim says. "You haven't said a word since I walked in."

"Nothing to say. Don't waste words or energy. Especially tonight. No one coming will be interested in a lot of talk, just serious talk. Do you understand me?"

"Sure, sure. Keep it to the point and simple."

"They are not simple men, and they will have their own rituals to follow this evening, things that may seem frivolous to you, but they are not. They are patterns this group has followed for at least three generations, much longer than I know about. But what they want from you is reassurance, not frivolous talk. So I will assist in steering the conversation in directions that may assist you, but what you say is your decision. Make good decisions this evening. It means success or failure of the project." With that Wang stands and pushes through the beaded screen, disappearing into the back. Jim takes the paperwork upstairs where he falls onto his pallet and begins reading.

Somewhere after the third page, he drops off to sleep, only to wake about 20 minutes later, temporarily disoriented then jerked back to reality. He just had a recurring dream of floating in the South Pacific Ocean, waiting for rescue, and not sure it was coming. The sudden awakening was from getting a dream wave in the face and choking until he was awake again. Rubbing his face vigorously, he takes up the papers and starts reviewing them again.

A total of 19 people are expected, but only eight are relevant to their cause, with Tamil one of the eight and Ahmad Basher another. The rest are there as a courtesy or because they will have a significant role in the project at a later date - people from transportation, customs, processing plants, and distribution sources. All are important but the amazing eight are essential, all growers who must immediately provide investment into the activities of their undertaking, Project Grape. A rather banal name but to the point, and understandable to those for whom English is a second language.

After reading, and rereading the biographies, Jim strips and bathes. When he comes back to his room with a towel wrapped around his middle, there are new clothes on his pallet. They are similar style to what he had been wearing during the day, but somewhat brighter colors and nicer material. "Leave it to Wang," he muses quietly, and starts dressing. He will obviously need help with the wrapping, but he can go downstairs for that.

Wang is standing in the front room, resplendent in a most elegant robe of peacock blue with dark red trim that slightly drags the floor in the back. The high collar meets in the front and there are gold nugget toggles buttoning the front. The enormous sleeves swallow his slender, sinewy arms, and his erect bearing tells Jim all he needs to know about the importance of the evening's proceedings. "I could use a hand getting wrapped up, if you don't mind," Jim says.

"Not a problem." And the finishing touches to Jim's costume are applied after which he steps to the side to the full-length mirror and just shakes his head in growling amazement or disgust, it's hardtotellwhich. Wang decides toplunge theneedleabit deeper with, "I have an appropriate oil lamp in the kitchen. If you would like, I can get it for you, Aladdin."

"Allah el Din to you, infidel. Let's go."

They are silent during the short trip to the club except for the taxi's engine. Wang speaks quietly to the driver. Then Jim and Wang get out and climb the steps to the club's front door where a beaming Tony, standing there in resplendent garb, greets them. "I hope you will find everything to your satisfaction, Mr. Wang. Hello, Mr. Jim."

Both men nod and walk to the fountain area where they can talk in private before the guests arrive. Jim gives a short summary of the dossiers he has read while Wang's head slowly nods in thought. "I suspect that while Tamil is the main object of our approach, gathering information by talking with the others will be more beneficial than a direct approach. For one thing, a direct approach would give Tamil, and the rest, the impression that his opinion is the one that must be taken into account. Our efforts must be to lower his influence, not raise it." Wang's nodding gets a bit more vigorous, but only the seriously astute would notice, and Jim notices. "Have I missed anything?"

"No," is all Wang says.

"You going to be any more verbal than that during the evening or am I getting hung out to dry?"

"I am not sure why you feel you are wet."

"It is an expression suggesting that I am on my own even with you present."

"No, no, no. Certainly not. I will be welcoming each attendee personally and will remain in control of the meeting throughout the evening, inviting your comments as necessary. Mainly I will organize our discussion, the question-and-answer period, if you will, so the earliest questions are from the friendliest guests, etcetera, etcetera. You will in no way be seen as in charge of this event, I assure you."

"Good, because I don't want it, and I am certain they do not either. So I will play to your lead, I mean, react to what you do and say, and be as helpful as I can to our fearless leader," Jim says with a slight bow toward Wang.

"I am in no way fearless."

"Another saying. I guess I am a bit nervous just anticipating events as it were and coming up with more clichés than usual."

"Not to worry. This meeting only represents several million pesos in investment and many more pesos in profit if it works to plan. Be calm."

"Yeah, right," and the bell for the door sounds on cue.

Tony answers the door and Ahmad Basher enters and Tamil follows. Ahmad has a half smile on his bearded face, while Tamil's face wears a ¾-scowl. Both men are a shorter than Jim, but Ahmad is darkly handsome with expressively mobile eyebrows. Tamil is on the verge of downright ugly.

Wang steps forward with a medium bow to Basher and a slight bow to Tamil. Jim's time in China lets him know that the games have begun. Wang shows the two men into the fountain area where Jim is waiting. Basher is first to approach Jim, take him by the elbow and escort him to Tamil for an introduction. Tamil's countenance does not change except for the slightly quizzical look as he takes in Jim's face. Tamil nods his head and Jim does the same. The doorbell sounds again and Wang returns to the front. Tamil says, "I hear some information about you, an American newspaper worker, but until tonight I have not met, not true?"

"Yes, as far as I can remember, I have not had the pleasure of meeting you. I welcome the opportunity this evening. I have heard many reports of your success as a businessman and am sure I will be able to learn many things from you, perhaps even this evening."

The flattery has the intended effect and the ¾-scowl become a ¼-smile, which Jim takes as 100 percent improvement. The atmosphere relaxes as Wang comes into the area with the next two guests. They seem to be arriving in pairs. He just finishes the introductions to Jim - the others are quite familiar with one another - when the bell sounds again and Wang is off.

The process repeats itself several times until all are milling about the fountain area with various non-alcoholic drinks in their hands.

Tony eventually appears and whispers to Wang, who claps his hands for attention and announces dinner. Wang leads the way down the short hall into a splendidly adorned room, which Jim does not recognize at first. Neither do the others, although they have been here numerous times. Tony and the staff have so enhanced the décor that it seems an entirely different space: lush tropical plants, songbirds in cages lining three corners of the room, the ceiling hidden above a tent-like structure supported by eight well-polished wooden poles and draped down the length of the poles. The floor is covered in many layers of hand-tied silk and wool carpets with five low tables surrounded by cushions, one in each corner and a larger one in the center of the room.

Wang efficiently and assertively sorts the seating among the guests and the last one as the first course is laid on the table. The fare is all Middle Eastern with rice, flat bread, lamb, goat, beef, and multiple types of boiled vegetables, all with a spicy kick to them. Conversation is muted as the guests begin eating from the communal bowls of food in the center of each table. They each have plates but there are no utensils. So hands are used to retrieve food from bowls in the center of the table to their plates. Large crockery bowls of lemon water are arranged about the tables so each guest has an individual bowl, as well as an individual towel next to the bowl. Right now the bowls and towels are ignored as the food is excellent and being devoured, not least of all by Jim. His appreciation of food and willingness to experiment with foods of various cultures has made him a favoured guest in houses from New York and Mexico to China and Micronesia. This is as good as any he has had.

Slowly the eating is less intense, the burps more plentiful, and the bowls of water cleanse the greasy hands of the guests. Conversation starts slowly around the room and at Jim's table in the center it is about the coffee crop that has started to be harvested.

"I do not believe we will see many more harvests, my friends," says Basher, who sits opposite Jim. Behind Basher at the next table, Matunkup huffs and nods in agreement.

To the left of Matunkup is the table where Tamil sits. "Again I tell you, my friends, to take down these sick trees and plant something that will survive and make a profit. I feel happy I did not plant coffee," Tamil says. With that, he sits back with a satisfied smile and Wang, at Jim's table, asks Basher, "So what is there that would be good to plant in place of the coffee, Ahmad Basher?"

"I have been thinking about this since the vintage opening, and I wonder if there is a way to make more money from grapes. Grapes have some difficulties with disease, but not nearly so much as coffee. And they are less expensive to plant and sustain."

Matunkup speaks up, saying, "I believe if we could agree on a coordinated plan that brought benefits to all here, as well as to many others in the Zamboanga community, that plan would be ideal. I think there is more strength in many working together than in many separate efforts." There are several nods to which Wang responds, "Perhaps our newest colleague, with whom several of you spoke the evening of the vintage opening, could offer some ideas on how grapes could become the replacement crop to coffee. Mr. Jim Tuck, can you offer any ideas?"

And with that Jim is off. He builds slowly, speaking in terms understandable by the several for whom English is still unfamiliar, outlining the main points of his paper, making eye contact with certain guests for emphasis and to make sure they are following him. His eyes slide by Tamil several times but never makes direct eye contact until he reaches the point in his presentation when raising the consumption of grape products in Zamboanga would change the local market into the primary one.

At that point, he locks on Tamil's eyes and the two seem to be in a staring contest. Finally, with the pause building into a significant silence, Jim makes an expansive move with his arms saying, "Everyone in this room could be at the top of the new Zamboanga economy if we systematically increase local consumption of grapes, pull out diseased coffee trees, leave healthy coffee plants, and plant grapes, thus adding to our incomes. I am sure with a few significant events to inform the local community about the changing economy, we can easily make Zamboanga grapes more important than coconuts and certainly more important than coffee. And each person in this room," and here his eyes stop roaming the room and land back on Tamil, "will succeed as he has never thought possible. He will succeed mainly because all parts of Zamboanga society will benefit, increasing the amount of money in the community, which increases the income of everyone here, and many who are not here. But it starts with increasing local consumption of grapes."

With that, Jim leans back on his cushion, takes a drink of juice, which happens to be grape juice, and allows the quiet to build. Finally Wang breaks the silence and says, "I think we have not heard such ideas before. Perhaps the members are not sure about this program?" That is said with a slight tilt and tip of the head, as if asking, "Are there only cowards in this room?" The effect is immediate. Everyone starts jabbering simultaneously, except Tamil who sits, eyeing Jim. His gaze does not seem malevolent, just intensely curious. Finally, with the slightest of nods, he indicates the archway out of the room. He stands slowly and retreats from the room. Jim waits 10 beats and stands, with a small smile toward Wang and follows. In the fountain area Tamil is sitting on a stone bench waiting for Jim to catch up. As Jim approaches, he pats the seat near him and Jim sits.

"I do not know you."

Jim is quiet, then nods and says, "Do you want to know me?"

"I am not sure that is possible. I know few people, and few know me. I like that. However this idea requires much thought, and I believe it is worth more thought. I think I must discuss the idea with my family, and for them to discuss it properly, they must understand it. You are best to explain it, but my family speaks very little English. Wang has never been to my house, and I suspect he never will. However, Ahmad Basher seems to agree with much that you say and he speaks English well. We will meet at my house at noon in two days - you, Ahmad Basher, me and my family. He can understand the English and tell it to my family, as you speak it. You have met him. Do you trust him?"

"I am not sure I trust anyone very much, but of those I have met here, he seems to be one of the easiest to talk with."

"I agree. I trust Ahmad Basher because he is my cousin and therefore family. And he has married my sister, which makes him more family. He thinks this is a good idea. I do not yet know, but will take the counsel of my family after we talk in two days. I will see you at my house at noon that day. Goodbye, Jim Tuck."

With that, Tamil is away from the fountain and out the front door.

Jim has not seen anyone else leave, so Ahmad Basher must still be here. Odd. But there you are. Now people are leaving in two's and three's, each sent cordially on their way by the ever collegial host, Wang.

Finally Wang, with Basher close beside him, arm in arm, comes into the fountain area where Jim is sitting on one of the benches. They make a lovely if odd couple, both resplendent in their individual finery. Basher walks right up to Jim and presents his hand for a shake. Jim stands and takes the proffered hand with a serious grip that is returned with ¾ of a smile on Basher's face. "I believe you have an appointment with our friend Tamil, do you not?"

"How did you know?"

Basher removes his hand with a bit of a shake, Jim's grip is serious, and says, "We were discussing options after your talk this evening. Your comments, along with my conversation with Tamil earlier, seem to have a calming effect on his worries about the consequences for his farm, if there is an overproduction at the next grape harvest. I believe he will cooperate as an important member of the project team, but needs a bit more time with you to himself. It is quite interesting that you received an invitation to his house at all. Americans are not at the top of his guest list at any time. As a matter of fact I do not remember any time he had an American as a guest in his house. The word will spread quickly in the community and the project will succeed, assuming you do not offend him day after tomorrow."

"I may need a bit of a tutorial about protocol with Tamil before I go to the meeting. Are you willing to give me some pointers?"

Basher nods, smiles and again gently takes Jim's hand in his; he suggests dinner at his place the next evening, to which Jim readily agrees. Wang is standing to the side, appreciating all their interaction. He then accompanies Ahmad Basher to the door for a last goodbye. Jim hears the, "Ma'a salama," from near the door and Basher is gone. Wang fairly springs into the courtyard and lightly dances around the fountain one turn before stopping in front of Jim. "This evening was better than I expected," Wang says. "You will bring prosperity to Zamboanga and to each of my colleagues, and, of course, to me. Luck continues to shine on us. We will go to the shop now and prepare for your dinner tomorrow night."

"What do you mean prepare? I am going to Basher's for tutoring is all. What else is there?"

"My friend, you are still a babe in this very dangerous wood and I must assist you around the danger points. We go home now, but do not expect to be asleep before midnight. I suggest a cold shower to revive you as well as allow you to smell better. Sniff, sniff." With that Wang curls his upper lip and shows Jim to the door, the taxi and home. Wang is, of course, right again and Jim's education in Zamboanga elite customs is detailed with many requests from Wang for him to repeat, summarize or restate the information to reassure Wang the information has penetrated. By 1 a.m. Jim is flagging badly, while Wang is pacing the floor ready to start another chapter. Jim holds up his well-scrubbed hand and says, "I give! Enough for tonight. If there is much more to this story, we'll finish tomorrow."

Wang stops pacing and looks down at Jim, who is sitting on his pallet in his room. Contemplating the scene, Wang nods, turns and heads out the door. "6 a.m. sharp, in the kitchen."

"Groan! What?"

"You heard perfectly fine the first time. Good night," and Wang is down the stairs. Jim flops back on the pallet, pulls the mosquito net down and tucks it under his pallet. He is asleep before he rolls completely on his back.

Coffee. The aroma is delicious and causes Jim's eyes to open ever so slightly to see Tony standing in the door with a tray. "What the hell are you doing here in the middle of the night? Come back tomorrow! Better yet, never come back!"

With his customary early morning growl, Jim rolls to his other side away from the apparition in the doorway. "It is 5:45 a.m.," Tony says, "and Mr. Wang sends his compliments with this coffee. He wishes you to join him for breakfast in 15 minutes. Thank you so much, Mr. Jim."

Tony places the tray on the floor just out of reach of the mosquito net and begins to step back when Jim launches himself upright on the pallet and tries to grab Tony, only to become hopelessly entangled in the net. Jim thrashes about as if possessed. Tony simply stands there staring in amazement, then exits the room. Jim stands still for a minute and listens to Tony's footsteps descending the stairs. He then finally sits still long enough to disentangle himself, raise the net and reach for the coffee. After the first gulp he puts on his clothes, splashes water on his face, drinks the rest of his coffee and heads downstairs.

At the bottom of the stairs he turns and enters the kitchen, which smells heavenly of rice and stir-fried shrimp in soy sauce and more coffee on the stove. He is suddenly ravenous and is ready to dish up a plate when Wang enters behind him with, "Good morning. Did I hear some difficulties upstairs?"

"No, of course not. It was just early morning banter. Holy shit! What in the world are we doing up this early, before the sun is shining at all?"

"As you have said, we are early birds, are we not?"

"Early, my ass! This is ridiculous."

"We will succeed, but only if we are diligent. True?"

Jim sits, huffs two huffs and accepts the offer of another cup of coffee. "A little steam releasing never hurt anyone, right? Well, let's get started."

With that, Jim's plate is laden with rice and shrimp. He takes a large swallow of coffee and they are off on a crash course in Zamboanga culture. By 7:30 Jim is ready to excuse himself to begin work at the paper, Wang is ready to supervise the seamstresses' work, and both are satisfied that the grape project is well under way. The day is only half full of calls on businesses to solicit advertising and Jim is pretty much finished with his newspaper job by 1 p.m.

Jim is sitting down at the café to enjoy Tony's "gentle ministrations". Today is a Tony day at the café that Jim has come to anticipate. When Tony arrives at the table, the morning's escapades are forgotten and the old reparte' is returned. Jim is under an umbrella to shade himself from the sun. The weather is exquisite and he is feeling fine, if a bit sleepy from his early start. After lunch, rather than upstairs to the paper offices, he heads back to the shop and heads upstairs for a siesta, a very important part of Zamboanga life he has learned to appreciate. The afternoon is lazed away with a short walk to Pershing Plaza, which happens to be a triangle. Then Jim returns to the shop to prepare for dinner with Ahmad Basher. The dinner with Basher is, of course, excellent, starting with soup held in bowls and drunk, lamb slices piled high next to a mound of rice, all on a platter in the center of the short table, multiple vegetables boiled and piled on a separate plate next to the lamb. Once they have had their fill, the main course is removed and tea is served with bowls of dates, the super sweet Middle Eastern specialty of baklava, and a large bowl of cut fruit.

Finally, the conversation turns to the upcoming meeting with Tamil, and starts with the many facets of Tamil's family and business. The fact that Tamil has all girls is interesting to Jim, but a serious matter to Basher. "You must understand that to many, girls are a burden, or worse yet, an embarrassment," Basher explains. "To have no sons at all means Tamil feels disgrace in his community. His girls are seldom seen in public. The oldest is 17 and the youngest of the six is five years old. His three wives have all disappointed him by producing only female offspring. Now he is in the difficult position of trying to find suitable husbands for them all. Of course, there are many families in Zamboanga who would like to marry into his wealth. So there are always bees buzzing around his hive. He protects his honey jealously, as well as fiercely.

"He may be embarrassed but, of course, he will never admit it, nor will he allow any disgrace upon his house. He is a very traditional man. If you happen to accidentally be faced with any of the women or girls of the Tamil household, avert your eyes and pretend they are not there. This is very important, Jim!"

Jim suddenly looks up at the earnest countenance facing him and puts down his fork to stop eating. "I do not want to annoy you, or burden you with unnecessary details, but this is one I must emphasize," Basher continues. "Tamil's family is hidden away from the public on purpose. He is ashamed that he has only female offspring and he is very protective of their virtue. Do you understand me?"

Jim nods and looks directly in Basher's eyes. Basher gives a perfunctory nod indicating the point is finished and they return to their meal. The last of the meal includes a fruit salad with a delicious caramelized custard. The dinner ends with a brusque farewell from Basher. Jim is quiet on the taxi ride back to the shop. He has the taxi stop a block short of the shop so he can walk a bit and think. He exits the taxi and turns at the corner to walk around the block before returning to the shop. As he approaches the next corner, a group of four toughs are headed in his direction. Two of them limp slightly and the other two are talking loudly - until they spot Jim. They stop suddenly and Jim recognizes them from an earlier stroll with Wang. As Jim approaches, they all suddenly shrink back against the storefront, leaving the entire width of the sidewalk to Jim, who walks slowly by with a smile. "Good evening, gentlemen. Glad to see you are well this evening. Lovely weather the past few days, wouldn't you say?"

The looks from the four are murderous, but Jim continues his walk uninterrupted and turns the corner whistling an out- of-tune melody and chuckling to himself as he approaches the shop. Jim muses as he enters the shop, "Bit of alright that Wang's colleagues certainly have a calming influence on the nastier element of Zamboanga." He heads to his room upstairs, exhausted.

Today is a good day. That is the mantra rolling through Jim's head as he moves rather mechanically through his chores the next day. It had a much more civilized start at 7:30, still with coffee and Chinese stir-fried leftovers. It is still hot, and he is back into his familiar clothes since he is visiting newspaper clients of various stripes.

At the newspaper offices he receives an envelope, sealed, addressed to him with no indication of origin on the surface of the envelope. Curiosity causes him to quickly rip the paper, nearly ripping the note inside as well. The note simply informs him of a change in appointment time at Tamil's, from lunch to dinner at 8 p.m.. That makes his day much easier and he lets Gus know the change, as well as having Gus call Matunkup with the information about the change. Jim will inform Wang while out on his rounds, which start now. And his day is underway.

CHAPTER 6

And The
Games Begin

Lunchtime sees him back at the café. But since it is a day that Tony is elsewhere, probably on errands for Wang and Matunkup, he dines without much interest until a car arrives at the curb just ahead of where his table is shaded under an umbrella. Being in the shade on a bright, sunny day allows him to observe the passengers of the automobile as they exit, and the first out is a lovely young woman, petite, with the typically round face of the Moro people. She is exquisitely proportioned and nimble. She turns back to the car to take the arm of a matronly woman, who herds two younger girls toward the café. Arm in arm the young woman and older woman follow the two younger ones, who look to be primary school age, up the steps and into the shade of the café's interior.

Suddenly Jim's rather uninteresting lunch has taken on some higher purpose and he concentrates on the windows of the café to see if he can tell where the females sit. No luck, the reflection of the sunny glare does not allow any view of the dark interior. Having finished his lunch, he decides to take the check to the counter and pay it inside rather than wait for the waiter.

He demonstrates his most nonchalant walk to the cashier's desk, which is just inside the door to the café, hands the bill over and casually turns to examine the room. There is the group of four females off to the right, away from the windows and heat of the sun. The openness of the room provides a constant draft through the building, typically back to front and the breeze constantly ruffles the table cloths. It also ruffles the large sleeves of the native dresses of the two women, but the younger girls' long dresses and tight sleeves remain undisturbed. All the females have their hair in tight buns so he cannot tell how long it is or what it would look like, but, if they are typical, it is likely to be quite curly and black through and through. Just as he becomes aware that he is staring, the older woman turns her head toward him and he simultaneously turns to pay the bill to avoid eye contact. Not being sure why he is acting this way, he is sure that the young woman has caught his attention. His lack of female companionship is playing a role in his interest, for sure, but there is something about the young woman, who has not even glanced in his direction, that is more than simply fascinating. Accepting the thanks of the cashier, he turns left and walks briskly out the door into the glare of the sun, feeling the stare of the matronly woman on his back. His afternoon becomes busy, but Jim has a constant buzz, remembering the lovely young woman and a slight apprehension about the older woman she was with. "Wonder who they are, what they are to one another." The phrase repeats in his head most of the day when he is not distracted with business meetings.

By five in the afternoon he is finished with his clients and has deposited his notes and order books back at the paper. Walking back to the shop his mind wanders again, and it is right back to the café and the young lady at the table. She is erect sitting there and has some sort of regal bearing, just like royalty. Her features are neither coarse nor refined, but she is obviously, for him, one of the more attractive local women he has seen. And she is aristocratic. That way of carrying herself makes a five foot stature seem like an elegant six feet tall beauty. What in the world has that girl got that is affecting him so? She is stuck in his head like an itch needing scratching. And she did not even see him. How can he be smitten by a girl who doesn't even know he is there? Oddest thing he has ever encountered.

Wang is solicitous, ever present in the evening to make sure Jim's costume for his dinner with Tamil is exact in every way. He is to be in one of the Aladdin outfits since Tamil is a traditional man. The tunic is tan with gold trim, understated yet rich. The pantaloons are tan with red trim and are gathered just below the knees, exposing his sizeable calves. The sash is red and gold braid and the turban is white. The silk shoes are black allowing all the attention to be focused on the upper body. His compact frame fills the costume well and he sees himself as handsome in an outlandish sort of way. Looking in the full-length mirror, he can't help the grimace that accompanies the deep-chested growl producing a, "Tsk, tsk," from Wang. "You will be successful this evening, and a certain amount of success will be from these clothes. You will control yourself, will you not?"

Jim steps back, puts on the wry smile that Wang has learned indicates resignation, turns and walks out the door to the taxi without a backward glance. The taxi is away and Wang slowly shakes his head, along with his version of a wry smile.

The trip to the northeast part of town is relatively short and Jim has barely sorted his demeanor before the large gates in the tall wall open to admit the taxi to the courtyard. A circular drive paved with crushed white stone lies around a lily pond with hyacinths in bloom and a black convertible Cadillac sedan parked halfway around the circle. The scent hovering over the courtyard is very similar to jasmine, one of Jim's favourites. As the taxi stops below the front steps, behind the sedan, the large wooden double doors open and a liveried house servant descends the three stairs and opens the taxi door. Holding the door for Jim he says, "Welcome to the home of Sheik Tamil." Jim nods and climbs the stairs where he is met by another liveried man, who motions him into the foyer of the two-story house. The foyer extends up both stories with a balcony overlooking the entrance and there are Tamil and Basher, high above. Both men turn from the balcony rail and walk slowly to the stairs on the right, descending deliberately. When they arrive at the bottom, Basher stands by the stairs while Tamil crosses the black marble floor to Jim. "Welcome," he says quietly. "I hope your trip was pleasant. I also hope your walks at night are pleasant, no problems."

Jim's eyes widen slightly, he nods his head and says, "Yes, the trip here was quite short. I did not realize Wang's shop was so near your home, and I understand we have you to thank for the safety of our neighborhood."

Tamil nods, Basher comes to join them and Tamil motions to the right, indicating an archway into the adjoining room. They stroll ever so slowly into the next room and, just as they enter, a form disappears through an open door in the far left corner of the room. Jim gives a slight start, then relaxes into disinterest as he realizes the person making the quick exit is female, heeding Basher's warning. Basher is engaging Tamil in small talk and gives no indication of having seen anything.

Turning to his right, away from the far door and away from the distraction, Jim gives the room a good look. The walls are plastered over stone and painted sandy light saffron with the floors pink marble, contrasting with the foyer. They are covered, nearly wall to wall, with multiple layers of rich hand-tied carpets that appear to be silk. A large one covering the center of the room, probably 9 by 12 feet, has many others placed over it that seem to complement the basic blues and red of the main one. There is fringe completely around the margin of the carpet with at least four feet of marble floor between carpet and wall. The center of the room is occupied by a low, round table surrounded by cushions, not unlike Basher's place. Three water pipes are placed around the table with a brass tray in the center of the table holding a sweating ceramic jug and glasses. "Please to sit there," Tamil says as he points to the opposite side of the table, then indicates a third spot to Basher between Jim and himself. The three men divide the table into three equal parts, a water pipe in the center of each part.

Jim circles the table, which is at least six feet in diameter, and sits on his left hip, leaning on the substantial pillow there. His right hand is free to the table and he notices that Tamil and Basher sit similarly. Tamil reaches and pours from the pitcher, then offers each a glass and a guttural salute. Not having a clue what Tamil just meant, Jim raises his glass and smiles. Basher takes a long pull on the cold juice, smacks his lips and returns the glass to the table.

Tamil asks Jim, "Is there some food you may not eat?"

"No, I enjoy all food, especially when I am hungry."

Tamil takes the hint, claps one time, and a large tray is carried into the room by two servants while a third shifts the drinks tray to make room. A plate is placed in front of each man along with a sizeable bowl with slices of lemon floating in water. Tamil motions to each man and then to the tray and says simply, "Eat."

Jim has gotten used to using his hands by now and does not hesitate to start the sampling of rice, vegetables, various meats, of which there are at least four, and the fruit that is cut in sizeable chunks adorning the far side of the tray. Each man is concentrating on his plate when Tamil suddenly stops, rinses his hand in the water bowl next to him and claps once. Instantly a servant is by his side and he whispers something to which the servant scurries away and another comes within thirty seconds with a plate of warm flat bread. Jim eyes the plate and Tamil motions for each man to help himself. It smells wonderful - round, flat and warm with a pocket in the middle. Jim opens the pocket and fills it with vegetables, meat, and a topping of rice to make a luscious sandwich. Tamil nods approvingly and makes one for himself. Basher uses his bread instead as a pusher to assist him in gathering his food, then raising it to his mouth.

Just before taking a bite, Tamil looks up and says, "After we eat, my family will come and you can explain, with Basher, the plan you have. First, we eat."

Jim's chewing slows and, just as he is about to reply, he hears a rustling behind him, sees Tamil's countenance cloud as he gives a quick wave of his hand as if banishing someone or something from the room. Jim's fatal curiosity gets the better of him and he turns to see a petite woman rush out of the room. He turns quickly back to the table when he instantly recognizes the young woman he had seen at the café earlier. Heart leaping like a drum that he is sure is heard across the table, he struggles mightily with his face, trying to maintain a calm, placid exterior. His insides are in an uproar. Tamil glances his way, but Jim calmly takes another bite and chews with more vigor than usual, trying to get rid of some of the instantly acquired energy. Basher has been watching while eating himself and gives the slightest of nods to Jim indicating that Jim's discretion is exactly what is needed at the moment.

Jim raises his head and opens his mouth to respond to Tamil, only to find his voice is significantly higher pitched than usual. He coughs vigorously, smacks himself on the chest, and tries to regain his composure. "I look forward to it. Basher's assistance will, I hope, make everything clear for everyone in your family."

The meal is completed fairly quickly, the trays removed, hands cleaned and dried. Then Tamil claps his hands and several young men, two ancient and one similar to Tamil's age, enter the room from the direction the food came. There are six men, no women, who all find places around the table. Jim was hopelessly anticipating the lovely young woman would be allowed in the room. Another tray of glasses and cold drink is placed in the middle. Once they are all settled, with no introductions for Jim, Tamil asks, "You like grapes very much. Why grapes?"

Jim clears his throat, checks Basher, then starts his short explanation, stopping frequently for Basher to translate. "Grapes grow well in Zamboanga. Right now a few plantation owners grow grapes, but find that their years of profit and loss are extreme. I mean, they frequently have years when they have too many grapes, and then other years when they do not have enough. It is because they rely mostly on foreign markets. As easily as grapes grow here, the owners could make much more money if they could be certain to sell their entire crop every year. And they could also make more money if they could sell more grapes every year." Tamil is nodding slowly and obviously following the logic easily. The other men show no signs of acceptance, misunderstanding, or even much interest. Their blank expressions seem painted on, but Jim and Basher forge ahead.

"So, it seems to me that helping growers sell more grapes will help them avoid years with less money. Concentrating on grapes allows us to start with a product that already exists, has a market and just needs a bigger one. Many people will benefit from selling more grapes, including you. If you want to plant more, I think I can show you that you will likely sell everything you grow, every year." Jim stops momentarily for Basher to catch up and for Jim to gather his thoughts. He is actually slightly proud of his ability to stay on task with the butterflies coursing in his belly. "The other growers will also sell more, but I think you are most interested in how much you sell and not so much in how much Matunkup or some rival grower sells. How much they sell, in a market that wants more grapes, does not matter. It only matters if there are too many grapes, or if they sell more than you. That would mean you would not sell enough. But that is not what we propose. We propose that when we finish, you will sell as many grapes as you grow, every year, no matter how many you grow." Basher completes the translation, the six new faces around the table remain blank until one of the younger ones smiles and glances at Tamil who nods. Then everyone smiles.

Tamil sits and looks hard at Jim, then leans back and takes a drink from his glass and nods at Basher. Resting one elbow on the table, he leans forward and gives the same guttural salute he gave earlier, which Jim still does not understand. Jim and Basher go ahead and raise their glasses in return. All three men take a sip, then Tamil smiles and claps for the platter of sweets. When it arrives, all nine men begin eating again. The sweets are just that, very sweet, creating the urge for more drinks. Tamil looks around at his relatives, says a few things to them in Tagalog to which they all shake their heads in the negative. Appearing satisfied, Tamil nods to the eldest of the six and they all rise as one from the table and depart single file, without a backward glance. It is the strangest thing Jim has encountered in a long time and he has encountered many odd things.

Throughout the meal, the conversation, dessert - the whole evening - no mention is made of the young woman Tamil had banished with a wave of his hand, and whom Jim had studiously avoided noticing. Finally the water pipes are lit. The tobacco is Turkish and black and strong. The water cools it and Jim smokes it contentedly.

The burble of three pipes fills the room until Tamil breaks the silence and says, "I will help with this plan. I will plant more grapes. My family will be happy, even if my daughter does not behave politely sometimes. Interrupting a father's dinner is not permitted. But she is a good daughter most times. I hope you were not too disturbed by her rudeness."

Jim takes the pipe mouthpiece out of his mouth and smiles his best half-smile. "No problem here, Mr. Tamil."

"Please, Ishmael."

"Ishmael? That is your name?"

"Of course! Do you not know this? All people know this! Basher! You do not tell him my name?"

"It is not my place to give information that belongs to my friends. If my friends want this information to be public, they will say it themselves." With a nod to Jim and Tamil, he returns to the burbling pipe.

Tamil turns back to Jim asking, "Why does not Wang tell you the important information?"

"I suspect he wanted me to be sure I was respectful. Ishmael it is, if it is permitted," Jim says with a nod to Basher and Tamil. "I think I will return to my room at the tailor shop now, as I am very tired from my day of work. We will be in very close communication with you while planning the next steps to this project." As he is rising, Jim says, "I have enjoyed this evening very much. Thank you for your generous hospitality. Thank you, Basher, for your valuable assistance." The double meaning is not lost on Basher.

Tamil rises and responds, "I thank you. Please come and visit my humble home whenever you wish. I am happy to accept your visit any time." All three men are standing and Tamil takes Jim's arm in his right hand, Basher's elbow in his left and they march three abreast. Jim's insides are squirming a bit but he walks alongside Tamil to the front door that opens out into the cool evening breeze scented with flowers that encircle the house. Jim stands a moment and breathes the air. Tamil notices and says, "Yes, it is beautiful, is it not?"

"Yes, it is. Thank you again." Jim leaves the other two men in the doorway, enters the opened door of the taxi and heads back to town. Tamil and Basher remain standing in the driveway as the taxi exits the gate. Jim waves his hand slightly and Basher smiles while Tamil returns the wave. That is the last he sees of them as the gates close behind them.

Jim asks the taxi driver to drop him a block away from the shop again. As he exits the taxi, he makes his way around the block, uneventfully tonight. Walking the deserted street he muses about the young lady he has glimpsed twice today. Now he is wondering exactly how little she had observed while he was there. Was he ignored as much as he thought? Delicious!

As the next day begins, Jim is assessing where the project stands and realizing their enterprise is well underway. Tamil has given his seal of approval for the project; the municipal authorities are issuing appropriate edicts; the paper now prints weekly special editions and regular stories concerning everything grape; posters adorn lamp posts, blank walls and fences; and conversations at clubs, pubs, beaches and street corners are all about grapes.

On top of all that progress, the sheiks are pulling in relatives from the hills and neighboring districts as growers add additional acreage for plantings. Commerce is rapidly picking up from construction, transportation, advertising, and all things agricultural.

Jim now focuses on the specifics of the upcoming chef's competition. He has frequent trips to Pettit Barracks, is arranging several luncheons at various locales. Hacienda Matunkup, Ahmad Basher's house and Wang's Club all serve as sites to introduce the local elite to the commander of the barracks. There are many wounds that need the salve of good food and amiable conversation and Connolly is eager to accommodate the competition at his officers' club kitchens and dining room. Security is able to be relaxed on the base since all sheiks have signed onto the plan and the word is out that the barracks is, for now, out of bounds for any violent acts by locals still harboring resentment for previous lost battles with the U.S. Army.

The qualifying chefs were chosen in a preliminary cook-off with the remaining five chefs now preening daily for the benefit of the newspaper and their fellow competitors. They have come from restaurants all over Zamboanga in order to represent as many sub-districts as possible in the finals. The energy around town is positive with little or no grousing from those who did not make the finals. The represented restaurants are proudly decked out in bunting announcing their qualifications to the passersby. The whole marketing scheme is designed to increase the status of locals, including the chefs, so Jim made sure arrangements were made so the barracks chef did not reach the finals, a situation Jim mentioned to Connolly prior to the cook-off. Connolly quietly met with his staff, and the officers' club was able to heartily welcome the winning locals to the orientation at the club prior to the final event. Wang and Julio both congratulated Jim for his diplomatic skills.

Gus has done a masterful job of keeping the news of the upcoming competition on the papers' front page and Jim writes weekly updates for the inside pages. Photos of the various finalist chefs appear on posters sponsored by the competing kitchens and printed by the paper's print shop for a modestly profitable fee. All in all, the build up to the day of the competition is going swimmingly.

The whirlwind around Jim is exactly to his liking and he bounces around Zamboanga from one end of town to the other. He is able to provide each of the sheiks and growers weekly personal updates on the progress of the competition. He particularly anticipates visiting Tamil's house. However, the three times he has made the pilgrimage he doesn't even get a glimpse of the young lady in question, although he discovers her name is Hanna. No H at the end, because the name comes to a sudden stop, like something that gets stuck in the back of your mouth. Like there is a sudden space available after the word comes out. Hanna. Sometimes he has seen it written Hanna', to indicate a sudden stop. He looked it up and it means full of grace, the gracefulness that comes from privilege. Like royalty are graceful. Anyway, the mysterious Hanna' fills his mind whenever he isn't working. What's going on here? He has never indulged in crushes on females before. Why in the world indulge in one now? It can't be the forbidden fruit syndrome. It's something else, but what?

The preparations are in place: the chefs are familiar with the equipment in the barracks' kitchen, the guest list is finalized and invitations are mailed to the city's elite, most having been on the list for the vintage opening. Wang is overworked as usual, and the seamstresses are making more money than they have ever made. Other businesses are flourishing - with more money than time - but enjoying it while it lasts.

Finally, the last week before the chefs' competition arrives and so do a myriad of small catastrophes, all needing immediate attention, which is Jim's forte. Chickens with heads cut off are less frantic, but Jim is enjoying himself more than at any time since his arrival. It may have something to do with the fact that he has his fingers in every part of the contest pie, knows the whole process inside out, and is able to assist several very influential people in the city. He makes sure the guest list has the flexibility to allow guests to invite family members in addition to the adults of their constituency. Jim hopes perhaps if Ahmad Basher and others bring their older children, maybe Tamil will bring Hanna' as well. Jim is anxious to have the opportunity to formally meet her. Machiavelli could take lessons.

The entertainment for the evening, other than the master of ceremonies and the chefs' performances themselves, consists of several prominent local musicians and performers, all of whom have been thoroughly vetted to allow them access to the barracks. The whole evening is likely to last into the wee hours of the morning, but that is more than fine with everyone he has talked to. Matunkup has agreed to be the master of ceremonies, keeping the evening on track, while Jim flits among the various guests making sure the evening goes without a hitch.

The remaining tasks are photography and advertising, making sure the elite are seen in the best light possible with no one coming out superior to anyone else. That would be a serious mistake. That is why Matunkup is the perfect choice for MC since most sheiks have few issues against him, that is, none that Jim has been able to find. That cannot be said for any of the other sheiks since their tribes are very competitive. Somehow, Matunkup seems able to get along with just about everyone, and Jim, using his coattails, is enjoying having some of that influence rub off on him as well.

Thursday is the day of the competition, the day before the next edition of the Mindanao Herald. Gus has reorganized the printing schedule so Friday's edition will publish the results of the competition and society photos of guests. It will have the largest printing and distribution of any paper ever, and Gus is obsessing on every detail, from printing schedule to mechanics. The newspaper employees will make more money this week as well. As frantic as Gus is, the excitement is getting to him even more. Great blue clouds of cigar smoke billow out of his office as he bellows orders out into the hallway. Jim stays out of the office. Too much to do anyway.

The usually tidy entrance and streets of the barracks are now festooned with lights of all shapes and colors, draping the archway leading into the barracks and leading to the officers' club, the site of the competition. The lights are lit before dark, just to make sure they are all working, and as the evening falls they become prominent in the increasing darkness. Jim arrives on the base at twilight, bringing his dress costume to change into after preparations are complete. He watches as the lights become more obvious in the gathering gloom of evening and realizes all his effort - the first event in the grape project - is about to commence with the cooking competition. He turns to re-enter the officers' club and sees Connolly enter dressed in his best uniform, pressed to sharp creases in trousers and sleeves, Sam Brown belt and all. The tan shoes are shined to a sparkle and his heels are clicking on the hard floor of the club as he approaches Jim. Jim almost, but not quite, comes to attention, smiles and says, "Well, Commander, your people have done well, very well, actually. I suspect there will be some reward available to them as a result?" That last remark is accented with a slight rise of Jim's right eyebrow.

"It is all taken care of. The entire barracks are up for leave, one unit at a time, following restoration of the status of the barracks. Certain amenities on Basilan Island have been secured and the manufacture of ice and spirits has been going on for a month already. They all know it, so the cooperation from the troops has been fantastic, as you see. Now how are preparations for the evening?"

"As far as I can tell, everything is ready. Matunkup will be here in half an hour. Gus and the photographer will be coming with him to take preliminary photos, one of you with the two of them I hope, and the contestants arrive half an hour after that. The first two music acts are already warming up and I expect the first guests in slightly over an hour. The secrets of the dishes to be made are here in my pocket, so I am certain there has been no advantage to anyone. There will be four courses prepared, as you know, and the quantities must feed the entire assembly. So the chefs are showing their ability to cook for large crowds. Everyone should leave sated as well as satisfied with the entertainment. Tomorrow afternoon you should have a news report of the entire event on your desk here at the barracks. The same reports will with the papers distributed in Manila as well as each major city north of here. We are arranging for the stories and pictures to be taken to Singapore, Kuala Lumpur, Penang and Bangkok as well, hoping the papers there will repeat some of the printing. It's big, Connolly, big."

"My, oh my. I'll say. Wonder what Central Command in Manila will think about it?"

"If you do not cast too large a shadow over them, they will be able to take credit for the marketing coup and the inevitable benefits to stability in the region. Be sure to let them have it. They will love you for it, as long as they look good."

Connolly just smiles, nods, takes one more look around the decorated room, and turns on his heel, clicking his way back out the far door.

With only three relatively minor screw-ups that evening, the chefs' contest is a monumental success. The officers' club is packed with glittering, colorful personalities. Even in the warmth of the evening they are chattering, table hopping among their particular cliques. Matunkup as master of ceremonies has an impeccable performance and Tamil's table is full of family, including Hanna'. Jim is everywhere - by the end of the evening he has visited every table, some more than once. The two occasions he stops to speak to Tamil he carefully avoids any eye contact with the women. Still he feels his face blush and wonders if his discomfort is obvious. He will have to express his gratitude for Basher's tutoring.

On his final visit to Tamil's table he catches a glimpse of Hanna' when Tamil turns in his chair to speak to a fellow guest. Hanna' barely makes eye contact, looking past him with a Mona Lisa smile. Little does Jim realize how this "encounter" will affect his future on Zamboanga.

In the kitchen he notices that the large wooden crate of grapes is ¾-empty and asks the barracks chef his opinion as to whether what remains is sufficient for the creation of desserts for the evening. Thoughtfully examining the supply, the sergeant then goes to the kitchen door and re-examines the audience for numbers, returns and shakes his head. "Need probably another 25 pounds." Jim is off immediately to see Basher, whose table is near the rear of the dining room. They confer, then Jim is off to the carpool where the guests' cars are parked, finds Basher's car, and explains to the driver what is needed and the urgency. The driver is away immediately and Jim returns to the kitchen. The chefs are about to start preparations for the desserts and Jim gathers them together to let them know the status of supplies and plans for compensating the shortfall. The remaining grapes are divided equally among the five chefs and they start their preparations. Suddenly there is a loud bang on the service entrance and the barracks chef opens the doors to find Basher's driver standing there with a crate of grapes in hand. The grapes are immediately taken to the sink and washed while Jim rustles up a full dinner for the driver, as well as a 20 peso note in gratitude. With food and money in hand, the driver returns to the carpool. Supplies replenished, the chefs are well into their dessert preparations.

The evening is coming to a conclusion with the judges from the municipal offices conferring while guests are having their coffee and conversation. Finally a loud "Ladies and Gentlemen" comes over the speaker system with Matunkup at the microphone. A hush descends over the crowd. "We have a winner and first runner up. First runner up is chef Amelio from the Zamboanga Club. Please help us congratulate him." There is appropriate applause as the chef comes forward for his small trophy and certificate. With his withdrawal, Matunkup again approaches the microphone and says, "Now the winner of this inaugural chefs' competition: Let us applaud chef Tito from the Club of Seven. This year's chef of the grape, chef Tito!" With that there is huge applause, in obvious agreement with the decision. There is much back slapping by audience members as Tito makes his way to the stage. A few scowls are scattered among the other contestants, but the positive atmosphere in the room overwhelms the losers, who eventually join in the applause.

"This concludes the evening's festivities. Please feel free to enjoy the hospitality of the Pettit Barracks for as long as you care to this evening. I bid you a fond good night." With that, Matunkup steps away from the microphone and down from the stage. He spots Jim at the back of the crowd and gives a slight motion of the head toward the exit doors. They meet just outside the doors and Julio reaches out to take Jim's hand with, "This was a wonderful evening. Only a few of us know how much of the success is your responsibility. I am one, and I thank you. We meet at the hacienda tomorrow at 5 p.m. for dinner, the entire committee. I will see you then."

Jim gives Julio's hand a firm squeeze, which Julio returns before he releases his hand and departs. Jim stands a moment in the jasmine-scented breeze enjoying his success, then returns to the room and finds Connolly smiling ear to ear. "Well, young fella, looks like we did it, eh? This went better than I could have expected. No one got too pissed at the results. Happens sometimes with winners and losers, but looks like we may have dodged that bullet."

"Looks that way, but looks can be deceiving. We'll know more tomorrow evening. Thanks a lot for your grand cooperation. Pettit Barracks was the perfect venue, particularly for the first event. We will probably spread it around to other venues over the coming years, but this one will have set the standard," Jim gushes. "Everyone I have spoken with was impressed with the facilities and the organization. The commendations will all come back to you in the end. Enjoy it. You deserve it. Been a pleasure, old sod."

With that Jim gives Connolly a whack on the shoulder and returns to the dining room where the guests are readying themselves to leave. A small, dark, female head peeks around a large Tamil, smiles very briefly and returns out of site. The peek is enough to set Jim's heart on edge and he makes an abrupt left turn to check the status of the kitchen. It is in excellent order due to the ministrations of the regular barracks kitchen staff. Knowing where things go once cleaned is a real advantage, and there is no shortage of cleaning staff. The kitchen is well on its way to being ship shape again so Jim exits the other door to quickly scan the room and notices that Tamil and his family are no longer there. Basher and his family are at the back about to exit. Basher waves him over. "I will see you again soon, correct?"

"Yes, probably at Matunkup's."

"Nicely done this evening. I am happy, are you?" With that, he scrupulously examines Jim's face and suddenly Jim blushes a brighter red than he has in years, getting the drift of Basher's comment. How the heck did he know?

"Yes, I am quite happy, actually. I think the evening went very well indeed." With that Jim smiles, shakes

Basher's hand, turns and exits through the kitchen, then out the service entrance. He finds his way to the motor pool area and the taxi that somehow has Wang sitting in the rear.

"Come in, young man. You are to be congratulated on several levels. Your self-restraint has been well-noted. Now we go home for a well-deserved rest. Seven a.m. will come soon enough."

"Seven a.m.? What the hell is important enough to occur at 7 a.m. tomorrow? I do not expect to be awake before noon!"

"How quaint. No, there is not time to waste sleeping. The full rounds of the participants must start first thing in the morning. I have agreed that you may sleep in until seven, but you will be at your first appointment by 8 a.m. So I think seven is late enough, don't you?"

"What the fuck!"

"It seems you are agitated a bit."

"Agitated? A bit? You gotta be kidding me! I gotta get home to a nice bottle of red wine, and eventually bed, and stay there awhile. Gus does not expect me tomorrow because the paper is set already. No one told me about visits to be made tomorrow!"

"You now know. A glass of wine will be by your bed when we arrive, along with a sample of some of the creations from this evening that you did not have the chance to eat because you were a bit occupied. I had some of the winning recipes saved for you to see what was won. But you will agree, I am sure, that to strike while the iron is hot is an important ability. And to miss the opportunity would not be in the best interests of our project. Seven a.m. it is. Here we are." As they exit the taxi, Wang gives Jim's arm a bit of a vice-like squeeze with a, "Good night, Jim." It is one of the few times Jim's name has ever passed Wang's lips.

The food is excellent, of course. How anyone could invent that many ways to cook with grapes is beyond him, but 7 a.m.? Shit! The glass of wine goes down quickly, and he pads quietly down the stairs to the kitchen to find the bottle and bring it upstairs to finish. The door to the kitchen, perpetually open, is closed and locked. "Shit, and double shit! Slimy whores await you in hell!" Then he stomps back upstairs as Wang smiles on his pallet and falls asleep peacefully.

The smell of coffee wafts up the stairs and helps Jim rise from the floor to stumble down the hall for his morning ablutions. Bathroom routine completed, he trods resolutely back to his room with the firm conviction that no one, especially Wang, will see him in any state other than alert, confident and proactive. Actually, he would prefer a lovely lie down for three days. Downstairs, the coffee is already in mugs, the frying pan is hot and several eggs are on the counter ready for breaking and cooking. A fresh loaf of bread is ready to slice and Jim looks around for someone in charge of the kitchen. No one is there. So he lifts the cup and takes a long sip of the excellent coffee. Jim himself starts cracking eggs into the frying pan. "Four ought to do it." With the eggs frying, he slices three or four thick slices from the loaf and extracts the marmalade from the icebox. Just as he starts flipping the eggs for over-easy frying, Wang comes through the door smiling. "A good morning to you, Jim Tuck. I see you have slept very well, or at least well enough to be able to cook me breakfast."

"Us, Wang, us. And I did sleep well, just not long. Longer would have been better."

"Not better for our enterprise though. I think you can see that easily. Anyway, Matunkup is awaiting your visit this morning. He will have several projects to discuss with you, and a few colleagues you have not met yet, at his place for a general meeting concerning stage two."

"What the hell is stage two?"

"We will, of course, use this excellent start to give the rest of the project momentum. The colleagues you will meet today will help in the planning, construction and details of the Miss Zamboanga Grape contest. All details will have to be developed and starting today we will need to keep the momentum going. As you know,

Gus will not be there as he must manage the distribution of the paper's special edition.

"But these gentlemen today will all have very important roles in each of the aspects of the plan, the plan that you developed. They will want to meet the person who started the process, as well as provide input into the plan's details. You will benefit from meeting the people most important to the next step in the plan."

"Ugh! First, we eat."

With that, the eggs disappear behind the bread and are washed down with coffee. Wiping his mouth, Jim rises from the table and stretches. Wang says, "Tony will be here this morning and he will take care of the kitchen. I will see you back here after your meeting with Matunkup and the group at the hacienda. We must be sure that there are enough resources applied to the next level of the project to produce success. Success is essential for our future, do you not agree?"

"Of course. Success. Hmm. I will have a better idea about resources after meeting Matunkup this morning."

"Exactly." And Wang turns and heads to the cutting room without another word, leaving Jim with raised eyebrows and a sardonic smile. "Touche'."

The hacienda is beautiful at 8:45 a.m. Coming around the final turn in the road, Jim views the buildings with the rising sun behind them as the morning breeze sways the palms. The gravel under the tires crunches in the morning silence. The taxi comes to a stop and Jim exits the rear door to see Julio waiting beside the open front door. Julio's broad smile is as genuine as Jim's is forced from fatigue. Julio opens a screen door, inviting Jim through the interior and out the rear door toward the gazebo. Jim is commenting on the weather when suddenly his steps slow as he sees five people already sitting under the gazebo roof. Julio gently prods him forward and Jim resumes walking, more slowly and slightly wary, until he hears Julio whisper, without moving his lips, "Friends, all, I assure you." With that, Jim's shoulders relax at least an inch as his head retracts, chin slightly forward and the blaze in his eyes focuses on the sitting group of five.

He, of course, recognizes all five individuals, but understands perfectly well that he knows very little about four of the five, the exception being Tamil. As he approaches the table, the five stand simultaneously, resplendent in their native dress. All five are planters. Gathered round the table they are: Arturo Basher, a cousin of Ahmad Basher's; Tamil himself; Mohammed Sulayman; Idi Ibn Mama; and finally Said Mastura. All five are influential individuals in Zamboanga society with significant investment in agriculture who can assist or sink the project as he likes. The stern, somber posture of each man demonstrates the fact that each knows his influence. The stares coming at Jim fairly turn his knees to jelly; Matunkup's thumb in the small of Jim's back reminds him of his mentor's whispered encouragement just 30 seconds before.

Since hand shaking is not the norm among the Moro people, they nod in unison. Jim bows his head slightly and they all sit, relatively simultaneously. Matunkup acknowledges the presence of each man, making certain each receives appropriate respect. Then he turns slightly toward Jim and presents, in simple English, appropriate accolades about Jim's performance the previous evening and all the planning that led to the successful evening. The occasional nods, slightly raised eyebrows, and hints of smiles provide the positive feedback Julio and Jim are looking for, allowing Julio to launch into the introduction of the next phase of the overall project.

This phase has two main sections: the investment in planting and vineyard development, and the province-wide contest to select Miss Zamboanga Grape. Basher, Sulayman, Mama and Mastura all make points about the additional construction and plantings, providing ideas, constraints, solutions and an energetic exchange that is quite animated for about 20 minutes. All this time Tamil hardly says anything. A couple of times Jim tries to bring him into the conversation, but he makes simple replies and appears almost entirely disinterested.

Finally Matunkup brings the conversation around to the contest for Miss Grape and suddenly Tamil is sitting ramrod straight, eyes directly on Jim's face and says, forcefully and quietly, "I am interested in the project. I will help." Everything becomes quiet, except for the birds in the nearby trees that provide the morning symphony, and the breeze rattling the palm fronds around the pond. No one breaks the silence for several seconds, which feels like an eternity for anyone whose heart is pounding as hard as Jim's. He is rapidly trying to calculate the meaning, subtexts and expressions on Tamil's face, looking for any possibilities for using Tamil's influence.

"Of course, your help is very important to make the project a success. Hmm, do you have some ideas already about how we should make this contest?"

Tamil sits, saying nothing. Jim shifts the position of his feet under the table, not wanting to give away his worry over the thought, "What the hell am I going to have him do? How can I keep him involved and out of the way?" Then Tamil gives a slight smile and says, "I am not having experience with Miss Grape contests. I do not wish to say what is best to do and what is not best to do. I will help as you say you need help. As you know, I have some people who will obey if I tell them what is needed.

I also have many people who know that I protect the honor of our women. If I help the contest, these people will trust the contest so the women of Zamboanga are honorable. Do you understand?"

Jim sits back, crosses his feet under the table, smiles the patented Jim Tuck smile, and says, "I understand perfectly, and I welcome you to the Miss Grape contest as perhaps its most important partner. There are many, many details we need to attend to in the next two months before making the public announcement, and your contacts will help very much. Also, if you are willing, we can use your name on many of the posters and advertising - the Miss Grape contest sponsored by Tamil Vineyards - open to all Zamboanga young women wanting to represent their community." Then Jim falls silent for a moment, brain in hyperdrive and looks at Tamil asking, "Is it possible for me to come to your house tomorrow, to discuss more of these ideas?"

Tamil is slightly taken aback but nods slightly saying, "Yes, it is possible. My schedule is small in the morning. Come at 6:30 tomorrow morning and we can talk for one hour. Thank you." With that, Tamil rises, nods to each of his colleagues and Matunkup and leaves the seated group without looking back.

Jim is half sitting, half standing as Tamil's exit did not give him time to stand completely. He sits back down and looks from one man to the next, then to Matunkup who says, "That's the way of Tamil. Am I correct?" Each of the others nods in agreement, then their solemn faces all crack into wide grins and a bit of a chuckle rises from three of the four.

Matunkup first smiles, then chuckles, then laughs out loud, holding the edge of the table. Once the hilarity calms he looks at Jim and says, "Tamil likes you. Enjoy your meeting in the morning." Then he breaks into another bout of laughter as the other four join in and the lemonade is brought to the table. Jim sits pondering the outburst, takes a glass and fills it and sits back again, pensive. "Wonder what I've gotten myself into," he muses.

After the lemonade, the group of five, with Jim as scribe and initiator, spend the rest of the morning planning the development of the grape plantings according to what each one can invest, then coming up with estimates for the other main planters not represented at the table. Matunkup, with the assistance of each of the four will be making personal contact with those colleagues not present in order to cajole cooperation. Having the best estimates of the four present will assist in negotiating. The scope of the development is impressive to all of them, most of all to Jim. The dollar value of the investment is more than Jim has ever contemplated, but stands to benefit Zamboanga society, and the planters even more, if all parts of the project perform as they should. Tomorrow's meeting with Tamil is going to be interesting for sure, but also important. Getting the entire community behind the project, using the contest as the driving force to obtain interest across the entire community is vital to the success of it all. Plus, Jim might just get another glimpse of Hanna'. The mind boggles at the possibilities.

Wang listens intently to Jim's narration of the mornings events while pouring wine for each at the dinner table in the kitchen behind the shop. Cold dinner with wine allows the full attention of each of them to the task of planning the next morning's meeting with Tamil, and setting objectives for the outcome. The energy coming from Wang is infectious and nearly overwhelming. Wang had no idea Tamil, of all people, would be interested only in this aspect of the project. Once his surprise subsided he got to work on the possibilities, started making lists of colleagues most likely influenced by Tamil, lists of possible candidates for Miss Grape, standing then sitting then standing again saying, "Did you get that one, that one?"

Jim maintains his composure with affirmative nods as Wang races on with the next names, not waiting to assist Jim with spelling, and with his mouth embarrassingly full - rattles off three more names and locations, giving their association with Tamil and the best ways to approach them. In the end, he and Jim agree that enlisting candidates for Miss Grape should be left to Tamil since having a foreigner approach a father requesting his daughter participate in some vague contest would not work at all. Wang is certain that his list of contestant candidates is the most appropriate, but they both acknowledge that Tamil is bound to have some of his own. Undoubtedly they will have to be included. Jim notices that Hanna's name is not on Wang's list. He keeps that information to himself, but begins developing his strategy for ensuring her participation. What better way to ensure contact with her than have her be a contestant in a program Jim is directing. The smile spreading across his face confuses Wang for a moment until he says, "Tamil has a lovely daughter, does he not?" Suddenly the smile is gone, and Wang simply nods sagely and wags a finger on his right hand indicating that caution should be employed in Jim's planning. Raised eyebrows indicate to Jim that Wang is fully aware of the temptations involved and the care that Jim must take in the face of the possibility of screwing up a multimillion dollar project for the sake of his carnal gratification. Jim's sheepish grin, drop of the forehead and overt concentration on the paper in front of him are all Wang needs to know he has hit the target directly in the bull's eye. The eyebrows drop, the inscrutable oriental face comes on and the comment, "Be cautious my young companion. This is delicate ground you walk on. It is dangerous ground. Tamil does not forgive, ever." Head down, Jim simply continues concentrating on the paper in front of him, as Wang takes up his wine glass and leaves for his bedroom. By himself, Jim takes a long pull on his glass, sits back, crosses his ankles and smiles half a smile. "Tomorrow it starts." Then he collects the papers and is off to bed. He has to be up early, again!

There is no sun to accompany the scent of coffee that fills Jim's room wafting through the mosquito net. Jim's eyes slide open as the smile slides up the corners of his mouth and he rolls to lift the edge of the net and make his way to the toilet and bathroom, avoiding the cup on the tray by his pallet. Ablutions complete he takes the cup with its remaining coffee down with him to the kitchen and frying eggs and buttered bread. Wang, the cook this morning, takes one look at Jim and raises one eyebrow saying, "You are visiting one of the most traditional leaders of Zamboanga society this morning, and you look like an American imperialist."

Jim stops in midstride, looks down at his outfit and nods, setting the cup on the counter. "I'll be right back." With that he climbs the stairs to his room and changes into his Aladdin outfit, as he and Wang identify it, returning in about eight minutes to a cold cup of coffee. Wang simply pours more hot on top and Jim takes a deep draught in appreciation of the gesture. Breakfast is short lived and Jim gathers the paperwork from yesterday evening - names, suggestions, ideas. He gets his turban wound by Wang, and heads out to the front room to the waiting taxi. "Go well, my young friend, and carefully," comes from Wang standing in the middle of the beaded curtain. Jim gives a slight smile and a wave as he shuts the door and steps to the taxi.

The ride to Tamil's is short since traffic has not built to its usual crescendo. They arrive at the gate in the wall surrounding the house at 6:20 and Jim insists they not announce themselves until 6:28 by his watch. The gate opens with the announcement, both sides swinging wide to open the entrance to the gravel circular drive with fountain in the center. The slow progress of the car around the circle allows the crunching gravel to sound as if the stones are crunching against one another one at a time. The gurgling of the fountain adds to the quiet morning music and Jim feels strangely calm as he exits the taxi, silk shoes first and turban last. The gravel pokes through his silk shoes as he strolls toward the large entrance door. As he reaches the flagstone entranceway the large door swings open and a servant beckons him to enter. As the door closes behind him, Tamil appears through the archway to the right, gliding on the polished marble floor. The quiet swish of his feet skimming the floor also soothes Jim's' nerves. He is actually feeling pretty good as Tamil greets him and indicates they should return through the archway.

As they walk, Jim tries his best at Muslim small talk, not knowing for sure if he is seen as blathering or polite. After passing through two rooms, they reach a rather small room covered with several layers of silk carpets of many designs and color combinations, a low table surrounded by large pillows and the welcome fragrance of coffee and jasmine. "Please to sit down here," and Tamil indicates a pillow on the near side of the octagonal table. He walks to the other side, sits and a servant is immediately present ready to pour the coffee.

Jim raises his eyes to the servant's face and nods that he would indeed like some, which brings a smile. The steaming coffee streams into his cup, coming to an abrupt stop just below the lip. There are no sugar or dairy containers on the table, and Jim waits for the pouring to finish in Tamil's cup before lifting his and giving a small salute that Tamil returns. The coffee is marvelously strong. Added to the caffeine he had at Wang's shortly before he is slightly wired and on edge, quite alert.

From his sleeve, out of his waistband, Jim retrieves his small sheaf of papers for the meeting and Tamil puts his cup back on the table, clapping his hands for the servant. The servant arrives and Tamil gives a short instruction which is swiftly met with a nod and the retreat of the servant. As Jim watches the servant depart around the corner, there is a slight movement he barely catches in the corner of his eye. He turns his head to the right but there is nothing there, and he goes back to his cup, relishing the strong coffee taste.

Tamil puts his cup down and starts, "So you have papers to start this project. What do I do?"

Jim glances down, reshuffles the stack of papers and holds up the first. "Mr. Wang gave me some names of people who either may support the contest or may have possible contestants for the contest. But he and I decided that finding the contestants would be the best thing for you to do. So I brought the list we made, or Mr. Wang dictated to me, so you could see it and make the best changes, as well as perhaps add other names to the list. In addition, this paper," and he lifts the next page, "has the names of influential people who can help bring the contest to all parts of Zamboanga society. We know, that for this project to succeed, all parts of Zamboanga must support it. Therefore, if we have enthusiasm in all parts, coming from people supporting one contestant or another, then the project will be well known everywhere. Here are the names of the contestants Mr. Wang thought of and here are the names of the most influential people who might be good supporters of the contest." With that he slides both papers over to Tamil who extracts a glasses case from his sleeve, puts on a reasonably ugly pair of horn-rimmed glasses and begins examining the two papers. While he is reading, Jim is sipping, enjoying his coffee and surreptitiously glancing around the room. Suddenly he sees a flicker of cloth near the door the servant exited, then it stops just before the servant strides around the corner, glancing back over his shoulder, bringing back sweets on a tray. He lays the tray on the table and retreats without the slightest acknowledgment from Tamil. Tamil looks up and gestures toward the tray, "Try these. I think you will be impressed."

Jim nods and reaches forward, retrieving a sticky item, which he suddenly recognizes as baklava. He sniffs it - sure enough it is baklava - and bites the corner off, savoring the honey and nuts, rolling it in his mouth - then a small sip of coffee to add to the flavor. Closing his eyes he realizes he has not had something this good in his mouth for ages and is wallowing in the sensation when he hears, "Is it not good? You seem quiet or not liking it."

"It is the nearest to heaven I have been in many years.

This is absolutely wonderful. I am really enjoying this."

Tamil puts the papers down, reaches forward taking a baklava from the other side of the tray and bites, chewing noisily, then agrees that it is fair.

"Fair! How can you call this fair? This is the best baklava I have eaten, ever! I have eaten it many times, but never this good."

Tamil flicks pieces of filo off his chin onto the table, finishes off the baklava and smiles a wide smile. "I am glad you enjoy it. Have another one."

Jim starts for the tray, but stops his hand half way saying, "Baklava this good must be enjoyed in small bits. I may have another later. For now I am satisfied."

Tamil's eyebrows lift, then descend immediately again and he returns to his papers with, "As you wish. Have more if you want."

Ten minutes later he places the two papers on the table and leans sideways onto the pillow, propping on his right elbow. "This list is very good. Mr. Wang knows our community well. There are two names that must not be on the list of contestants, but I know of four more that are not listed here. I will write their names and contact them myself. I will contact all families of candidates myself, as you suggested. I will contact the most important person in each neighborhood and ask for his help in giving information about the contest to people in his neighborhood. These people know the neighborhood better than anyone." With that he sits up more erect and takes his coffee cup in the palm of his hand. "One problem is there that I do not have a solution."

A small set of worry lines appear in Jim's forehead and he quietly asks, "What problem?"

"I agree I must contact families who have contestants for the contest. They will listen to me. But I have a very beautiful daughter also. I think she would be the best Miss Grape, but others will not agree if I say my daughter will enter the contest."

Jim's heart is pounding its way out of the front of his waistcoat and color is rising up his cheeks, causing his head to drop down into his papers. He whispers something about solutions available. "Are you not well, Mr. Jim?"

With a bit of a squirm, Jim rubs his face and growls out, "Need the toilet, please."

"Oh, of course." Tamil claps his hands and whispers to the servant who beckons to Jim and leads him down a wide marble-paved hall to a closed door. Jim mumbles "Thanks", enters, rushes to the sink and splashes water on his burning cheeks. For show he urinates down the porcelain hole in the floor, takes a bucket of water and pours it down after, does another quick splash to his face and dries it with the small towel hanging beside the sink.

There is no mirror so he cannot check his countenance before leaving the room, but after running his hand through his hair, he replaces his turban and retraces his way back to the room where Tamil is speaking with the most beautiful young woman that Jim has ever laid his eyes on, and his heart takes off again. He feels the crimson rising again while Tamil is saying, "Mr. Jim, this my daughter Hanna', who is old enough for the contest, only next month. Today she is 17 years, next month she will be 18 years. Do you think she is good contestant?"

Jim's mouth is moving but his vocal cords only squeak. "Of course!" he is able to blurt out with just a tad too much force. Tamil smiles, bows to Hanna' and indicates she is to leave the room. Jim's gaze is fixed on her back as she rounds the corner of the opening at the far end of the left wall, where the coffee and food came from before. Suddenly he realizes his mouth is still open and breaks into a wide smile as he sits and re-stacks his papers, saying, "I think she would have a wonderful chance of succeeding in the contest." The voice quality has improved considerably so he can actually be understood. Tamil smiles a knowing smile and raises his cup to Jim who responds with his own. "There are certainly many ways to have your daughter participate without irritating your colleagues. I will think about this with Mr. Wang and Julio Matunkup and perhaps they can give you a suggestion you will agree can succeed. I will talk with them today and come again tomorrow if I can."

"I will begin speaking today with my colleagues who are without daughters. I can see you tomorrow at 2 p.m. I hope you enjoy your day today. Goodbye." With that Tamil rises, turns and is out through the archway to the right before Jim has time to react, rise, or say anything. His brain is boiling with projects, possibilities and plans as he exits the room behind the servant that had guided him to the toilet. At the door, Jim smiles his most engaging smile and says thank you to the servant who nods, gesturing Jim out the door and closing it behind him. The taxi is right where Jim left it and he enters ready to head back to the tailor shop, when an idea hits him and he tells the driver to drive to the hacienda. Matunkup may be very helpful with the development of a plan for Tamil and Hanna' without the extra hassle of fending off the knowing looks and judgmental innuendos that he is bound to collect at Wang's.

Traffic is intense now so the trip to Matunkup's takes at least half again as long as usual with Jim simulating a worm in hot ashes most of the way. Not able to sit still, he sits first on one side of the back then the other. Then he slouches then onto the front edge of the seat, then back again. The driver catches his eye in the mirror, winks and Jim immediately calms with the idea, "What the heck?" Then he says, "What you looking at smiling? Watch the road, OK?"

The driver simply nods a smiling nod, faces forward the entire time, and begins singing some local tune that Jim suspects is lascivious. As the taxi driver is nodding, singing and keeping time on the steering wheel, they make their way up the hill to the hacienda. The taxi arrives but for the first time Julio is not there at the door to greet Jim. Explaining to the driver that he likely will not be over half an hour, he bounds up the steps and raps on the door jam. After several seconds one of the servants that Jim has not met arrives, opens the door and asks, "Can I help you?"

Jim explains who he is and why he is there. The fellow says that Mr. Matunkup is away until the following Tuesday, to which Jim says, "Bullshit. I saw the cars all there out front."

The servant rises a bit taller, frowns and is about to offer Jim the opportunity to exit the property when Julio passes behind the servant crossing to the dining area and lets out a small whoop, which startles the servant into a quick turn that causes a full frontal collision with Matunkup. Once they disentangle, Julio reaches for Jim and provides a large abrazzo that startles the servant more than the collision. "Jim, I see you have met Hermano who joined us yesterday afternoon. The man is a magician with a spoon and you will have the opportunity to try some of his specialties at lunch, assuming you can stay that long. OK, Hermano, I am glad you were able to greet my good friend, Jim. I can take it from here. See you at lunch," and with that Julio bustles Jim through the door and left into the living room where three elderly gentleman are sitting in three corners of the room.

As Matunkup and Jim virtually spring into the room, the three men rise simultaneously and Julio introduces them sequentially, each time using the expression "good friend" for Jim as well as for each elder. It becomes abundantly clear that Jim has stumbled into a planning meeting between Matunkup and three planters Jim has not met yet. Matunkup briefly explains Jim's role in the development of the overall plan and asks Jim to give a quick overview of the full project and what developments have occurred to date. Clearing his throat to give himself a moment of thought collection, Jim glances at Julio and sees the broadest smile ever and realizes that Matunkup expects that having the originator of the project provide the background information gives credibility to it that Julio as another planter might not be able to provide. So, standing relaxed in the center of the three seated men of his audience, Jim waxes his most eloquent about the basics of the three-part plan and the progress to date.

He watches the three faces as he is talking and notes the nods, unstated queries and half smiles as he keeps on going, backtracking to explain possible questions and restate the points receiving nods and smiles, so that by the time he finishes all three men are sitting forward on their chairs.

When he indicates he is finished, Matunkup springs to his feet slightly before the other three and all five join in a five-way handshake in the center of the room. Then Julio escorts the three gentlemen to the front door offering farewells and plans for their inclusion in the next full-group meeting in a week. Walking back into the living room, Julio is fairly bouncing with each step and lets out a larger whoop, saying, "That was as lucky as I get in life! Your showing up at the expressly right moment and making the presentation you did was perfect! They loved every bit, my friend, and they are sold completely. Aah!" And with that he flops back onto the sofa with pillows all around and laughs the longest, loudest, largest belly laugh Jim has ever seen.

Once Matunkup calms himself, he suddenly sits up and looks at Jim, asking, "What in the world are you doing here anyway?"

"Thought you'd never ask. That did go fairly well, didn't it," and a slightly cheeky half smile graces Jim's face. It is the smile that has melted more than one feminine heart, but simply causes another burst of laughter from Matunkup.

"Yes, fairly well, indeed. Now, how did you happen to be here? I do not believe in Providence, so what caused the happy accident?"

"OK, here it is. I met with Tamil this morning about his involvement in the Miss Grape contest. Oh, by the way, Miss Zamboanga Grape was way too long, so it will be Miss Grape. Anyway, Tamil will be the recruiter of contestants from among his acquaintances and colleagues, but today he mentioned that he thought his daughter might be a good candidate. I happen to agree. Have you seen her? Never mind, anyway, he is worried that his recruiting of other contestants might not look too good if his daughter is automatically in the mix. Nepotism and all that, and he does not want to piss off his colleagues or give offence. So, how do we get his daughter in as another contestant and have Tamil as emissary recruiter of contestants?"

By now, Julio has shifted from hilarity to thoughtful demeanor and comes to sitting on the edge of the couch. He shifts from chin resting in his hand to slowly raising his eyes to meet Jim's. Then a slow, wicked smile spreads across his face, one that is all lips and no eyes. "Yes, I have seen Tamil's oldest daughter from a distance. She enjoys accompanying her mother to the café below the newspaper offices in the municipal building. She is stunningly beautiful, I will have to admit. And you say Tamil wants her as a contestant in the Miss Grape contest? Tamil can be very persuasive, can't he? Well, lets us put our heads together to see if we can find some way to help Tamil out, OK?" The eyebrows come up with that last sentence and Jim squirms a bit but maintains his cool in the face of such insightful and sardonic observations.

"Let us retire to the gazebo where it is cooler. I suspect we can think more clearly there, agreed?"

"Agreed," says Jim, who has started another round of blushing, albeit less than he displayed at Tamil's.

The lemonade arrives as they sit at the gazebo and Matunkup pours for them both. "Now, as I see it, Tamil is critical in his role as a go-between in obtaining contestants, correct?"

"Correct."

"So, how to keep him in his role and accept his daughter as a contestant without irritating his fellow planters and others who also have daughters in the competition. Hmm." With that, Matunkup swirls the clinking iced lemonade rapidly in his glass and stands to walk the circle of the gazebo. Suddenly he stops, looks over at Jim from the other side of the table and says, "He must be seen as acquiescing to the demands of his colleagues who put forward Tamil's daughter as another contestant."

Jim puts down his glass, scratches his head and deposits his silk shod feet onto the chair beside him, legs fully stretched out. He has not been this nonchalant with Matunkup or Wang since he arrived, but he suddenly appreciates the political acumen of Matunkup like he has not before. His half smile is back as he says, "OK. That makes perfect Machiavellian sense. How? As in, how do we pull that off?"

"Tamil's colleagues must appreciate the fact that he has a beautiful daughter who is not in the contest, and why she is not, and that will generate the feeling of generosity of spirit as well as the public magnanimous attitude each tries to show. That attitude gives the public appearance of strength, shows confidence in the beauty of his own daughter, assuming he has a daughter who is a contestant, and provides each generous individual temporary supremacy at the top of the pecking order." Matunkup starts slowly strolling around the gazebo in a counterclockwise circle, gently rubbing his right temple and continues, "For this to work, the demonstrations of magnanimity must take place in front of all the others, and facing Tamil. Everyone must be trying for one-upmanship in their attempts to convince Tamil to enter Hanna' into the contest."

Jim sits there, feet up, lifts his glass and raises it in an appreciative toasting motion, asking, "Any idea how we can get them all together?"

"Wang and I will organize a dinner at the club after each of Tamil's colleagues has been contacted by either me or Wang. We will point out the unfairness of Hanna' not being able to participate and I suspect it will not take too much convincing to bring them around to the idea that they can solidify their place in Zamboanga society by assisting to bring justice to this situation and right a terrible wrong, insisting Hanna' participate alongside all the other beautiful daughters of Zamboanga society. I will talk to Wang this afternoon and we will get started. I think it would be best to have this issue put to rest by the end of next week. So late next week we will have dinner at the club. How does it sound to you?" That last question is with one eyebrow raised and lips slightly pursed as if he knows the answer already. Jim simply nods, puts his glass down, stands and walks over to Julio. They are at least one generation apart in age, roughly the same height, looking eye to eye. Jim says simply, "Thank you."

"I feel certain that we will all benefit from this little exercise. I hope that the project survives." With that he claps Jim on the shoulder, calls Hermano, and they sit down to a three-course early lunch with wine and vanilla ice cream with cointreau for dessert. Slightly soused, Jim slides into the taxi after lunch, sits back, lights a cigar and puffs all the way back to town. It has been a great day so far, and he plans to take the rest of it off.

He exits the taxi at the municipal building heading to the newspaper office when he glances across the café to the far corner and spots Tamil's family, including Hanna'. Avoid staring at all costs, he veers from his course toward the stairs and heads to a small table near the cashier's desk. As he sits, Tony arrives smiling and asking about his health - in quiet tones - about the progress of the project. Tony diplomatically avoids mentioning Jim's attire. Jim gives his most enigmatic smile and assures Tony all is well and then orders an unneeded coffee. When the coffee arrives, after five minutes of studiously avoiding looking across the room, Jim asks Tony, "Do you know the family that is sitting across the room?" giving a nod of his head in the appropriate direction.

Tony glances in the direction and returns his gaze to Jim, then begins smiling ear to ear saying, "Of course, it is the family of Tamil, the vineyard owner and leader of the southeast section of Zamboanga. They are very well known here, and come often. It is a very old Zamboanga family, many years here, and very important. It is also a family well known for having beautiful women, at least when they are young. I think you may not have noticed how beautiful some of the young women at that table are, but I tell you, they are very beautiful." Tony's voice has gradually increased in volume during this soliloquy causing Jim to look him in the eye with deadly intent that creates the intended effect and Tony is suddenly silent.

"Thank you very much for your detailed information. You are quite correct in assuming I have not closely examined the features of the women at the table, but I may in the future." Taking a sip, he says, "The coffee is excellent as usual. Thank you." With that, Tony takes the cue and exits stage right in a hurry. Jim spends the next 20 minutes sipping tepid coffee and secretly watching Hanna' over the rim of his cup. Never once does he notice her looking at him, but he realizes from the chef's contest that she must see everything he is doing. He hopes against hope that her ears are not as good as her eyes. After 20 minutes, Tamil's family of five leaves their table and exits the café with Jim watching their silent parade. Hanna' is the last out the door and just as she exits, her rear hand gives a small backward wave without turning at all, just a flick of the fingers by her hip, and she is gone. It sends Jim to the moon.

Tepid coffee finished, he bounds up the stairs with a tad more energy than he has any right to demonstrate and into the office that he has not seen for awhile. Gus is not obviously present so he goes behind the desk and down the hall to Gus's office where the grey head is turned away from the door, feet up on the bookcase looking for all the world like he is sound asleep, although Jim can't see his face. "Bout time you made it back here. I was wondering if I still had any staff. Sit down." He's not asleep.

Jim sits in the folding chair, tilting it back on the back two legs and propping his knees on the front of the wooden desk. "So, what's the latest around here? I miss anything lately?"

Gus's feet come back to the floor and he swings around to face Jim, the countenance on his face darkly disapproving. "What the hell have you got on?"

"Don't get your knickers in a twist. I have been working since 6:30, first at Tamil's - thus this garb - then at Matunkup's, and then I came straight here. No time to change. Thought it best to get here as soon as possible."

"Well, get yourself home, change and get back here. Are you worried you might have missed something? Gosh, I appreciate the concern. Hell yes, you've missed a few things! I have had exactly five hours sleep in the last three days. Look at these bags under my eyes, they have bags of their own. This grape project is killing me!"

"So, wanna call it all off, do you?"

"Shut the hell up! Of course we can't call it off. But I need help or I'm a casualty of the project!"

Jim's feet hit the floor as the chair falls back into a four-legged stance. As he stands he leans his hands onto the desk and looks Gus fixedly in the eye, "Look, I have been up late and then early the next day for nearly two weeks now. I just got back from Matunkup's from my second meeting this morning. This tiger we are riding ain't easy to dismount, but I suspect Wang and Matunkup would be able to find a way to ease your exit from participation if you are finding it a bit much."

Gus holds Jim's stare, neither of them blinking for at least 30 seconds. Then Gus exhales deeply, leans back and says, "Thought I might invest in another staff member. Got any ideas or recommendations?"

Standing again, allowing his shoulders to slack, Jim shifts to one foot and says, "That's about the shortest fight I have ever had. Yes, I have a suggestion. Get Tony full time from the café and pay him twice what the café owner pays. He is worth four times as much so you are getting a bargain. He is already in on the details of the project so no need to keep secrets and he is thorough, silent and efficient. Couldn't get better."

"Send him up here, will ya? I gotta get this copy to the printer five minutes ago. Thanks, and nice to see ya." With that Gus is out the back door of his office and down the hall. Jim exits the office and heads downstairs to the café.

It is mid afternoon and business has slowed so Tony is able to spare a moment. He lets out a whoop when Jim tells him there'a a job waiting for him upstairs if he wants it. Off comes the apron, which he formally hands to the cashier, writes a quick resignation note with his unpaid hours noted, and leaves it with the cashier. Jim tells him that Gus is out of the office at the moment, but will probably be back soon. With a wave and a chuck on Tony's shoulder, Jim leaves the café through the door used by Hanna' shortly before and heads for the tailor shop. His half day off has suddenly gotten much shorter, but better. Wang listens intently to Jim's report about his meeting with Tamil, the conundrum presented by Tamil, and Matunkup's skillful solution. Wang seems pleased to hear Jim's visit to the newspaper office resulted in an advancement for Tony. Things seem to be going swimmingly well at the moment, but Wang's face is not light. It seems to maintain the heavy expression brought on by worry or indigestion. "And Matunkup is able to assist the enlistment of Tamil's daughter into the list of contestants?"

"He thinks so, but we don't know yet. We will know in a few days. We need to schedule a meeting at the club soon, and Julio will take care of the rest." Jim delivers the information with just a hint of reserve or chagrin or deference that he has not typically shown in the past.

Wang responds, "I will make the arrangements with Matunkup so there is no double scheduling." With that he just sits and looks at Jim with a knowing look, slightly skeptical, that is beginning to get under Jim's skin.

"You look a bit funny, Wang. Is there a problem?"

"I certainly hope not." With that, Wang stands and slowly exits through the bead curtain into the back room where one sewing machine is going and the sound of scissors cutting on a hollow wooden surface resonates. Jim is left sitting in the front room, wondering what he is getting himself into. As if he doesn't have enough potential risks, Jim plans the next step he can take toward direct contact with the forbidden fruit.

The next week is filled with regular newspaper business for Jim, plus the extra details of logistics for the all important meeting at the club. Each day is strenuous, hectic and at the end of each Jim wonders exactly what he accomplished with all the running around. The advertising contracts are easily enough accounted for and show on his pending commission paycheck. He has been doing fine the last couple months, financial wise, and has a sizeable nest egg set aside for a rainy day or his departure. Rainy days are likely to arrive sooner than his departure, but it is just a cliché anyway. The larger nest egg, the one he brought in from Manila, continues to lie dormant in his pack upstairs. It is as safe here at the tailor shop as anywhere in the world, and is what he plans to use to re-enter his life back in the States. His earnings here in Zamboanga have developed to the point that he not only won't need to touch his stash, but actually will likely add to it by the time he is ready to go. Going is for the future, not today. Today is time for meeting Tamil again to assess the progress toward a serious Miss Grape contest.

He is actually welcomed at the door by Tamil himself. A nod of the head precedes their walk through the marble corridors, Jim for the first time in his "normal" clothes. Tamil has given no indication of a personal reaction to having a western clad white man in his house, but the staff seem a bit more reserved than usual as Jim and Tamil settle themselves onto the cushions at the low table. The tray of drinks arrives immediately followed by a bowl of diced fruit and two small plates. Ivory picks are on linen napkins beside the plates and Jim helps himself to a large glass of orange juice and some diced papaya while Tamil simply rests on his elbow on the pillows opposite. Before drinking, Jim asks, "I understand that you have had several visits to colleagues already, many with beautiful daughters who might participate in the contest. How did they react to the idea of entering their daughters in the contest?"

"You are correct. I have visited eleven colleagues, eight of them have daughters. One man is very, how do you say, old fashioned, and he refuses completely. The other seven agree. I have four more visits to make, all to homes with daughters. I will visit these tomorrow and will have information for our group tomorrow night at our meeting at the club. The information I will give only to our group because the fathers do not want to embarrass their daughters and want to discuss how the contest must happen so their daughters are safe. But they agree now. I think we will have eleven daughters in the contest."

"That is very good, but I think we will actually have twelve daughters in the contest, don't you?" Jim says this with an earnest smile on his face, but with a nervous knot in his stomach. What if it gets screwed up and Hanna' does not get into the contest? Ugh!

"Yes, of course, twelve. Perhaps we have twelve. My friend Wang is, I think, a very clever man and perhaps he and Mr. Matunkup can help with this question. We will see. Whatever comes is the will of Allah."

"Of course, the will of Allah. But, if others feel that your daughter must also be part of the contest, I think you will be happy, won't you?" Tamil is quiet just long enough to make Jim slightly squirm on his pillow, hopefully not so much that Tamil notices. But Jim knows that Tamil notices everything, or so it seems. Jim tamps down his squirming while Tamil ruminates until he finally says, "Happy, yes, because I think my daughter is happy to try."

Neither Jim nor Tamil have used Hanna's name through the entire discussion, but no matter, all Jim has to do now is make sure the coup this evening comes off and Hanna' is in the contest. Yess! Just then she enters the room, walking straight to her father's side, giving him a slight peck on the cheek. She whispers something in his ear. Tamil smiles and rises, motioning Jim to stay seated, as he exits the room, telling Jim, "I am needed for a moment. Please eat some fruit. It is very good."

With that he heads to the archway behind Jim with Hanna' following him. As she passes Jim her thigh grazes his shoulder, sending an electric shock through his entire body, nearly causing him to collapse. Luckily his glass is still on the table and he has no food in his mouth that might fall out of his slack-jawed face. She exits the room without the slightest recognition that he is there, but he knows she knows he knows.

Suddenly he begins trying to remember where the bathroom is. He sits up straight and, taking up his glass, chugs a huge swallow, wishing for all the world that it was Jack Daniels. With the next swallow, the glass is empty and he looks around the room expectantly, causing a young servant to slide to his side. "Bathroom?" Quizzical look then, "Banyo?" Sudden recognition and energetic motioning that Jim should follow. He rises and follows out the opposite side of the room and down a short hall where a closed door is indicated. The servant raps lightly on the door with no response, opens it for Jim and motions him to enter. Jim smiles, enters and closes the door behind him.

"Get ahold of yourself, old boy. What's gotten into you? It is just a girl, a beautiful girl, but just a girl." He continues the self talk along these lines while relieving himself, sprinkles water on his hands, dries them and leaves the toilet to find the servant patiently waiting outside the door to escort him back to the lounge. Jim offers his slightly meek smile and follows three steps back. Around the corner Jim enters the room where Tamil is back on his pillow sipping a mango juice with ice. The day is hotter than usual, thankfully, because Jim's sweating now has a plausible explanation. He resumes his seat, nodding to Tamil.

"Simple problems seem to overcome my wives and require the calming hand of the father, no?"

"They are lucky to have a father that can calm issues so quickly."

Tamil nods and takes some of the diced fruit on his plate. They both eat quietly for a few minutes then Jim says, "I have several more stops to make today, but I am very happy to have this talk with you and am pleased that it looks so good for the success of the Miss Grape contest. If it is successful, much of the praise must be for your efforts. If there are no contestants there is no contest, yes?"

Tamil sagely nods and says nothing other than a slight smile and small shrug of the shoulder. Then Jim says, "If you don't mind, I will let myself out and get on with my schedule for the day. I am very happy today." And he is, but not entirely because of Tamil's recruiting so many contestants. Jim rises, nods to Tamil who returns the gesture. Jim turns and heads toward the front of the house. There is an open door on the right, which Jim glances behind, where he spies Hanna' sitting at a front window reading a small book. She stops reading, turns her head toward the door, and smiles at Jim, who stumbles, obviously smitten by her. Hanna' smiles even wider and slightly waves her hand, which Jim returns. It is the first full communication either has had toward the other and, rather than call attention to himself, Jim immediately dashes down the hallway and out the front door. It opens immediately as he approaches, with the small boy who opens it barely reaching the knob. Jim smiles and waves at the little fellow and heads to the taxi. Realizing that he is at the front of the house, he looks down the façade a few windows and spots a familiar drapery pattern, the one framing the window Hanna' was sitting in, but there is no Hanna' in the window now. He is surprised at the degree of disappointment he feels, but stifles it and folds himself into the car and closes the door behind him. There is enough to do today without the distraction of the disappointment of not seeing Hanna' in the window. Still, why in the world is he feeling this way? He slumps into the seat and bumps along to the next appointment. He has to keep this sensation hidden from Wang's clever wit or he will have hell to pay.

The meeting at the club is almost anticlimactic. Matunkup had obviously done his advanced caucusing work very well, Wang is the consummate host, the chorus of voices encouraging Tamil to enter his daughter in the contest obviously impresses Tamil, and impresses Jim even more. What a show these guys can put on! At the breakup toast with juices, Tamil thanks his colleagues and expresses his admiration for the honor of the members of the group. As people are filtering out of the meeting room Tamil takes Jim aside to inform him that he is expected for breakfast at Tamil's house, 6:30 tomorrow morning. Jim is expected to provide Hanna' the details of the contest and her obligations, as well as the expectations of the contest committee. Smiling very deferentially, Jim accepts the command performance and Tamil turns and leaves without a backward glance. He obviously knows who is in charge. Jim whispers the information about breakfast to Matunkup before Julio leaves for the hacienda.

As they are driving back to the tailor shop, Jim informs Wang of his breakfast appointment. "Jim, this is quite important. Do you understand just how important?"

"I think I do, but you had better tell me what you are thinking."

"This contest will spread the information about the Zamboanga grape project throughout the province, and beyond. Since we will use judges from Manila to assure impartial results, even Manila will know about our project. The project must succeed. Failure will set back Zamboanga business and society for many years. Many years. Nothing must threaten the success. If Tamil becomes an enemy of the project, it will not succeed. If Tamil's daughter dishonors the family, Tamil will be most upset. Do not allow yourself to seduce Hanna' and dishonor Tamil's family. Is this very clear?"

"Crystal."

"What is crystal? I do not understand. Is this not some kind of glass for drinking or making fancy containers?"

"It is very clear glass, which allows us to see clearly. So, crystal means so clear that it seems like looking through glass made of crystal. In other words, I understand very clearly."

"Good." And the conversation is finished as they turn the corner and stop in front of the shop.

"Good night, Jim. Coffee will be ready in the morning." Wang touches Jim to give his arm a squeeze in the small vice of his fingers.

Jim winces ever so slightly, smiles at Wang and, once his arm is released, walks just behind Wang to the door. Wang fishes out his keys, opens the door, and waits for Jim to follow him through, closing it after. With a nod, Wang departs through the beaded curtain and Jim makes his way into the kitchen and pours a glass of red wine with an ice cube. He walks on out through the back door and stands in the damp moonlight, enjoying the neutral temperature of the air, no breeze. It is almost like there is no air at all, just calm. Before the storm? We'll see. Glass into the sink, up the stairs and off to bed.

The coffee smells marvelous the next morning, allowing a semblance of civility as Jim descends the stairs. He is in "normal" clothes again since it seems Tamil accepts the fact that he is a friendly invader. Wang pours his cup full and says, "Matunkup wants a personal report once you finish at Tamil's. Please go straight to the hacienda when you finish. Gus knows already, is not happy, but accepting. Tony will fill in a few of your duties this morning."

With that Wang turns and heads to the cutting room where the treadle machines are just starting up as the day begins. Jim sits quietly with his cup in his palms contemplating the far wall, and nothing at all. Slowly the caffeine catches up with his consciousness and he is sitting a tad straighter, beginning to tap one foot; then he stands and pours half the cup down the drain, depositing the empty cup in the sink. It is now 6:15 and time to find the taxi. Find is not the right word since it is undoubtedly out front as usual. Off he goes.

The taxi pulls up at the gate, one honk and the gate opens to the courtyard and fountain. Jim exits the cab and is walking to the door when it opens to Tamil's smiling face and welcoming nod. "Come in, come in. We go to the back of the house where we will eat. Come, come." Hustling Jim along, they stride swiftly along with Tamil's robes swishing side to side and brushing one wall. Jim nearly jogs to keep up. Suddenly they are in a kitchen and eating area at the very back of the house. The smells coming from the room are exquisite.

Tamil stops in mid-stride, indicates the other side of the table to Jim, who walks around and pulls out the heavy chair. No sitting on the floor this time. Tamil sits on the near side and the food immediately comes to the table via three different servants, with a fourth bringing the silver coffee server and cups. Jim looks at the food with saliva filling his mouth. He is hungry, but before he allows anything to be served on his plate he asks, "Are we not eating with Hanna' so I can tell her about the contest?"

"Hanna' has eaten already. She always awakens at 5 a.m. and eats with her mother and sisters at 6 a.m., always." With that explanation, Tamil simply returns to observing the filling of his plate and Jim acknowledges with a nod to the servant, who starts filling Jim's. They eat in silence, finish with juice and coffee. Tamil rises first, indicating Jim should follow. They move more slowly this time, through the kitchen, back toward the front of the house to a small room with no windows along the long corridor. Inside the room is the omnipresent low table and pillows with a water pitcher and glasses in the middle. Tamil invites Jim to enter, which he does, and Tamil turns to the nearest servant and whispers something. Off goes the servant and Tamil and Jim settle themselves comfortably on the pillows. Their elbows have no more than touched the pillow tops when there is a tap at the door and Tamil voices something Jim figures means enter, or something similar. The door opens and in slides Hanna' in traditional dress with her head encased in a turban-like wrapping. Her high-waisted skirt reaches the floor and the blouse is long-sleeved and has a high stiff collar that keeps her head up by pressing under her chin. It gives her the imperial look that Jim has noticed the other times he has seen her.

Tamil makes the introduction, "Jim Tuck, this is my oldest child, Hanna'. She is, in one month, 18 years. She knows English language. You may speak to her."

"Hello, Hanna'." Jim is working as hard as he can to prevent any squeaking in his voice. He is nervous as a whore in church, but does not dare to show it. A slight smile in the left corner of Hanna's mouth, the corner her father cannot see, demonstrates that his heroic efforts are useless; she sees right through him.

"Hello, Mr. Tuck. It is so nice to meet you." This is followed by a small curtsy and a genuine smile, full mouth, which her father can see. "You can call me Jim, if you like. Most people do. Your English is quite clear."

"Hanna', this is Mr. Tuck, as you said. He will remain Mr. Tuck. Hanna' has had many tutors of English language, and two girls who are her American friends. That is enough American friends, I think. They are enough for learning to speak."

Jim has turned toward Tamil during his explanation and does not see the frown that flashes across Hanna's face. It disappears as quickly. Jim then turns toward

Hanna', who by now has returned her sunny disposition to her face. "Would you like to sit with us while I explain about the contest?"

"Hanna' will stand there where she can easily hear what you have to say and can ask any question if she wants. Tell her, please."

Again, the flash of attitude comes and goes before it can be detected by her father. Jim begins the lesson. He sits erect instead of the semi-reclined posture he had before, but Tamil remains nonchalant on his pillows. Hanna' pays rapt attention, asking a few questions. Then there is a tap at the door. Tamil sits erect with a scowl at the interruption and calls, "Who?"

A muffled voice comes through the door and Tamil gruffly orders the door opened. A servant comes meekly into the room, eyes averted, head down and mumbles something Jim does not understand, but which causes Tamil to stand and march off, giving the servant a firm push forward as if the messenger needed a reprimand. Just as he is leaving the room he turns and says, "I apologize for this interruption. I will return soon. Please wait for me." Then he is away and Jim is left sitting erect at the table with Hanna' standing between him and the door. Five seconds after Tamil leaves, Hanna' gently pushes the door mostly closed and launches herself at Jim, causing him to fall back on the pillows. Her turban falls off and she wraps her arms around him in a grip that he has not felt since Wang held his arm last night. Her face is next to his, her eyes blazing as he lies on his back, arms away from his sides, wondering what in the world is this. Suddenly Hanna's mouth is on his. Breathlessly she presses her voluptuous chest against Jim. He finds himself wrapping his arms around her. His groin is aching like never before, and he starts to gulp for air as the lip lock Hanna' has him in seems permanent.

Then, just as suddenly, Hanna' is up, places the turban on her head, smooths her skirt and straightens her blouse. Within five seconds she is exactly as she was before that volcanic eruption. Jim is still lying on his back with a dazed expression on his face, a swelling in his pants, but no trace of lipstick or makeup on his person. It is not allowed in Tamil's house. Just as his senses start to realign and he sits upright, Jim hears footsteps in the hall and Tamil barges into the room in a gruff manner. "Continue!" he growls. Not looking at either Jim or Hanna', he finds his cushion and resumes his semi-reclined posture with a furious countenance that unsettles Jim.

"Is there a problem, Tamil?"

"No. Idiots in the world! Idiots who call me and then hang up the telephone with no messages! The new servant will certainly not do this mistake again."

"What happened to this servant who just came and delivered the message?"

"He is not here now, not anymore. Continue. We are wasting time."

So Jim clears his throat, glances at Tamil's furiously dark face and resumes the lesson. It takes about 10 minutes total, including the beginning, excluding the extracurricular activities. Hanna' remains unperturbed throughout, slightly smiling, asking three questions, which seem more polite than clarifying. When Jim finishes, Tamil nods at Hanna' and she dips a small curtsy, turns and is out the door. Sweating profusely, Jim announces his need to report to the hacienda and Tamil escorts him to the front door. As they stand there, Tamil examines Jim minutely, to the point that Jim is sweating from places he has not sweated before. Then Tamil softens his gaze, takes Jim's right arm and leads him to the taxi. "Please give my dear friend Matunkup my greeting. Thank you for your help to Zamboanga. We will have a very prosperous future together." With that he claps Jim on the back, opens the car door and Jim slides in with Tamil shutting the door behind him. A quick wave from Jim, returned by Tamil, and the car is out the gate headed to the hacienda. Jim slides his butt forward in the seat, reclines against the back and lets out a long exhalation for relaxation.

By the halfway point, Jim has calmed himself almost to normal levels of energy, but remains agitated. As the car rises up the hill to the hacienda he does not view the magnificent scenery simply because all he can see is Hanna's face close to his. All he can feel is the exquisite sensation of her body next to his. Noting that his breathe is becoming faster, he forces his attention outside the car and finally notes the number of workers on the next hill erecting trellises for the new plantings of grapes. High up the hill are more workers planting the trellises that have already been erected. In all he counts about 60 workers actively engaged with construction and planting and four others supervising. Ox carts are making their way up the hill bringing more materials for trellises and cart loads of seedlings for planting. The scale of the industry underway is impressive and Jim stops his Hanna' musings long enough to contemplate the overall scale of the work going on all over the province. It is one thing to plan it on paper, quite another to see it actually happening.

The car arrives to a crunching halt at the bottom of the stairs and Julio flings open the wide hacienda screen door, holding his arms wide in a wonderful Mediterranean welcome. "Hello, Jim. Come, let us discuss your success and our success, and peer into the future. What has been your success today?"

Jim swallows his first response and smiles as genuine a smile as he can as he exits the car and climbs the stairs. "Tamil is fully involved now. I instructed Hanna' this morning under the watchful eye of her father and I suspect she will do quite well in the contest. I could use some lemonade. You have any?"

"We have gallons for the conquering hero of the moment. Come, come, let's go through to the back. It is becoming hot already so the gazebo is the best place for us. Come tell me the details. As you know, the devil is in the details."

Jim's muse comes in from the back of his mind with a silent, "Don't I know it." The thought brings an ironic smile to his face and a questioning look from Matunkup. "All the news fit to print. Let's go to the gazebo. Come on." Jim waxes eloquently for the next half hour over exquisite lemonade. Matunkup leans back into the dialogue with the occasional nod, murmur of recognition and then, "So, Tamil's daughter is quite the beauty, is she not?"

Jim stops is struck dumb, shifting uncomfortably in his chair and asks, "You've been talking to Wang?"

"Not recently, no, just making an observation, one man to another."

After a relatively short pause, Jim replies, "Yeah, she's a knockout actually. Why?"

"So, you think she has a chance of winning the whole thing?"

"Of course, especially if the emphasis of the judges is on looks. The criteria cover other items as well, as you know, including how much she comes across as a Zamboanguena, ability to think on her feet and so on. But if the emphasis is on looks, wow, she is the likely winner."

"I have thought the same thing, sitting out here on my own the last few days. Getting the cooperation of the other growers, particularly the ones with daughters in the contest, was a good strategic move. I am wondering what the outcome would be should she win. Maybe good, maybe not. In any case, I think she does not need any help with the competition, do you? Just your tutorial this morning should be sufficient, don't you think?"

Jim is sitting, looking at Julio, his face suddenly more mask than openness. "Not sure what you're getting at, old boy. Where would she obtain help to boost her chances?"

"We organized the contest, set the rules, know the process inside out. If there were any further assistance it would have to come from one of the three of us, right? I am too old, Wang is too Chinese, so, leaving us out, you remain the most likely, if it occurred. Personal time assisting her would not be all that onerous, would it? Got any plans for extracurricular instruction time? I only ask because should you get caught playing at any funny business with the contestants, it would not result in the best outcomes, that is a certainty."

Now Jim's countenance is unequivocally cloudy, bordering on volcanic.

"Struck a nerve, have I? Settle down, settle down. I'm just waving hypotheticals in the wind, trial balloons as they were, to see what pops. I suggest that I have struck several nerves along the way. Sounds like Wang may have had a similar conversation with you recently as well. We are more than business partners by now, are we not? Tell Uncle Julio what's up. No pressure, just empty it all out here and we'll see what to do with it."

Jim's countenance rapidly changes from stormy to chastened puppy. He leans back in the chair and asks, "Got anything stronger than lemonade?"

Matunkup raises a hand and the servant is at his side in seconds, nods to the quiet request and hustles away, returning with a bottle of Jack Daniels, two glasses and an ice bucket. Matunkup offers his thanks and pours generous portions over ice and hands one to Jim who swallows, leans back in his chair and starts his tale from his original sight of Hanna', when he did not know who she was, to this morning and their passionate embrace and kisses under Tamil's own roof. Julio is sipping, listening, nodding and remaining silent as the tomb, his face not betraying any of what is rolling around in his head. Jim swallows again, and finishes his tale, placing his glass near the bottle, which Matunkup takes as the suggestion to refill it. The first round went down so fast there is no need to replace any ice.

After obtaining his refill, Jim slows his imbibing to a more sociable rate and sits back waiting for the wisdom. "Shit!" is all he gets to begin with. He has never heard Julio swear and it takes him aback a bit but he waits for the rest. Matunkup puts down his now empty glass, looks at Jim, the bottle, and refills his glass before commenting further.

"You know, this could just sink the whole operation, depending on how we work it. Tamil's cooperation is critical. If he finds that Hanna' has a crush on you, you being a white face in fact, we have trouble."

"I doubt she is about to bare her soul to him. They rarely speak to one another, she is an object in his household and she knows it. I see no filial relationship there at all."

"Don't underestimate your opponent, my friend. Tamil, like most people here, has eyes in the back of his head and tentacles in all parts of town. That is his survival necessity. Ever find yourself wondering about Wang's information and influence around town?"

Now the smile of recognition rises on Jim's face when he says, "All the time. The man is a wizard, Never saw anything like it in my life."

"They all can do that; maybe not as well as Wang, but they all can. There are few secrets in Zamboanga. We, and I mean you, are treading on very dangerous ground. Millions can be lost overnight if you get caught with your pants down."

Now he is getting angry. "They won't be caught down because they are not coming down! You think I am some sort of weak-kneed kid or what? I know what the score is, what's going on, as well as anybody. I only told you about this morning's events because I needed someone to let it out with and thought you were it. And what I end up getting is lectures. Blow it out your ass!"

Before Jim can get all the way to his feet Matunkup is at his side, hand firmly on his shoulder preventing him from standing. A few wriggles and an "Oomph." Julio gently says, "Calm down."

Jim settles slowly, then looks away as Matunkup takes his seat across the table. "Jim, I am sorry if I seemed to be lecturing. I am worried, as you can imagine, but you are important for more than making the project a success, at least to me." At that, Jim's head comes back around and he examines Matunkup's face for any sign of dishonesty. There is nothing but earnest caring coming from Julio across the table. Jim's shoulders relax and he sags back in his chair.

"I am worried, too. I have honestly never had these feelings happen to me before. Women come and go, no big deal, so why am I all out of sorts over this one?"

"Forbidden fruit, young man, forbidden fruit. That and the fact that there is adventure involved, risk, which makes it potentially tastier. It forms a desirable object almost impossible to resist. Do you think you can resist? I am asking because you are obviously being drawn in purposely by a very clever girl who, by no means, has given up. As a matter of fact, I believe she may have just started. Has she communicated further with you in any way since you were there this morning or any other time?"

Jim sits back and recalls the furtive wave at the café and her thigh brushing against his shoulder at Tamil's house. Matunkup is sitting, nodding, then stands and begins to pace. "You are being pursued, no doubt, and do not doubt the likelihood of her success. Tamil's family is known not only for conservative Muslim traits, but also for intelligence. Tamil's grandfather was sultan further north from here, and negotiated land trades to provide space for his family to grow. The old man was noted for being extremely clever, outwitting Pershing in the earlier conflicts. He died a revered man of great wealth and still in administrative control of his sultanate. The government tried many times to unseat him but he succeeded in frustrating all their efforts. Tamil is every bit as clever as his grandfather, and I have no doubt that his daughter is as clever as he. Beware, young man. Resisting will not be easy."

"You still underestimate me, Julio. I am now much better equipped with information. The next foray will not catch me unawares or off guard. Thank you for all your support. I am sorry I flew off the handle earlier."

"No apologies needed. Let us get you back to town as there is much to do to prepare for the contest and you cannot get it done out here." With that they both rise and exit the gazebo to the house. Matunkup stands at the open double doors, waving as Jim's car exits the parking circle and heads down the hill. A hand comes out the window returning the wave and Julio reenters the house, slightly shaking his head and mumbling to himself, "I have an uneasy feeling. The boy is too certain of his skills with women. Mm, mm, MM!" The last is said with a vigorous shake of his head.

Jim arrives at the municipal building in time for afternoon tea and the café, indoors and out, has every table full. As he steps up the first step of the staircase to the newspaper offices, there is a sudden chill between his shoulders and he is certain he is being watched. Resisting the urge to turn and look, he bounds up the full flight of stairs and only looks back once at the top, stopping to run his fingers through his hair and re-button two buttons on his shirt that he had opened on the drive. While concentrating on the buttons, he quickly scans the room and there they are, Tamil's family, at the table by the windows where they usually sit. Hanna' has her eyes locked on his; her mother is fully occupied with the spill Hannas' sister has just made. The contact is no more than three seconds but it seems a lifetime and Jim's gut begins to churn. His fingers suddenly are too uncoordinated to button his shirt, his mouth abnormally dry. He breaks the eye contact first, turns and walks down the corridor to the newspaper offices. Entering the office door in full flight, he nearly bowls over Tony who is carrying an enormous stack of posters. As Tony staggers backward, Jim leaps forward to steady him. "Sorry, mate. Sorry. You OK?"

"Yes, Mr. Jim. I am fine. Are you fine too? You look very excited."

"I do? Oh, shoot. I just have urgent information for Gus, that's all. Glad you are OK and sorry again for nearly running you over." With that, Tony is out the door and down the hall toward the municipal offices for whom the posters have been prepared. Jim heads to Gus's office, but finds it empty. Sitting outside Gus's office, he contemplates his situation and decides on an immediate course of action. It is out the back entrance of the offices, down the back stairs and to the tailor shop. He needs some peace of mind to think a bit.

Just as Jim reaches the bottom stair, a young woman steps forward with an envelope in her hand, asking, "Are you Mr. Jim Tuck from the newspaper?" Jim looks at her, never having seen her before, but suspecting she knows perfectly well who he is.

Stepping back, he nods saying, "Yes, that's me. I do not think I know you, do I?"

"No matter. Here, this is for you. Goodbye." With that, she is gone through the doors to the kitchen and immediately out of sight.

"What the heck?" He exits the back door to the building onto an alleyway, and starts walking left toward his street. As he walks he rips open the envelope, which has "Jim" hand- printed on the front, and extracts a single sheet of blue paper. Handwritten on the page is, "I will be at Plaza Pershing by the monument at 8 p.m. this evening. I must see you. Believe me, I have made it safe for us."

His walking slows until he is at the corner ready to turn right. He comes to a complete stop. "Son of a bitch! Julio is right. How in the world did she know I was coming down the back? She isn't just covering her bases.

Wow! This is tough. What the fuck am I into here?" With that he refolds the paper and starts walking back to Wang's shop. His pace is definitely slower than usual as his mind is running way ahead. Getting to the tailor shop, he does not stop to chat but heads immediately upstairs, where he strips and heads to the shower. After a long soak, he dries off and is back in his room, lying on his pallet under the net. There is almost no breeze so he sweats gently under the sheets. He lies very still, thinking. Modestly he has wrapped a towel around him like a kilt; involuntarily it begins to rise. He rolls on his side with a "Shit!" and tries his best to reset his thinking. He fails, but does manage to have a nap.

It is dark when he wakes up from a great two-hour nap. Sitting up, he stretches, climbs out from under the net and puts on clean clothes. Checking his watch on the way downstairs, he notices it is just after 6 p.m.. Feeling energetic, he goes into the empty cutting room to find Wang concentrating on piecing together a garment. Wang looks up, smiles and indicates the outfit, "Tamil's for the contest. He will likely be one of the best dressed there."

Walking over for a closer look, he stands over Wang's right shoulder to examine the silk fabric. It is absolutely gorgeous and Jim can imagine Tamil in it, imperious, distant, and absolutely malevolent. Standing up, Jim clucks his approval and stammers something about going out for the evening. Wang stops sewing and looks up at Jim. "I was hoping we could talk awhile. I have a brand new bottle of wine, still corked but needing attention. What do you think?"

Jim hesitates, looks at the earnest expression on Wang's face, then his watch, and back at Wang with a nod of his head. "A little red wine would be just about perfect right now. Sounds like a great idea."

Wang folds the garment, places his sewing apparatus in the lacquered wooden box on the table and leads Jim into the kitchen. He opens the bottle and generously pours the wine into two glasses. "How about the small table on the front walk? It will be cooler there."

"Fine," and they exit through the beaded curtain, through the front room that acts as the display room, and out the front door. Jim sits down with a nice long sigh, takes a sip and leans back, causing the folding chair to creak ominously.

Wang takes a long drink, then sits and leans forward on his forearms. Then he observes Jim with a determined gaze that is not unfriendly. "I think I may have upset you this morning. If I did, I apologize. My feelings of peril need not intrude on our relationship."

It is the first somewhat vulnerable thing Wang has ever said to Jim and he sits himself more erectly with a look of mild wonder on his face. "No need to apologize, Wang. You have a great investment in the project and I understand how unpleasant some of the possibilities are if we, or I, act foolishly. I do not intend to be foolish."

Wang leans away from the table, lifts his glass in salute, to which Jim responds. And they both take a large gulp of wine in silence. The small breeze snakes its way along the street, barely ruffling the leaves on the tree in front of the shop, but it feels glorious to both men. They are lost in their own thoughts for several minutes until Jim drains his glass and says, "I need a relaxing walk this evening. I will be back before too late since I have several visits to make tomorrow and must inspect the hall for the contest. Thanks for the drink."

Jim rises to his feet, turns and walks away in the direction of Pershing Plaza, slowly, since it is only 6:45. Arriving early, he might be able to examine the area and decide whether it is appropriate to meet Hanna'. Crap, he knows it is inappropriate, and here is the moth headed straight for the flame. He reaches down to make sure his fly is buttoned closed all the way. It is and he continues to wander toward his doom. Two streets down he turns left and heads toward the main thoroughfare, slowing down as he goes. Two long blocks later he is looking across the street from behind a large palm tree into Pershing Plaza. He feels like a fool, but he isn't going anywhere.

The evening is one of those magical ones in the tropics when the breeze is gentle, the palm fronds clacking quietly in response, the temperature neutral so it rewards inactivity and promotes sweating if you decide to get even a little active. Standing behind the palm, Jim enjoys the breeze through the palms and drifts into a mild meditative state.

Suddenly he notices a young woman in a blue shroud making her way toward the corner and the park bench by the footpath. Just as she comes into view under the street light, another shape turns away to walk behind the Pershing statue in the plaza. The blue clad young lady looks vaguely familiar and Jim's curiosity is piqued. Gazing at her as she sits, head covered and face only slightly obscured, he suddenly stands erect and hides behind a tree to completely hide himself. She is the girl who gave him the hand-written envelope this afternoon at the municipal building. Hanna' must be nearby, using her as lookout. He peeks back around the tree just as a person comes around the slab holding Pershing's statue. She also is partially shrouded but obviously Hanna'.

Petite, erect, and proud, she is searching systematically in all directions. Jim's side of the street has no street lights so he is in the dark and not likely to be seen by someone standing in the light across the street. Settling into the trunk of the tree, Jim examines Hanna' at his leisure, a luxury he has not had to date. She can't be over five feet tall, perfectly proportioned, which can be seen even through the scarf she is wearing. Her face is slightly round, owing to her Moro heritage, but finely chiseled with high cheekbones and alert, dark eyes. Her hands are constantly moving, the only indicator of her nervous energy. A golden belt cinches her tiny waist. Interesting that she can get away with emphasizing her waist, given the conservative nature of her family. Then Hanna' removes her belt, stowing it in a small bag hanging on her right arm. Then she takes it back out and puts it back around her waist. Another fidget.

Mesmerized, Jim watches as Hanna' leans into the statue's base, her tiny left hand a foot from the hoof of Pershing's horse. She continues to scan slowly, first right then left and back again. Finally, Jim decides he has had more than enough of this delicious torture and steps out from behind the tree, keeping his light colored khaki outfit behind the tree and his eyes focused on Hanna'. He reaches the edge of the street and turns and walks away, heart thumping like a bass drum, breath coming in fits and spurts, his footsteps solid but light. He takes one last glance to assure him he has not been noticed. The walk to the shop is four long blocks. It takes what seems like one and a half lifetimes. The last block of Via Lobos is deserted until two doors from the shop, where a slightly inebriated large man suddenly steps out and blocks Jim's path.

"Where you go in my city, white face?"

Jim stops two steps short of the fellow, who sways slightly. He is a head taller than Jim. "Home, asshole." Jim takes one long step forward, dips to his left, fooling the oaf to make the wrong postural adjustment - a slight weight shift in the same direction and the drunk's head tilted right. Jim's right open hand instantly comes over the top and the heel of his hand contacts the oaf's left ear. Jim's coup de grace is a left elbow making contact to the bridge of his opponent's nose.

The sidewalk is suddenly full of comatose oaf, face down and bleeding profusely from his left ear and nose. Poor bugger picked the wrong guy to harass on the wrong night. Jim steps over the body, breathes out a nice long sigh and walks through the shop's unlocked front door.

Inside, Wang is leaning with his right shoulder on the window frame, his inscrutable face on. Jim stops and says, "You saw?"

"Yes. I think there is no need for Tamil's assistance, correct?"

"Correct. Good night."

"Good night."

Upstairs, Jim undresses and heads to the bathroom. He turns the water on cold, which means tepid, and pours the splashing water to wash away the rest of his excess energy, what's left after releasing the huge tensions of the day. Back in his room, plopped on his pallet under the net, he is asleep by the time his head hits the pillow.

Next morning is the first day of the last two weeks before the Miss Grape contest. Jim is back into the clothes he wore last night. Gotta get as many days wear as possible out of each outfit to avoid excessive washing. Washing reduces the lifespan of clothes tremendously. Downstairs he smells eggs, toast and coffee, not necessarily in that order. Wang is, again, flipping over-easy eggs and buttering toast. Jim never ceases to marvel at the menial tasks he takes on, given the fact that he is undoubtedly one of the wealthiest people in Zamboanga. Jim is offered a plate soon after entering the kitchen, which he takes with a forceful gracious, "Thanks," and the coffee is half gone with the first gulp. He attacks the plate with gusto finishing before Wang has his toast buttered, then goes over to the sink to wash up the plate and get another cup of coffee.

Now that his mouth is available for discourse, Wang asks, "You slept well?"

"Like a baby. Never better."

"You dispatched that poor fellow on the street quite without remorse, it seemed. Your energy was quite impressive. Did you have any particular motivation for your violent attack?"

"The guy was aggressive, blocking the walkway, called me names. Couldn't let that go, not in this neighborhood, now could I?"

"But, we both know that Tamil is all we need. A simple telephone call would suffice, eh?"

"And how do I get to the phone, past that guy?"

"You could simply call out and I would be available, or better yet, mention Tamil to the fellow. He may be drunk, but even in a stupor; he is not ignorant of consequences. It seemed you were very ready for combat as soon as he appeared. Am I not correct?"

"Always have to be ready. What are you getting at?"

"Nothing, nothing. Do not become agitated. I was simply curious about your aggressive nature last night, given what I have seen from you in the past. No conversation, no warning, just boom, and he is gone. Very efficient. Tamil's cleanup squad came by this morning at about 5 a.m. and scooped him up, by the way. I doubt he will return to this part of town, ever. He comes from Sulu, and as you noted, does not like foreigners and had made a bit of a nuisance of himself by the port. Someone there gave him the idea about a "white face" living above the tailor shop. They have now convinced him to remove himself. Why, I do not know. Some people are always interested in no-good works.

"Anyway, I received a call at about 8:30 last evening from a friend who overheard the conversation about white faces. Realizing the fellow may be a problem for me, or us, he called and I waited for you to warn you. But, he was already here, on the other side of the shop, so I did not see him arrive. You both surprised me, but I was not surprised at the outcome, just how quick it was. You are fine?"

"Fit as a fiddle. Gotta go and get some more organizing done. Thanks for breakfast; I'm off." With that, he is out through the beaded curtain and out the front door walking to the municipal building. Looking back over his shoulder he notices the dark splotch in the middle of the sidewalk, all that is left from opening his steam valve. The morning walk is quite pleasant, except for the 5 minute shower that soaks him. His cotton shirt and shorts are slow to dry, but the heat of the day helps and by the time he sees Gus in the office he is comfortable. They plan the day splitting his duties between his next level of contest planning and his rounds of advertising clients so that by the time they finish 30 minutes later his schedule is made for the next 8 hours, with a half hour for lunch. And, away he goes!

Twelve-thirty rolls around and he is back at the municipal building for lunch at the café. He misses Tony's smiling face and conversation, but is hungry enough to let the new waiter take his regular order, request for iced fruit juice and a copy of the newspaper that just came out that morning. Waiting for his food, he is reading the paper when suddenly an envelope is dropped into his lap inside the paper. It startles him enough that he nearly tips over his juice when he jumps forward in his seat. He looks up quickly and just catches the back of a small woman as she enters the café and turns right. Jim leaps up from his outdoor table and runs after her, carrying the envelope. In the door he turns right, but the café is full and there is no one standing inside the room. He is sure there was not time to pass completely through the room and out before he entered so he begins systematically examining the bodies and faces of people seated at the tables. Some notice his attention and return it briefly as he scans through the room. Nothing. He can't remember exactly what the person had been wearing, and it probably wouldn't matter anyway. Shoulders slumped, he returns to his table and begins retrieving bits of the paper from around the courtyard where they have blown after they fell to the ground during his emergency leap to his feet. Last piece gathered, he resumes his seat, places the paper under the food plate that just arrived, sits back and opens the envelope. It is blue again, so he suspects the author.

"Dearest Mr. Jim," it starts. God, that sounds too funky, "dearest Mr. Jim." Who says that shit? Don't be silly, you know who says it. "I was too sorry to miss seeing you last night. I will wait each night, at the same place, until 9 p.m., when I must again be at home. Perhaps you will be able to come one evening, before the contest. H"

What the fuck? This girl is diabolical in the exact sense of the term. He re-reads the note, then tears it in very small pieces before eating his lunch. Finished, he heads to the cashier's desk and, while change is being counted, he surreptitiously examines the room. Nothing. Who the hell dropped this thing in his lap? Change in hand, he heads out for his afternoon schedule. He has the taxi stop at the edge of the road just before the first bridge out of town and drops the torn pieces of the note into the slow-moving, sludgy river below, where they quickly flow away and drop out of sight. Mollified, he proceeds through his afternoon, returning to the newspaper offices at 5:30 to find Gus already gone and the rooms empty. The place is relatively quiet, given the street noise below, and Gus's door is locked shut. He progresses down the hall to his office, which is never locked, opens the door and there on his desk is a huge single hibiscus, still damp with dew and orange as orange can be. It is floating in a large shallow blue bowl of water with the edge of a note peeking out underneath.

"What's with this girl?" He folds the paper and puts it into his pocket and heads out the door, out of the office, down the stairs and out to Calle Voluntario. Turning right, he walks straight into town on this main thoroughfare, passing the parks on the right and Pershing Plaza on the left, using the opportunity for a bit of espionage on the way. Two blocks past the plaza is his destination, the falafel shop that is his favourite eatery away from home. Inside it is cozy, with tables and chairs jammed in, people's loud voices adding to the crush, and the owner throwing his arms wide and exclaiming, "Jeem!"

Jim smiles at the welcome and squeezes past a few tables full of people to a rear less occupied one and yelling "Eat!"

"Yes," is yelled back at full smiling volume and Jim sits at a table already occupied by two men who nod and motion to the empty chair, the last one Jim sees in the place. He sits, acknowledging their welcome with a nod and a grin. The other two resume their animated conversation, ignoring Jim from then on. Their tea glasses empty, they motion to the mustachioed owner, who sidles near the table and delivers another small pot of astringent, also known as chai to the locals, in honor of their Muslim background. The owner is back about three minutes later with Jim's meal of falafel and tea on a highly engraved brass tray. He puts the tray on the table, which barely has room for it. That is when Jim can see the orange hibiscus on the tray. His mouth drops open, the owner smiles his most wicked smile and Jim's appetite vanishes. His mind racing, he thinks, "How in the world could she know where I am, or am going?" Then, Matunkup's words come flooding back full force, "Never underestimate your opponent." Jim is thinking furiously, "But she is not my opponent," which has little or no effect on his stomach; he sits quietly, with the interrupted conversation of the other two crashing in on him. The owner is still standing there, as if awaiting further instructions. Jim puts on his most winning smile and says, "Thank you so much. Is the flower extra money?"

"Is all paid for already, Jeem. No extra."

Jim continues to think to himself, "She sure knows how to organize and control things. Probably is more than a match for her father. Is there a possibility we could pull off a liaison with no one knowing? Doubtful, Matunkup and Wang both know this place better than I do and they say the same thing. That settles it."

The owner in his slightly grubby apron shrugs, smiles, and says, "Eat. You are a lucky man so eat!"

Jim keeps the winning smile on his face and forces falafel into his mouth despite no appetite. Crunching the hummus, he smiles even wider, gives thumbs up to the owner. Satisfied, the owner leaves Jim to his meal.

The meal half eaten, Jim pays at the door and decides to walk awhile. Eight o'clock is awhile away and he has to think. This girl is getting his nervous system into a jangle, something he is not used to, at least never by a female. Flying cargo runs through enemy territory was one thing, but this is another thing entirely. What would Julio recommend? What would Wang suggest? Never mind, he knows what Wang would tell him to do, or not do. "Guess I have to tackle this head on and let her know we can't play this game anymore. It's way too dangerous. Isn't it? Hmmm."

Jim's walk continues, but at a slightly faster pace since he has settled the matter, right? Swinging back toward the sea, he walks back streets until he is again across the street from Pershing Plaza. He takes up his station behind the palm tree again and settles in to wait. He doesn't have to wait long.

The blue-draped young woman from last night is now in forest green and comes to sit on the park bench at the corner as Hanna' reappears from behind the statue. Jim develops a strategy of flanking the pair and coming up behind Hanna' in the shadows, so he is out of the light and can watch her and the space around her while he approaches unseen. He backs away from the tree, walks one block extra each direction until he can approach Hanna' from behind and to her right. He is 10 meters away and can see her clearly even though she is not directly in the light of the street light. As he takes his next step, a very large hand reaches out from the shadows and grabs his left shoulder. Just as he is about to raise his voice, the shadows say, "Quiet!" in an unmistakable tone that causes Jim to stifle the shout and avoid wriggling. Hanna' makes her way from beside the statue and gestures the restraining hand to leave. Jim rotates his shoulder blade and arm to restart the interrupted circulation. He is just about to complain when Hanna' signals him to hush then whispers, "My friends love me very much and protect me constantly. I am sorry if you were not treated kindly but he did not know you. Please, Mr. Jim, be calm."

Jim is still massaging his shoulder and appreciating the force of the grip that had held him. He nods and says, "No harm done. You are certainly well-protected."

"Yes, I am, so you have nothing to fear from my father." With that, she moves closer, then against Jim, front to front, puts her arms around his neck and pulls his face to her. Jim resists momentarily, glancing over his shoulder into the dark and she whispers, "He is away. He will come when I call." Then she kisses Jim, who relaxes and returns her kisses, which quickly become frantic.

Finally disentangling himself, Jim can only gasp out, "I have to get back to Wang's."

Hanna' pouts a bit then says, "We can meet here again. I will come in two nights, same time. My father will have a meeting and the housekeeper is my friend. She will help me, I am sure. My mother is always asleep by 8 p.m. Come in two nights." Then, with the largest, most expectant eyes Jim has ever seen, she looks up into his face, one of the few times a woman has had to look up at him. She is irresistible and he agrees, but warns that if Wang becomes suspicious he will not be able to come. "Please do not worry about Mr. Wang." And she turns and leaves, not looking back.

Jim is left standing there as if he was expected to do something. He passes through the plaza, going around Pershing and his horse, crosses the street and heads home. No hoodlums tonight, and probably never again. His heart and stomach in tumult, he climbs the stairs to his room, undresses and crawls under the net, no teeth brushing tonight. He is exhausted and he only had met with a beautiful, but dangerous woman. Perhaps nervous energy takes it out of you as much as physical effort. That is the last idea before he is awakened again to the smell of coffee.

The coffee is, as usual, magnificent. Eating no breakfast, he is off to the newspaper office. His day is full; he has five new advertising clients to visit who need marketing strategies, three of whom are new businesses anticipating growth from the grape harvest. Finishing at the paper, Jim tells Gus goodbye, is down the stairs and out the door where he is met by his usual taxi driver. "I didn't call you, did I?"

"No, Mr. Jeem. Mr. Wang he waits, in the car." And the driver points down the street to a car where Wang waves Jim over.

Wang leans partly out of the car window, saying, "Matunkup is requesting a short meeting at the hacienda and asked me to bring you along. It is short notice, I agree, but I am hoping you are available." Wang's inquisitive eyebrows raise and Jim nods assent. What the heck, he passes behind the car and gets into the passenger seat on the other side. Wang can't add any details about the meeting, but says Matunkup was rather insistent. Then he asks about the day's activities. Jim lists the new accounts and Wang gives his enigmatic smile and says, "The project is working, is it not? Business activity in the area is increasing very well. All my colleagues report good results, in their own ways. No one is willing to give open reports, but listening carefully we can see that everyone is doing well. Does Gus agree?"

"Of course! The paper has never had this much revenue coming in. It has a positive bank account for the first time in 20 years, and Gus is happy as a clam, busy as a bee!"

Wang just shakes his head with, "The American comparisons are very strange to my ears, that is certain. But, having all this early success makes this urgent meeting at the hacienda even more mysterious. I will be very interested to hear Matunkup."

Jim simply nods. They are mostly silent the rest of the trip. Julio is at the edge of the front porch, eager to greet his compatriots, noting the rather dour look on Wang's face and the quizzical one on Jim's. He smiles and says, "Come, gentlemen, we have a short meeting before a lovely dinner Mr. Song has created in marvellous Cantonese style. All will be well, I am sure, but we need to make a few decisions. This way," and they march quickly through the house front to back, straight out the back door to the gazebo, which has become the standard meeting place over the past few months.

The tray with lemonade is already sweating on the table. While Matunkup pours the lemonade, Jim, slightly impatiently, says, "So, Julio, may we begin?"

"Of course. To be efficient, I will get straight to the point. Tamil and two of his colleagues seem suddenly reluctant about some of the activities of the Miss Grape contest. These people are growers, as am I, but I also realize that they sometimes respond well to Wang's influence regarding business. I want to be able to nip this potential disagreement in the bud, so have arranged a short meeting, at the Club, for tomorrow evening. Yes, Wang, I know scheduling the club is usually your prerogative, but I was speaking with these three in person and decided to strike while the opportunity presented itself. All three have agreed to the get together. However I feel that the meeting will go better if it is just Wang and myself there. We have the longest relationship with these men, we are local and not foreign white faces, so to speak. I believe the best strategy warrants a restricted meeting. The three of us know the strengths of one another well enough that I believe you, Jim, would not be upset with any decisions Wang and I would make concerning the contest, any decisions needed to make sure it is smoothly produced. Am I correct, Jim?"

Jim is quiet for about 10 seconds, long enough to reinforce the appearance of decision-making, then smiles and agrees. Matunkup then provides some of the concerns of the three leading growers and Wang and Jim provide their opinions about how to deal with them. Jim has a few concerns about diluting the impact of the contest, wanting to make certain the publicity continues to emphasize the importance to the whole of Zamboanga province, Wang advocates for caution in how the girls are presented on stage, the three quickly clear up the details so each is satisfied he has been heard and there will be no surprises at the debriefing after the gathering tomorrow. Julio's raised hand brings the Cantonese meal that Wang samples, then sighs over. Jim's previous experience with Cantonese is limited, so he takes Wang's reaction as confirmation of high quality, Matunkup smiles at Song, who is watching from the kitchen window in the house. Song beams as the men dive into the meal. Talking has ended.

After they finish and have the obligatory Turkish coffee, Wang and Jim take their leave and the drive back is quiet, each with his own thoughts. There is not even much talk on arrival as Jim mentally reorders his next day's events. Arriving at the shop, Wang proposes they finish the bottle of red wine. Jm agrees and asks for a couple of ice cubes in his glass. This puzzles Wang, but he brings the glass with the ice already in it and says nothing. Jim does not even notice the slight grimace when he pours red wine over the ice, swishes the glass and downs a large swallow. By the time he focuses on Wang again, his flat, amiable expression is well in place. The bottle a dead soldier, the two are off to bed.

On his pallet, under the net, Jim is lying on top of the sheet completing his post-shower drying process. Allowing his mind to wander a bit, he suddenly sits bolt upright on the pallet. "That little vixen. She has instigated this emergency meeting. What a woman!" With that, he slowly lies back down, resetting his understanding of

Hanna' and her influence, her Machiavellian tendencies. "Wow!" and he rolls onto his side and sleeps.

Next morning, Jim is out before coffee is started, excusing himself, bright-eyed and bushy tailed. His walk is more than a bit jaunty on the way to the office and he doesn't even mind the incessant noise of the street: car horns, animal complaints, human traffic noisess, shouts from drivers as he dodges between cars. Everyone gets a smile this morning. "What snuck into your coffee this morning, young fella?"

"What do you mean, Gus. I am my normal, jovial self, old fella. Just lovin' life as usual."

"You have something up your sleeve, I can tell. Out with it."

"Look, Gus. Short-sleeved shirt, too hot for anything else. No, I'm just sprinting along this morning, anticipating a wonderful payday end of next week. How about you? You are looking pretty good yourself. What do you have going?"

"I am just enjoying this excellent tropical morning, son. Also, I visit the bank this morning. Get to put more in than I take out, again. That makes just about everyone smile, does it not?"

"I will be in the east province for most of the day so I'll be out of communication for awhile. Hardly any phones over there, but I want to check on how far they are building the new road, what farms now have access, and maybe hit up a couple for ads. I'll be back this afternoon, but don't know when. See ya later!" And he is out the door, down the stairs and waving at the taxi.

The ride is constantly interrupted by construction in odd places, none of it seemingly connected to the next section. Twice the car is nearly stuck in an unmarked graded area that is soft from the regular rain. Jim finds his sunny disposition rapidly dissipating until the end of the road is reached and the headlands blocking passage are viewed. It is magnificent scenery and there is an obvious donkey trail that has been used for hundreds of years for travel and commerce. He follows it to the top of the headland. The view back toward the city, which is nowhere in sight, is just endless green with the brown scar of the new road below, wending its way in the direction of town. The foliage is too dense to be able to sit and look out, so he stands, leans against a banyan root and examines the area for about half an hour. Then he returns to the taxi and they make plans for a few stops on the way back to town. His placid condition returned, Jim is almost uncaring about writing up new advertising for the paper, almost. His Zamboanga-based income depends on it, and his ego requires a certain amount of success.

These new contacts result, in a majority of cases, in positive outcomes for the paper and for himself.

The ride back is without incident and he arrives at the paper shortly after Gus has locked up. He deposits his paperwork, records the contacts and sales, and heads down to the cafe for dinner. It has been a good day and may get better. "Hmmm, gotta be careful, boy. Gotta stay calm." That gets the patented Tuck smile, rueful at his own foibles, at his tendency to self destruct. "Not this time, OK? OK!"

Jim arrives behind the statue, in the shadows, a little after seven and leans against the nearby building to wait. The wait lasts about 45 minutes and he notices the lookout girl walking toward the corner. Right behind comes Hanna', crossing behind the statue in front of Jim. Close behind Hanna' is the hulk who managed to immobilize Jim the last time. She is careful, and as safe as anyone, anywhere. Of course, being Tamil's daughter, she would have been safe anyway, assuming the tentative threat was from a local. Should an outsider happen along and she were alone, it might be another case. Hulk stops directly behind the statue plinth, muscle-bound arms akimbo, standing relaxed and ready. Hanna' continues to the side of the statue nearest Jim and around the corner where she can see the street and where she can be seen from the other side of the street.

Jim's dilemma now is how to attract Hanna's attention without being mutilated by the hulk. He is beginning to wonder if he has some sort of magnet implanted somewhere in his body that attracts giants. Finally he realizes the direct approach is likely the best. He straightens up and walks out of the shadows directly to Hanna'. The hulk is immediately alert but Jim preempts him by saying - in his best stage-whisper voice - "Hello Hanna'."

Hanna' gives a slight yelp, turns quickly, sees Jim and immediately holds up her hand to stop the hulk before he has taken more than three giant steps toward her aid. Smiling, she says something in Tagalog to him and he returns to his post, but with his attention concentrated on the couple. Jim stops his approach and Hanna' walks to him, slowly, with a slightly wicked smile. "You are clever, Jim Tuck. You hide from me. Maybe sometime you are too clever. Yes? My protector can be very strong and upset if I am in danger." By this time she has closed the distance between them, and reaches her arms up and around his neck. "I am not in danger, am I, Jim Tuck?"

"Not from me. I could not hurt you, ever." That brings a long, slow, non-frantic kiss that is not seen by the hulk or the lookout girl. The hulk has adjusted his posture to look back the way they came and the girl is in front of the statue watching the street. Both Jim and Hanna' are relaxed in the fact that they know Tamil and the rest are at the club talking about possible difficulties with the contest. Jim has realized that the coincidence of the meeting at the club with the appointment at the Pershing statue was no coincidence at all. His appreciation of Hanna' and her spirit has developed into early affection. That is a surprise to him since he has typically taken females for their more superficial function: service to his libido. He has to admit that he probably provides the same service to the women and girls, but it has never been more than that, until now.

Kissing inevitably leads to touching and exploring. Jim is not used to leaving it there, but realizes that more here isn't possibile. With his mind racing, and breath in short supply, he whispers, "Is there someplace we can go?"

Hanna' breaks off the embrace, leans back and looks at Jim, then shakes her head slowly. She sees the disappointment on his face and it touches her heart and her lower belly, at about the same intensity, but she repeats the negative and Jim relaxes his embrace slightly. She literally clambers onto his chest, gripping the back of his head and delivers a fierce kiss that eventually hits every spot on his face. She then steps back, smoothes her outfit, touches his cheek and walks back toward the hulk, who suddenly becomes animated. They exit the back area of the Pershing statue where they are automatically joined by the lookout girl and turn left up the street toward the car and home. Jim walks with a wide-based gait, trying to avoid his thighs making contact with his swollen testicles. Never have blues balls hit him as hard, so his return to the shop is laborious most of the way, increasing in speed as the pain subsides.

By the time he walks upstairs to his room he is nearly back to normal, except for the memory of the encounter and the constant calculations in his head of how to get Hanna' alone. It is consuming him right up until his body gives in to fatigue. He is sound asleep when Wang peeks into the room on his return from the club. He is satisfied that his energetic charge has behaved himself, and erroneously goes to bed happy.

CHAPTER 7

Consummation, Escape, Home to Salvation

Jim's next two weeks before the contest are hectic in the extreme, combining regular newspaper duties and contest preparations. It is unusually hectic simply because the newspaper activity has increased significantly as a result of the grape project. So far the goals of the project have exceeded expectations, and there are many business leaders in Zamboanga who are excessively happy as a result. The commander at Pettit Barracks is happy, the governor and the council are happy. What a lovely time to be in town.

Because of his busy schedule there have been no other nighttime rendezvous at Pershing Plaza. Jim and Hanna' have had several contacts during the rehearsals at the exhibition hall to smooth over the details of the contest and make a coordinated show. Each contact in this public setting they have had to ignore one another, except for necessary contact; each comes away slightly wounded as a result.

Finally the day of the contest has arrived. It is 5 p.m., the sun is low, the temperature is starting to go down ever so slightly, and Jim is sitting at his desk, having finished his postings for the day. He also has reviewed for the umpteenth time the evening's schedule. As he puts the paperwork down, there is a light tap on his door. He growls, "Come in." He is about to put the paperwork in the filing cabinet drawer when he turns to find no one there. He puts the papers away, then opens his door to find no one. On the floor is an envelope, the familiar blue-colored one. He just stands and stares for a minute until Gus yells from down the hall. It startles him and he quickly bends to retrieve the envelope and heads to Gus's office. Poking his head in, he asks, "Yeah?"

"Posted your day's activities yet?"

"Just finished, why?"

"I need a drink. Got time?"

"Always." And they are away down the stairs, Jim quietly slipping the envelope into a back pocket. They head to the cafe where they can get a wine or something stronger. As they relax under an umbrella near the front of the veranda that overlooks traffic, Gus casually observes, "Well, tonight's the night, eh?"

"It is indeed. Everything seems ready, which is probably a bad sign. But I honestly can't think of another item that needs to be done. The entire town is sold on it it seems, which is exactly what we wanted. The locals of each district around town are bursting with grape competition and the word is that the harvest next year - the first year - will be strong. The whole project has had the added effect of growers paying more attention to the grape plantings they already have, and that is improving yield as well. So even though the new vines won't bear until next year, the yield is up. Grapes are going to be everywhere."

Gus takes a long sip on his Jack Daniels, then says, "It sure seems like everything is going according to plan, even better than that. It always makes me nervous, to have things going so well."

"Gus, you gotta learn to relax. You're going to stroke out if you don't."

Another sip and Gus just leans back in his chair, looking askance at Jim and speaking out of the corner of his mouth, "Guess you're right. Still, I get these premonitions."

"Premonitions of what?"

"Disaster!"

Walking to the tailor shop, Jim opens the mysterious blue envelope. "Dressing room door at 6:15." He stops, re-reads the note, then slowly resumes his progress toward the shop. In the shower he concentrates on winding himself down, as his internals are constantly trying to wind him up. His flight to Shanghai gave him close to this level of adrenalin rush. And escaping into the toilet in California was fun, but not this exciting. This feeling is delicious, a mixture of anticipation and danger. No wonder gamblers get addicted to large betting. Scrubbed and dressed in his finest western gear, he descends to the kitchen where Wang is waiting with dumplings, fried rice and prawns for dinner, Jim's absolute favourite. Jim sadly has absolutely no appetite. Feigning hunger to appease Wang, Jim should've won an acting award. For his efforts all he got was a stomach ache and a fond farewell from Wang, who would not be attending the beauty pageant. Not his thing in the least.

The taxi is, of course, outside on the street and Jim asks the driver to head to the exhibition hall, which takes all of five minutes. He exits the car, walks to the entrance and waves the driver off, having arranged for pick up at the conclusion of the event. The driver pulls around the corner and Jim veers off to the left, turning the corner of the building at 6:05, walking down the alley toward the back of the building. Darkness is setting in, especially in the confines of the alleyway, so Jim is carefully picking his way around debris as he walks, looking at the ground most of the time until he reaches the back of the hall. There is a small courtyard, a place to turn motor vehicles around between the various building walls surrounding the open area. Along the back of the hall is a porch, or elevated decking, with individual wooden stairs to each of four doors in the back of the hall. There are lights over each door, but they do not seem to be working, not turned on yet or just not working. Standing there he checks his watch and sees 6:12, so he knows he is in time but does not know which of the four doors he should be moving toward. Two minutes later, by his watch, the second door from the right cracks open, slightly emitting a sliver of light onto the deck outside of it and Jim is off like the tightly wound spring he is, leaps the four steps to the deck and is in the room, door shut, in less than 15 seconds.

Stepping back from the door is a miniature apparition of pure beauty. Hanna' has her hair up, tied on the top of her head thus accentuating her neck, which is long for a tribal woman. Her petite body is shrouded in a long caftan-like garment that she will obviously not be wearing for the competition. She is not dressed yet for the stage. Jim is frozen in place looking at her, then notices that the fairly large dressing room is deserted except for them and the door to backstage into the hall is barred. Hanna' sees his glance toward the door and says,

"All are visiting their relatives, for at least half an hour." While she is explaining, she is also lifting the flowing caftan up and over her head revealing the absolutely perfect body Jim has imagined time and again, and had hints of from their brief physical embraces.

It is exquisite, a work of art, and he is mesmerized into inaction until Hanna' approaches him and reaches her arms around his neck. That breaks the trance and his clothes are off with a few buttons popped in the process and the next 10 minutes are rushes to paradise and back and back again. Both are caught up enough in the moment to ignore the fact that the most animalistic sounds are emanating from each of them. Then Hanna' stiffens, buries her head into Jim's chest and squeaks a long note while shuddering, which causes the ground to shift under Jim and he loses himself. They are standing throughout, and remain clinging to one another for countless moments, until noises coming from the hallway startle them simultaneously. They unwind, Hanna's smile could not be wider. Jim's half smile comes from the realization that he has to get his ass out of there now. He dresses, maintaining constant eye contact with Hanna', who has nonchalantly reclined, still nude, on the chaise in the room. A mild groan arises from Jim and when he finishes dressing he stoops and gives her one last kiss before exiting the room the way he came.

Hanna' pulls herself together, dons the caftan, straightens her hair back into the style it held before, and begins the final preparations for the stage. Five minutes after Hanna' removes the bolt from the door, the rest of the contestants begin returning to the dressing room, each glancing suspiciously at Hanna', a few giggling in a knowing way. Hanna' remains placid, her typical expression that she need not abandon now. The girls notice her poised, calm demeanour and slowly return to their preparations, beginning to wonder what the fuss was all about.

Jim makes his way unnoticed back to the front of the hall and sees several of the dignitaries who will be recognized this evening. Making his way over to them, he effusively shakes a few hands, slaps a few shoulders and once again is the organizing captain of industry, not the lovestruck whelp of 10 minutes earlier. His heart still has not slowed entirely, but he is able to channel that energy into his official duties, carrying off the evening in grand style.

In the end, Hanna' does not win the competition, but Tamil's closest colleague's daughter does. So Tamil and Hanna' celebrate the success of one close to their hearts. Even though Jim is prominent throughout the event, with all the contestants in full view, there is never even a hint of recognition between Hanna' and Jim. Each of them privately revels in the secret of their illicit liason. The evening ends and the hall empties out. The crowd disperses - the elite from the balconies and the common folk, who filled the audience, from the floor level. The streaming humanity exiting the hall overwhelms any conversations, but the buzzing excitement gives Jim his second rush of the evening. Not quite the level of the first, but good nonetheless.

The evening definitely deserves a drink, which he finds waiting for him back home in the kitchen at the shop. The table is set with all sorts of snack foods, oriental and western, and a red wine bottle has been opened with a glass poured, ice cube in place. How Wang manages to time these things still amazes Jim, even though it has happened countless times. He sits, with a truly weary sigh, lifts the glass to Wang, who is having sake, and exclaims, "Saludo, my friend." Each drains his glass, and Jim lets out a half whoop, half sigh with a huge smile on his face. No half smiles here, it is pure joy.

"It seems you feel the evening was successful."

"Was it ever! The place was packed, everyone who was anyone was there, including common folk from every district of town, whooping and cheering. The contestants were beautiful, even the round faces. The judges did us a favour and crowned the daughter of Tamil's friend rather than his own, so he saves face in town. Grapes are established in Zamboanga. I think your colleagues will hold you in high esteem for many years to come."

That last comment brings the first blush Jim has seen on Wang's face, and Wang dips his face toward the table in recognition of the fact. They raise their glasses, once again full, and toast again before plunging into the feast. Their private celebration is most satisfying and they each stagger toward their beds at sunrise, neither expecting to be functioning the next day. What the heck, it's a holiday.

The buzz around town is effectively maintained for at least two weeks through the efforts of the newspaper, the town council and the small conclaves in the various neighbourhoods represented in the contest. Greetings on the street typically recall the outcome of the contest or something grape-related in their neighbourhood; wine is suddenly the drink of choice among the non-Muslim population, and quietly among many of the Muslims as well. Every cafe is trying to outperform the others in new and interesting recipes including grapes, most of them represented in the chef's cook-off. Grapes are in such demand that some are actually being imported from other parts of the Philippines and from Malaysia. The notoriety of the contest has spread to Manila and three other larger cities, mainly because they were the origins of the judges. The news of the project continues to spread nicely as well.

The paper is back at work, so is Jim, and the visits to Matunkup's hacienda are sporadic, mostly for celebration. His travels around town allow for frequent message drops from Hanna', but the only visual contact in the past three weeks after the contest has been at her father's house. Tamil hosts a celebration breakfast for Jim the week after the beauty pageant. Tamil is unusually effusive in his praise of Jim's work, and Jim finds himself relaxing in the comfort of a somewhat familiar place, given the number of visits he has made in the past few months. Hanna' delivers one of the courses of the breakfast meal and whispers something to her father who nods. Tamil does not rise or leave, just mumbles a response, which brings a fleeting expression of disappointment across Hanna's face. Tamil does not notice her response since he is concentrating on his food. Hanna' disappears around the corner behind Tamil, allowing herself the briefest glance at Jim, accompanied by a sad smile. Jim instantly realizes that her latest ploy has just failed, bringing his own sad smile. Tamil gives him a questioning look. Jim becomes self conscious and blurts out that he was just thinking about the results of the contest, wondering if Tamil was disappointed.

"Not at all. The result could not have been better," Tamil says. "My relationship with my colleague, whose daughter was successful, has never been better. I make very much profit now. It is good."

With that, the conversation moves to upcoming agricultural happenings, leaving Jim's mind to more pleasant memories and a secret, wistful smile.

That breakfast was nearly two weeks ago and Jim has not seen Hanna' since. Ten weeks after the contest Jim remains busy, yet still longing for Hanna'. Then another envelope arrives on his desk at the newspaper office. It is just before lunch, so he heads to the cafe for lunch. Tony is just returning from the municipal offices and they meet at the top of the stairs, agreeing to lunch together. Jim has occasionally invited Tony to lunch, again revelling in his irrepressible optimism. It is similar to a tonic for Jim during those occasional down days. Today is not one, but happy accidents need to be exploited and here they both are, ready for lunch at the same time in the same place.

By now Jim has staked out a territory that many recognize as "his table," at the street edge of the outdoor courtyard, under the large umbrella providing welcome shade. They order their usual lunches on the way to the table, secure in the knowledge that everyone will know where to find them, and then they settle down to their noontime lemonade. After the usual pleasantries, Tony asks, "So, Mr. Jim, I hope I do not offend you, but how is your girlfriend?" That brings Jim's head up from the lemonade, the glass firmly returning to the table.

"What do you mean? What girlfriend? I don't have one, remember?"

"I know what you told me many months ago, but now there is talk around town that Mr. Jim has a girlfriend, but that she is not well. I was surprised, but also I worry about her health, because I think you will be worried also. Are you not worried about her?"

"First, there is not a her since I do not have a girlfriend, and so how can I worry about her?" The tone in his voice alerts Tony to the fact that something is not right, so he backs off saying something like it must have been a mistake, not to worry, and other soothing phrases designed to defuse the conversation.

Jim settles down and the conversation shifts to Tony's shuttling between the newspaper office and the municipal offices, how he now nearly runs off his feet juggling all the new projects, contacts and details he has to manage. Jim talks about his latest visit to the hacienda and about his trip up the east coast as far as the road extends. There is quite a bit of development there with new vineyards started, old ones expanded, and the new and established planters becoming either competitors or cooperatives. Tony listens attentively, nodding occasionally, and then offers an observation or two that bring relationships among apparently different planters into focus, again providing Jim with insights that had eluded him. He always comes back from lunch with Tony with valuable information. Lunch finished, they part company. Tony heads upstairs, and Jim steps out into the street to signal a Wang taxi for his next visit.

After about 10 minutes, he discovers his usual typical ride, the driver in a fine sweat having a bit of a siesta behind the municipal building. Jim bangs on the roof of the car and climbs into the back. Sitting in the back seat, Jim feels the crumpled blue envelope in his back pocket, retrieves it and reads, "7:30 p.m." Remembering that he has dinner plans with Wang, he begins to plan the necessary escape for the rendezvous. He finally arrives at the shop at about 6 p.m. after a long, hot day of business visits behind him and what seems a fool-proof strategy for avoiding the dinner and making the Pershing Plaza appointment. He waves off the driver and comes in the front door of the shop. Just as he is closing the door, Wang appears through the beaded curtain behind the counter, greets him and asks, "If you are not too disappointed, I would like to change our dinner appointment to a different day. I have an invitation to see several of my closest colleagues this evening and they want to meet at the club at 7 p.m. Is this a problem for you?"

Jim's self control is severely tested as he puts on a semi-disappointed face, ponders a moment and then agrees to another day, all the while appreciating the Mata Hari nature of this young lady he has developed such a fond attachment to. Wang nods, returns through the curtain and Jim heads upstairs for the necessary shower and short nap before heading to the Plaza. What a delightful anticipation, especially after all this time. How to keep his libido in check is the next question, but first seeing Hanna' again is the priority. "I bet Tamil is at the club this evening." Fear runs through Jim's head as he showers and he is still shaking his head slightly as he changes into drier clothes.

At 7 p.m. Jim is heading to the Plaza. Walking at a slow speed, he can cover the distance in 20 minutes, but he is not walking slowly and he arrives at 7:15, behind the statue as before. Five minutes later, the lookout girl passes by on a side street, heading for her post at the corner. Hanna' strides purposefully into the alley behind the statue leaving the hulk at the street. Out of the corner of his eye, Jim sees another hulk, taller by a significant amount, take up station at the other end of the alley where it comes out onto the neighboring street. The alley essentially cuts across the corner of the block isolating Pershing Plaza in a triangular space and the alley crosses the diagonal from one street to another.

Just as Hanna' reaches her usual waiting place, she looks into the shadows and Jim emerges, smiling ear to ear, arms wide open. Then he stops abruptly half way there. Hanna' is facing him, and in the dim reflected light of the street lamps Jim sees her face distorted in anguish, tears running down her cheeks, wetting her whole chin. Jim drops his arms, the smile vanishes from his face and alarm takes its place. "What is the matter? Are you sick? Someone told me today you are sick. Are you? What's the..."

Hanna' holds up one hand to stop his questioning, then simply says, "I have a baby here," pointing to her belly. Jim's knees buckle, he nearly falls but catches himself and sputters, "Are you sure? How do you know? It can't be!"

Hanna' looks down, in abject despair and simply says, "My godmother can tell. I have no bleeding for two times, she can see the signs here (pointing to her breasts) and here (pointing to her belly). It is true, I know it now also. Tomorrow, my father will probably know. But he will not know before the afternoon. My godmother has agreed to not tell him until after the noon meal. Here, take this. It is the schedule of ships from here tomorrow. You must go. If my father can catch you, he will kill you, and he will know soon that you are the one. I will never tell, but he can discover the information. You must leave, I am so, so sorry. I will miss you too much. But, if you stay, you will die, and it will be a hard way to die." With that, she thrusts a paper in his hand, flings her arms around his neck and holds on as if he is preventing her from drowning. Then she releases him, turns and leaves the way she came, never looking back, just like before.

Jim is standing in place, unable to move, unable to think, barely able to breathe. Finally, one foot precedes the other and he is on his way back to the shop, not seeing much of anything on his way, missing collisions with lampposts by the smallest margins, barely getting his feet off the ground. Four long blocks later he is back at the shop; he steps inside and sits on a chair in the lobby area and stares at the floor. Finally he looks at the paper Hanna' thrust into his hand. It is quite wet with sweat by now, but still legible, and he notices that the Eastern Star sails at 12:30 tomorrow. "No shit! Eastern Star!" With that, he heads to his room, starts sorting his life, packing for a trip home. "Eastern Star. This is way too much. There are no gods, no heaven, no hell, but this sure beats all." By 11 p.m. he is sorted, his passport and merchant marine papers carefully stowed, and the Aladdin clothes carefully folded and put aside. Then he is able to take a stiff shot of Jack Daniels and get under the bed's netting. He does not hear Wang returning, but is not relishing tomorrow morning. Maybe he can get out of this with his skin intact.

His thoughts shift to Hanna' and he solemnly recalls their brief affair, if you can call it that, with more than a little regret and a whole lot of concern for her. How did he become so attached to such a distant target? Forbidden fruit, Matunkup said it. He just never saw himself as self-deluding as that, or as susceptible to manipulation of his feelings. Impatient, maybe, appetites slightly too large for practical matters, for sure, but not gullible. Was he manipulated? No, actually, he wasn't; he just was unable to control his appetites. "Gotta keep my wits about me, now. No slip-ups or I am up shit creek without a paddle." Then his vision is filled with Hanna', the most beautiful being he has ever seen, and sadness sets in, holding sleep at bay for what seems an eternity.

But the smell of coffee wakes him again the next morning. He lies there trying to reorient himself, slowly comes to full awareness and sits up slowly. He just sits there, maybe five minutes, head down, cross legged on his pallet, still under the net, on the floor. Finally he pushes out from under the net, stands sweating in the middle of the floor and eventually takes his towel down the hall for a tepid morning bucket shower. Slightly refreshed, he checks his gear, pockets the important papers and puts his backpack by the door, ready to depart.

Wang is frying eggs and has a pot boiling ready to receive dumplings. The kitchen is warm and the sense of the room is joyful when Jim walks in. Wang takes one look at Jim, flips the eggs, deposits the dumplings into the boiling water, then turns and asks, "What is wrong? You do not look happy."

Jim takes a step into the room, looks straight at Wang and says, "Hanna' says she is pregnant."

The joy in the room vanishes. Wang removes the cooked eggs onto two plates, dips the dumplings out of the pot into a bowl then sits himself at the table, elbows resting with his chin on his hands. It is his classic meditative position. "Sit down, please."

Jim sits across from Wang who looks up and asks, "Does Tamil know of this?"

"I think he does, according to Hanna'. She told me yesterday evening. She thinks Tamil will know by this afternoon who the father is. Hanna' told me to leave right away. I am booking a berth on the Eastern Star that leaves at 12:30 today. I think I will be safe until then."

Wang's head does not rise from his hands while he says, "Perhaps you will be safe until then. You will go now, after eating, to the newspaper office, take your things with you, and when it is time, leave through the rear of the building. The taxi will be waiting for you at noon, behind the building. Where are the plans for the project, the records of the meetings?"

"All the paperwork is at the newspaper. A bit is at the barracks in the commander's office. I do not think any of our paperwork is with any of the colleagues. Matunkup has some, of course. I do not think we kept any at the club, but you might check there."

Wang's head comes off his hands and he looks balefully at Jim so that there is no doubt about the consternation behind Wang's eyes. "I am sorry this has happened. I enjoyed our work together. We did a good thing for Zamboanga. Matunkup and I must work now to prevent the project's collapse. I believe we can do this. Your time in Zamboanga has been short, but important in many ways. Now finish your coffee and go to the newspaper. Gus must know about this also because the newspaper may be helpful in saving the project. How the city hears about this trouble, what information gets out, will be most important for saving the project. I will start with my colleagues and will telephone Matunkup. Gus must also help with the newspaper. All together we can perhaps be effective. Go now, Jim Tuck."

With that, Wang stands and retreats to his room, leaving Jim alone to finish his coffee. There is no breast-beating, no handshakes, no long wistful good-byes.

Wang is gone, now Jim has to go. Coffee finished, Jim heads back upstairs, two steps at a time, collects his bag, which contains his nest egg from Manila, and returns downstairs, sort of hoping Wang will be at the bottom of the stairs, or in the front room, for one last farewell. He's not. Out the door, into the cab and he is at the newspaper in five minutes.

After dropping his bag in his office, he returns to Gus's office where the man is wrestling with a stack of invoices that suddenly tips and scatters across the floor beside the desk. "Shit, and goddammit, son-of-a-bitch!"

"Here, let me help you get them back in order." Jim stoops and begins pulling the papers into a pile, check dates and invoice numbers, with Gus opposite him, squatting, doing the same. After about five minutes the stack is back together with a paperweight holding it down. Gus leans back in his chair with a sigh. "Great way to start the day, eh?"

"An even better way is with the information I have. I have to leave today. I am booking on the Eastern Star. She happens to be the same ship I arrived on. Funny that, but that is the only funny thing about it. Tamil's daughter, Hanna', is pregnant, Tamil knows, and I am the father. If I stay, I die a rather unpleasant death. So I am away at noon, if not before. Wang said to tell you the facts of the situation. He is calling Matunkup and the two of them will make a plan to circulate information around town that might help save the project. Wang is counting on you to do the same with the newspaper. He thinks that with a concerted effort from the three of you, the project can be saved. I hope so. Seems I fucked things up in more ways than one. Sorry, mate. But the closer we keep this among ourselves the better, OK?"

Through this small soliloquy, Gus has sunk further and further back into his chair, finishing in a full slump. "Goddammit, Jim," he says without yelling. Then he looks up at Jim, who is standing there in front of the desk, almost as a supplicant, and shakes his head slowly, emitting a long low whistle. "We will need a lookout to see if Tamil or his boys are coming to the building. Hold on a minute." He picks up his phone and clicks the cradle a couple of times and says, "Irene, is Tony down there in the municipal offices? Yeah? Good. Would you please have him come to my office for a moment? It is a tad urgent, OK? Thanks." He puts the receiver back and looks up at Jim, "He'll be here in a minute. He knows everyone involved, but does not need to know details to be able to tell us if Tamil or his gang are on their way."

Tony bounces smiling into the office. "You called for me, boss?"

"That was quick! I like your work, Tony. I have a slightly odd assignment for you for this morning, but it is important. You know Tamil and his family and his workers, do you not?"

"Sure. I know Tamil and his brothers and cousins, all of them. I do not think they know me, though."

"That is not a difficulty. I want you to plant yourself on the balcony outside the office where you can see out the front doors. And, if Tamil or any of his relatives or employees are coming from the street into the building, you tell me quickly. Do you understand? I need to know immediately"

Tony stands quiet for a moment, looking quizzically at Gus, then turns and with a face that has a tragic smile, he looks at Jim saying, "So the rumour is correct? Hanna' has a baby?"

Gus flops back into his chair, Jim sits on the one next to him and Gus asks, "Where did that rumour come from?"

"It is true, yes?" Jim simply nods, and Tony sits on the remaining chair, shaking his head. "It is a very dangerous time, Mr. Jim. The long knives and spears have been sharpened. The street is a very not safe place for many, but mostly for the one who did this terrible thing to Hanna', Tamil's daughter. Many, many people have heard, and I think it is time for you to go away. No one knows who did this to Hanna', not yet, but soon they will. Please go away, Mr. Jim.

I will watch for Tamil, but I hope you will go away soon."

"I will book a place on the Eastern Star. I was planning on going to the booking office at the port from here."

"The captain of the ship eats breakfast in the cafe now, Mr. Jim. Perhaps he could help you so you do not have to go outside yet."

"Where is he sitting?"

"He is inside, just near the far window. He wears a white uniform. I think I heard that this is the first trip for him on this ship. The old captain no longer works."

"I'll go check him out. Probably best it is a new captain, since I stiffed the other one."

"How did the old captain become stiff?"

"Just a phrase, Tony, just a phrase. It means I cheated the old captain a little bit when I did not stay on the boat the first time, and came into the city. He was supposed to take me to the U.S.A., but I did not stay on the boat."

"Oh, I understand."

"Gus, I'm going down and see what I can arrange. Tony, if you could start watching now, that would be helpful. That way I won't have to keep looking over my shoulder while talking to the captain."

"Yes, Mr. Jim. Right now." And with that, Tony is up and out the door, taking a chair with him to watch at the balcony railing that overlooks the lobby, the front doors and the cafe interior.

Jim rises with Tony, nods to Gus, and is out the door. He makes a brief visit to his office before heading to the stairs. He stops at the top of the stairs to scan the cafe and immediately spots the sea captain in his spotless whites, engrossed in a breakfast plate. Slowly descending, Jim reaches the bottom and makes his way to the captain's table. Suddenly sensing the presence of another, the captain stops eating and looks up. He is a large man, probably in his late thirties. Wearing a white short-sleeved shirt with epaulettes that is opened at the neck, white trousers with white twill belt and brass buckle, and black shoes, he has a no-nonsense air. His ethnic origin is indeterminate, but may be Pacific Islander, which accounts for his size. He is not fat at all, but broad-chested with dark well-muscled arms and thick hands. He is obviously someone who works most of the time outdoors, rather than in the confines of the ship's command post.

"Yes? Can I help you?" The question is asked as if he has little intention of helping anyone, least of all the fellow before him who has interrupted his breakfast.

"My name is Jim Tuck. I understand you sail at 12:30 today, for California. Is this information correct?" The question allows Jim time to further assess this man whose assistance is critical. Jim attempts to put a little more confidence in his voice.

"I am the captain of the Eastern Star, and my ship sails at 12:30. That is accurate."

Not making much headway here. The guy seems a hard ass. Hmmm. "I require transport to the U.S.A. and must depart as early as possible. I want to book a berth on your ship. I also can assist with many of the duties of a typical deckhand as I am certified with the merchant marine. Here is my certification booklet." With that he drops his seaman's ticket on the table and continues. "In addition, I can pay full fare, plus an additional amount that you might feel suitable for the late booking." With that, he drops $1000.00 onto the table in front of the captain. The typical steerage fare for the trip is $79.00, so the bundle on the table gets the captain's attention. "Of course, since this a late booking, the passenger manifest may not have the full details of my passage, might it not?"

The captain sits back in his chair, gently resting his knife and fork on the edge of the plate and examines Jim, who is in his best khaki outfit, knee socks and all. Then he takes a long look at the seaman's ticket, closely examining the picture and details, ruffles the wad of bills. He sits back again, then nods once to Jim. "I do not wait." With that, the money disappears from the table into a small white bag on the floor and the captain resumes eating, as if Jim was never there. Jim turns and walks briskly to the stairs, heels clicking on the concrete and tile floor, climbing the stairs two steps at a time. Back in Gus's office he relates the interaction. Gus nods and says, "He knows something is up. Do you trust him?"

"Do I have any choice?" Both smile and Jim heads to his office to write a summary of the status of all aspects of the project for his three partners. Some of the information only he knows and it needs to be on paper for the others to carry on the project without him. He sits back a moment, pondering that fact. How in the world did he get to this point? He knows exactly how. Some of his efforts he is immensely proud of, but he still is having a hard time coming to grips with the fact that he messed up so badly in the end. And he cannot spend time thinking about Hanna'. There will be plenty of time to contemplate that on the ocean.

Having finished the summary, handwritten on about eight sheets of paper, Jim writes a quick letter to his former lover Chayo in care of the aerodrome in California. He lets her know that he is due back in about three or four weeks, on board the Eastern Star. She can get updates of the ship's progress through the maritime offices at Long Beach, which is its destination. He asks, in his most humble and diplomatic fashion, for her to obtain a fast, seagoing boat and meet him off the town of Avalon on Santa Catalina Island where he plans to disembark the ship, prior to its arrival in Long Beach. That way there are no embarrassing reunions with U.S. immigration or customs, since he has a sizeable wad of cash, and never arrived as he should have the first time.

He is hoping the original captain did not press the issue, not wanting to return the fare paid by the embassy in Manila for a passenger that he did not deliver. He is also hoping the embassy folks have plenty to do, with the Japanese war in China heating up as it is, and do not have time to pursue the outcome of his original expulsion. But better safe than sorry he thinks. Folding the letter, placing it in an envelope with the appropriate stamps - extra for air mail - he deposits it in the outgoing mail of the post office in the municipal offices. Just as he is walking back toward the newspaper office, Tony rushes up to him from the balcony whispering, "They are here!" Tony's stage whisper is loud enough to carry down the corridor and into the room below. Jim asks, "Who?"

"They are five people, two cousins and three employees. They are the big people of Tamil's family and business, big, like, not small. They hurt people for Tamil. Do not look over the edge of the balcony. They are still outside, but may come in quickly. You must go now!"

Jim hustles back into the newspaper office, puts his head in Gus's door and says, "Summary is on my desk. Tamil's folks are downstairs. I am gone." A quick salute from Jim, a nod from Gus with a look that would break a hound dog's heart, and Jim dodges to his office and grabs his bag. He looks at his watch. Only 11:30, the taxi won't be there yet. "Shit!" Down the back stairs, he peeks out the back door both ways before exiting and heading toward the port on foot. He has taken no more than five steps than he hears a car behind him and the hackles go up on the back of his neck. He looks back to see Wang's taxi pulling up to the back door of the building. Jim stops, looks hard at the windshield and sees his most familiar driver's face, who is looking toward the building, not down the street where Jim is standing. Retracing his steps, Jim gets to the taxi, opens the passenger door by the curb and startles the driver, who is looking slightly back toward the building. "To the port."

"Quickly, I think so, eh?" The wicked smile says it all to Jim. Is there no one who does not know what's going on?

Jim mumbles to himself, "I must have been so naive, or stupid, or what?"

"What do you say? I cannot hear you so well," the driver says as the taxi lurches forward and down the alley toward the corner.

"Nothing, just talking to myself. So it seems the whole city knows I have trouble with Tamil."

"Not the whole city, but many, for sure." With that he has reached the second corner and turns right, heading along the wall separating the port from the city. Two blocks and he pulls up across the drive to the pier, almost blocking the entrance. Jim bounces out of the passenger seat and runs around the front of the car with his backpack in his grip. When he gets to the driver side he puts $200 in the driver's hand, gives a wave and says, "Leave the car there. Pick it up later, either there or at the impound if it gets towed. Wang can sort it. He won't mind. You go away for awhile. Thanks."

Jim is away down the drive toward the pier and the ship. The driver gives a wave back, looks at his hand, smiles and gives another wave just as he hears the quickly approaching mob. Looking over the top of the car toward the municipal building, he sees at least 20 or 30 men, running toward the port, each carrying a weapon. Many have spears, more have the local long sword that was made famous in the local Moro resistance wars against Pershing. Pershing's efforts to confiscate Moro weapons were more successful against firearms than against hand combat weapons. These swords carry much more personal significance to each man, and each man running toward the port is screaming for blood.

The driver slams the door, leaves the car where it is and heads toward the fishing village alongside the port. A sailboat will do him nicely just now, and his uncle on Sulu could use a visit from his favourite nephew.

The mob racing toward the port is stalled momentarily at the car that blocks the opening to the drive leading to the pier. They crash headlong into the side of the car, clamber over the top of it, around the front and rear, screaming in rage as Tuck runs ahead of them. The mob races toward Jim waving their weapons overhead, their bare feet pounding dust into the air. A glance back over his shoulder convinces Jim he needs to speed up. The bastards are gaining on him. His bag is slowing him down, but it is vital and can't be discarded; so he gets a tighter grip, pulls the bag closer to him, and lengthens his stride to pick up speed. A quick glance over his shoulder is not encouraging. The ship is still at least a hundred yards away, the gangplank still out of reach. Just then a lance thudded into the dirt behind his right leg. "Shit, shit, shit!" Jim struggles to run away, his lungs are on fire, his feet feel like lead weights, and sweat burns his eyes. Jim wipes his face, glances back just as another lance flashes past. This one thuds to the ground barely missing his left shoulder. Thirty yards to go and he can hear the mob gaining on him. He looks up and there is a crowd at the taffrail of the ship, enjoying the show. They haven't had this much entertainment the entire trip so far. Jim yells at the top of his lungs, "Start pulling in the gangway, start pulling it in! Now!"

With that, two of the onlookers head to the top of the gangway and begin winding the crank used to pull in the gangplank. Just as the end lifts off the ground, Jim makes a leap and lands in full stride on the elevated walkway. It continues to rise as he is running full speed along its length toward the ship. Suddenly Jim feels a sharp stinging at the back of his right arm. A lance careens off the railing of the gangway and clatters onto the rising gangway. Jim looks at the back of his arm and blood is everywhere. He leaps off the gangway onto the deck of the ship as three more lances clatter against the side of the ship.

Looking down, the crew can see the raging mob waving their swords, shaking their lances furiously at the side of the ship. Then emerging from behind the crowd is Tamil, slowly making his majestic way toward the ship. The mob quiets when he arrives, parts so he can approach the edge of the pier. Tamil stands and addresses the ship's crew: "I speak to the captain of this ship. Where is the captain?"

The captain has been watching the proceedings with his crew and steps toward to the rail. "I am the captain."

"You must send me the one who came now. Send him to me now. I am Tamil, I am Moro. He has offended my family. Send him now."

The captain looks down the 30 or 40 feet to the pier, sees the mob, the weapons and the seething Tamil. He places his white captain's cap on his head, stands slightly more erect and says, "No." With that he turns and barks the order, "Make way to sail. Bow and stern lines in, now!"

"But, Captain, it is only 11:45. We are not scheduled to sail for another 45 minutes." The sailor making the objection is just to the captain's right, not quite far enough out of reach. The captain's right hand swings from his side, catches the sailor on the right side of his head with a back hand that sends the sailor head over heels to the deck. Without breaking stride, the captain repeats, "Now." The crew shoots off to their stations. The captain glances over to Jim who is sitting on a coil of rope trying to staunch the bleeding on his right arm. "The ship's sickbay is a good one," the captain says. "See the attendant there. Down this hatch here, one deck," and he points to the nearest open hatchway.

Jim nods, "Thanks."

The captain turns and is up the stairway to the command post. The crew is concentrating on their myriad duties. Jim hitches himself up with his bag, clutching the back of his arm in an attempt to stop the bleeding. Before he heads downstairs, he walks back to the rail and looks over the edge at the mob below. When his head becomes visible, there is another roar and half a dozen lances clatter onto the side of the ship and onto the deck. One even sails through an open portal, clattering to a stop in the room below. Stepping back from the rail, Jim turns toward the door and notices a multihued sail unfurling from the fishing village, heading out into the harbor away from the city. He turns away, into the stairwell and heads downstairs to get his wound stitched up.

As the medic patches him up on the exam table, Jim thinks, "That was a close call. Wonder how many I have left in this ol body?"

Before the Eastern Star is out of Philippine waters, a small fishing boat arrives at Sulu Island with its passenger headed for a cloistered life at her uncle's rural compound where her infant truly will be raised by a village, and her shame limited to a community that rarely communicates with any society outside its confines. She is beautiful, intense, pregnant and out of sight, gone.

At the end of the second week at sea, Jim is able to join most of the deck routine activities. The long haul across the Pacific would be so boring if he had nothing to occupy himself, so he makes use of his merchant seaman's qualification while his arm continues to heal. Nights are full of freighter night sounds, from the continuous rumble of the engines to the creaking of cargo and swish of the sea passing. His routine returns to early to bed and early to rise, while accepting his share of night duty rotations. He regularly accepts some of the less glamorous or more onerous jobs, which helps ingratiate him to much of the crew; his refusal to accept pay, since he really does not need it, helps his status with the captain. By the middle of the third week he has the run of the ship and is accepted by most of the crew, the exceptions not worth caring about.

At the end of the third week at sea the ship is closing in on the California coast. Jim makes arrangements with the radio operator for a ship-to-shore call using the last phone number he had for Maria Rosario when he left what seems like eons ago. As he slips a $10 bill under the edge of the console, the call is completed and he hears what sounds like a phone ringing on the other end. The radio operator has the headphones on his head, but Jim has his ear close to the right ear piece and listens as the ringing continues. At the seventh ring a low male voice gruffly answers, "Que!" Jim motions to the operator to cut the connection, which he does immediately and Jim straightens up behind the operator. He places an additional $10 bill on top of the other one and says,

"This afternoon, 2 p.m." He figures that will be 4 p.m. in Los Angeles and Chayo's husband should be gone by then. Why he is there at 2 p.m. is a mystery, but whatever. Try again at two. His request is answered with a nod from Ignacio the radio operator, and Jim exits the radio room for cooler air on deck.

The noontime sun is fierce overhead so he finds shade under a tarp. Four others are already there, two in hammocks and two sprawled onto straw mats. One fellow moves to give Jim room on his mat, Jim accepts and offers cigarettes all around. The act receives smiles all around and the conversation restarts with the topics all revolving around shore leave, and what each man expects to accomplish. The braggadocio is almost humorous, but no one is laughing for fear of giving offence. Jim is careful as well, appreciating the fact that he is just now healing from his most recent exploits and has no wish to repeat such stupidity.

Two o'clock rolls around and Jim returns to the radio room to try another ship-to-shore call. Ignacio acknowledges Jim as he comes through the door, holding up a finger as he talks to someone at the docks in Long Beach about their berthing arrangements and writes notes for the captain. Signing off, he asks Jim to take the message to the captain while he retries the number Jim has given him before. Taking the slip of folded paper, Jim exits the room and climbs the stairway that leads to the command center where the captain is examining charts. Glancing at the charts Jim realizes they are still too far west for Santa Catalina to be shown on the charts, which means he has about another day on the ship. Glancing up, the captain smiles and Jim hands him the folded paper. "Courtesy of the radio room. I got enlisted to bring it up. Guess it must be reasonably important to need hand delivery."

The captain smiles again, thanks Jim, and glances at the paper. He makes a note on the margin of the chart then returns to examining the waters they are in. Taking his cue, Jim returns down the stairs to the radio room and enters just as Ignacio is saying, "Correct. Can you connect it now, please?" As Ignacio nods his head, he beckons to Jim to come closer to the set where he can hear the earphones and make himself heard over the microphone. Leaning over, Jim hears the phone ringing. On the third ring he hears Chayo's voice, "Hallo, hallo!"

"Chayo, it is Jim."

"Jim! Jim! Where are you? This telephone connection is muy feo."

"I am on the Eastern Star freighter, west of Santa Catalina Island. I will be passing south of the island tomorrow morning. Can you get a fast boat and meet my ship and take me to Los Angeles?"

"You are working as a waiter? Where are you?"

"No, no, no! Freighter. I am on a ship, coming to California. Come and meet me south of Santa Catalina Island. Tomorrow morning. Ship is Eastern Star. Do you understand?"

A seemingly interminable silence with a fair amount of static then, "Ship? You are coming? Tomorrow. I am coming. I am coming."

"Near Avalon City, on the south end of Santa Catalina. Wait tomorrow morning. Goodbye!"

"Yes, yes, yes! Tomorrow! Maybe at night time?"

"No, morning! Morning!"

"Yes, yes. I will see you."

The connection is broken and Jim stands slowly with a most perplexed expression, "Jesus, I may be stranded on Santa Catalina."

Ignacio looks at Jim and says, "You leaving us, Jeem? How do you leave us? Why?"

"Gotta meet a girl, Ignacio. Plus, there are probably a few people at the immigration office in Long Beach who might enjoy a chat, at their leisure. I am not interested in chatting with them, you understand?"

Ignacio looks quizzically at Jim, shakes his head, then says, "You are leaving the ship before arriving at the port. I think maybe the captain is not happy with this one."

"I am going up to talk to him now. Kind of keep this quiet, OK? Don't want to worry the boys, eh?" Ignacio draws a finger across his lips, sealing them shut, and Jim is back outside, climbing the stairs again.

In the command center the captain is about to exit the door to the walkway that skirts the exterior of the room when Jim bounds through the door from below. He takes two giant steps toward the captain and blurts out, "Got a minute, Captain?"

"Sure, come with me. I have to check the radio antennae out here." The two of them exit the room and walk single file around the perimeter between the wall of the superstructure and the railing. The wind is brisk and requires Jim to raise his voice to make himself heard. "Tomorrow morning I think we will be passing just south of Santa Catalina, correct?"

"Correct."

"I want to get off there, being met by a speedboat. And I want to use my own transportation to get into L.A. Any trouble with that?"

The captain stops in mid-stride, puts the forward foot down and turns back to Jim with a somewhat perturbed look on his face. "Highly irregular. Highly. How can we keep you from being missed at immigration?"

"I am not on any passenger manifest, right?"

The captain suddenly smiles half a smile and nods his head. "So that is why you suggested not logging you into the books, and "volunteered" your deck time. What do the authorities in Long Beach want you for?"

"As far as I know right now, nothing. I want to keep it that way. You saw my going away party at the Zamboanga pier, right? Well, what if the big fella decides to broadcast his displeasure to the U.S. embassy who might put out the word to Long Beach. I am just not keen on taking the chance and have arranged alternate transport from Avalon tomorrow morning."

The captain gives Jim his most menacing stare, and for a full minute they are nearly chest to chest. Then the captain abruptly turns away toward the bank of antennae and says, "Fine. Tomorrow we will keep watch through the morning. But if there is no boat, you stay with us."

"Fine." And Jim returns to his place under the shade tarp to occupy a few of the remaining hours available onboard.

The night is long, warm, rolling and he is awake with nerves, anxiety and anticipation. After dozing off for a couple of hours, Jim awakens to relative quiet, just the usual rumblings of an active ship. He lies motionless on his back, staring into the dark toward the ceiling he knows is there. The gentle rocking and occasional rolling of his bunk indicates calm seas, which he is glad for. But he just lies there, not moving, trying to get back to sleep, which does not happen.

His thoughts are all over the place: Hanna' in her dressing room; his narrow escape up the gangplank; his first meeting with Tony; and his first visit to Julio Matunkup's hacienda. He can feel the humid climate, almost hear the sounds of the street, the farm, the municipal building. He sees Gus standing there, glaring at him because he's screwed up again. Hanna's hulk morphs into Mighty Joe Young. Then he hears a whack on the cell door in front of him and he jumps. His eyes open, and there is another whack on the other side of the wall that gets him out of his berth, shaking his head with sleep. After pulling on a pair of shorts, he exits the door and stands in the hallway, looking for the source of the noise.

Beside his room is a storeroom with no light showing under its door. He turns the lever to open the door; the door swings open and Jim reaches in to turn on the room light. The dark grey walls impair the effect of the light fixture hanging in the middle of the room. But Jim sees a mop in its bucket swaying to and fro with the rocking of the ship. As the ship rolls slightly more, the mop handle falls and hits the empty drum next to it, causing a loud boom. He reaches in to remove the mop from the bucket and lays it on the floor. Back in his room he climbs back in bed and drops almost immediately to sleep. Then an incessant knocking on his door awakens him, muddling his restless dreams and the reality of waking up. Finally he is able to growl: "What!"

"Jim, there is a yellow speed boat off the port bow causing an unholy racket with its fog horn. You may want to come up here now!"

He is out of the berth, on his feet fighting with his shorts, pulls a T-shirt over his head, and exits his berth, leaping upstairs barefoot two steps at a time. From the command center he looks out the window over the port side of the ship and sees a yellow cigar boat with a woman driver in the rear. The boat produces a nearly constant cacophony from its fog horn. Jim goes out onto the walkway outside the port door of the command center. Looking down over the side of the ship, he waves toward the boat and the fog horn stops. It's been two years since he and Chayo were together. He can't help jumping up and down, and waving. Then he re-enters the command center and descends the stairs to his berth to gather his bag, put on his sandals and double check his room for forgotten items. Madly climbing back up the stairs he steps out on the small deck and waves to the yellow boat. He looks back at the captain, who motions, "Go, go, go!" Jim smiles and they clasp forearm to forearm. Hastily he heads down the external stairs to the deck railing where a rope ladder is being lowered over the side.

Jim notices that the ship has slowed and that the yellow boat is bobbing close to the bottom of the ladder. Both boats making slow headway. Quick goodbyes and claps on the shoulders and Jim is over the rail and starting down the ladder. A sudden cross current causes Jim to swing away from the metal side of the ship and come slamming back into it. He grunts from the impact then continues his descent, stopping for two beats to look at Chayo. His timing just right, he releases his grip on the ladder and jumps, landing in the bottom of the yellow boat. Just then the boat starts rising on a swell that causes his knees to buckle. Jim falls heavily on his right shoulder, but he bounces back and stands up, swaying and waving to his shipmates above him. At least eight or nine heads are leaning over, yelling and waving, and Jim gives them a thumbs up sign. There are a couple of wolf whistles that Chayo acknowledges with a smile and a wave. Then she shoves the throttle forward.

The cigar boat leaps forward and separates from the Eastern Star, at least tripling the speed of the ship. The boat dodges a rocky outcrop and then goes around the south end of Santa Catalina Island, heading north toward Los Angeles. They lumber on in a somewhat straight line toward Long Beach pier and the berth that awaits.

Two hours after boarding into the cigar boat, putting distance between it and the ship, they finally enjoy a long embrace and passionate kisses. Soon the cigar boat pulls into a jetty and a concrete slip on the California seashore. Home again. Once the boat is secured at the jetty, they hop unsteadily onto the firm surface of the pier. Jim and Chayo walk hand in hand toward the exit of the sailing club. In the relative quiet Jim asks, "Whose boat?"

"Cecelia, a friend. She is a member here, and a very long friend. It is good, no?"

"Good, yes. Where we headed now?"

"It will be good for you to have a safe place to stay, and Cecelia is away for one week. She gives me the key to her place, a small apartment near here. You may stay there until you are ready."

"Ready? For what?"

"For starting your next life. Are you ready now?"

"No. You are, as usual, very clever. Thank you. But, first, I am hungry, didn't have breakfast. Can we eat?"

"Of course! Let's go. I know the best place, and I have a new friend working there. Come on!" With that, she is off, dragging Jim toward the parking lot and a powder blue Cadillac convertible with its top down.

"Some things never change." With that, his bag is in the back, he is in the passenger seat and smiling ear to ear, anticipating any post-breakfast activities. Hanna' is no longer in the forefront of his memory.

The Mexicali diner is just east of downtown L.A., and Jim has good vibes for the food since the parking lot is full. "I have a back way in and am pretty sure there will be a table," Chayo says.

Jim looks sceptical and asks, "Even when there are all those folks trying to get in the front door?"

"Even then. Trust me!" Big smile, she guides them around the back of the building that is a classic single story stucco, southern California style. They make their way toward the swinging door that leads them into the restaurant itself. Just as they step through the door, one of the waitresses, a stately, tall (for a Mexicana) woman wearing a flamenco style dress comes directly to Chayo and gives her a large hug right in the busy intersection of the restaurant. As they unclasp, Chayo turns to Jim and introduces Marta, her best friend in California who grew up in the same region of Mexico as Maria Rosario. Jim and Marta stand about four feet apart, just stare quietly at one another until Jim's wits return and he says, "Mucho gusto." Marta extends herhandinaconfident, assertive manner, taking Jim's in a firm grip and returns the greeting in Spanish. All the while they do not take their eyes off one another, as if they spy something in the other that they have never experienced before.

Chayo takes a short step back to get out of the firing line and smiles. Without Jim or Marta noticing, she goes over to the telephone on the wall, picks up the receiver and makes a very short call. She hangs up and returns just as the spell is broken. Marta's attention returns to the kitchen. Marta turns and retrieves an order from the shelf and is off toward a table. Chayo turns to Jim and says, "Wow, that was intense. Do you know each other?"

"Never saw that woman before in my life. But you are right, something happened. I don't know what. Who did you say she was?"

"She is a friend from Mexico, who has had a very hard time but managed to make it up here away from back there where it is very difficult. She is a good woman, is strong in her heart, and, I think, beautiful, yes?"

"No, she is not beautiful, like on the cover of Life magazine. She is different than that. She is striking, for sure. Has she always been so straight, so erect?"

"Always, even when she was small. She had a few years when she was stolen away to work in the house of a wealthy person but her mother never stopped trying to find her. She did not go to school for several years, and her family had little money so some other children were mean to her. After her mother found, Marta stayed with her family for awhile. Then she came to the states, and the word went out that she was looking for me. Everyone in that village knows I am in L.A.; I was able to find her a year ago last month. She has been working here for awhile, learning more English, making some money, but not very much. I think they do not pay her a lot because she does not have proper papers and she cannot complain. Most of the time she seems happy."

Just then one of the restaurant staff came up to Chayo, saying there was a telephone call for her. "Excuse me." She takes the call while Jim's head swivels back toward the room where Marta is working. Chayo comes back looking flustered. "Someone who knew I would be here called and needs me to come instantly. Always instantly, people have no patience anymore. So I will go and come back for you in one hour. OK, Jim?"

"Sure, not a problem. I better get my bag out of the trunk of your car."

"No problem. You stay here, take a seat at the table over there or it will be full soon. I will get you in one hour. Do you have money to pay?"

"No worries, Chayo. I'll take care of it." Chayo exits out the front door to avoid the chaos of the kitchen. Jim makes it over to the table and sits. One of the waiters comes over to take his order, but Marta is immediately there at his side, saying, "This is the table of mine, please.

Thank you." The formality of her speech lets the fellow know he has no other options, so he moves to the next customer.

"You are hungry? What do you eat?" The questions are succinct, but her stance says he has quite awhile to respond if he wants.

"I want huevos rancheros, muy hombres, por favor."

Marta produces the biggest smile he has seen in a few weeks and twirls her flamenco skirt as she turns to place the order. "Oh, y cafe negro." That gets a nod as she continues on her way. Jim's Spanish pronunciation is not all that bad, and she is obviously delighted.

The hour is almost up, Jim has finished his meal and asks for "La quenta, por favor." Marta is back in a moment, presents him with a very modest bill, which he pays for with some of his U.S. money. When she returns with his change he places a generous tip under the edge of the water glass and ventures a question. "I do not have any business tomorrow. Do you know where I could go for fun during the day? What is your recommendation?"

"Oh, I do not have working tomorrow either!" That brings a dusky blush to her walnut cheeks and she drops her eyes momentarily, only to gaze back at Jim and say, "That was poor manners for me. I should not be so strong. Chayo tells me always to be more gentle." She finishes with a shy smile.

"Not a problem. I am glad to hear you do not work tomorrow. Perhaps you could show me the best places to go around here. I could meet you where you are staying, or somewhere else and we could visit the places you like the best. Would you like that?"

Marta is quiet, not taking her eyes off Jim for a moment, to the point that he is beginning to be a bit nervous. "I like that," she finally says. "Meet here at 9 a.m. tomorrow."

"Marta! Order is up!"

"I must go. See you tomorrow, correct?"

"Correct. See you tomorrow. I will find you here, OK?" Marta heads to kitchen shouting back, "OK," just as Chayo comes through the front door.

Jim stands and says, "Now that is something. How long have you known Marta?"

"I think 15 or 18 years, off and on. Why?" "Did you know her when I was here before?"

"No, well, yes. I knew her, but she was not here. She did not come to L.A. until after you had left. I knew her in Mexico. There is another thing, you did not say goodbye, or anything! I did not know anything about you until your letter came. I should be very angry with you."

"Maybe, but you're not. Come on, let's go put my stuff up, go to a bank, then to the merchant marine offices. I have some chores to get done during the daylight. Tomorrow Marta is going to show me some of her favourite places around here. Oh, could I use your car tomorrow?"

Chayo takes a step back, looks Jim up and down and says, "Why do you think I want any competition for your attention? Eh? Why should I give you my car, risk my husband seeing you driving it around town, so you can take Marta for a date? Is that not crazy?"

"Basically, because she is your friend, your husband is out of town, and I am sure you have more than your share of male companionship available. That's why."

Chayo's smile broadens as he is talking, then she clasps onto his arm saying, "Where to first?"

"The bank. Gotta get this money safe. Went with little and managed to come back with a lot more. I suspect the word will be out, sometime, that you have a gringo "friend" and someone is going to ask for it."

"If that happens, then whoever is that foolish will have great trouble walking for awhile." There is no smile with that notation, and Jim has a small involuntary shiver of recognition and of remembrance. Off they go to the bank.

Money deposited, new clothes purchased, unpacked and set up in temporary digs, Jim sees Chayo off to do her chores and takes a walk around the neighbourhood.

Being only three blocks from the ocean, he takes himself to the beach for an afternoon of quiet and reflection. There are park benches up and down the boardwalk and he sees several couples sitting, enjoying the sun, a few with baby buggies with their sun shades up, all quietly taking in the California sun. As he walks up the boardwalk he overhears conversations, bits and pieces of local gossip and scoldings from parents to their wayward kids who are challenging the edge of acceptable behaviour. As he passes a group of four young toughs at the end of the sidewalk, he overhears insults aimed at him as they discuss the merits of Anglo society, demerits actually. He does not react, does not break stride, since he has no interest in challenges to his person. He has been feeling too good. But his disregard of their taunts does not sit well with the thugs, who jump down from the wall they were sitting on, and start trolling along behind him about three yards. Their voices slowly rise, the insults in Spanish becoming more salacious. Jim keeps walking, not reacting to their insults. Finally, one of the larger fellows sidles up to Jim's side and bumps into his left shoulder, as if he has just lost his balance, which he hadn't. Then the fellow challenges Jim saying, "You are in the wrong place, whitey. This place belongs..."

That is as far as he gets before he finds himself flat on the ground, his three buddies suddenly stopped in their tracks. Then another is flat on his back, holding his ears. The final two decide that maybe there is something to do somewhere else. Jim steps back, unloads a string of Spanish epithets that could curl the leaves off any tree in the neighbourhood, and turns to walk on, his serene mood destroyed for the moment.

At the next corner Jim crosses the street and walks down the street perpendicular to the one he was on and continues two more blocks before he turns right, heading back to his temporary home. That was enough excitement for one day. Along the way, he picks up a newspaper and a Life magazine, and spends the rest of the day and evening listening to American radio and reading the paper and magazines. Immersing himself in the U.S.A. atmosphere after being away for a few years allows him to get his footing on familiar soil.

A quiet night, a bath next morning, and new clothes that are more in style than shorts and long socks, Jim is ready to head to meet Marta at the restaurant. He looks outside and realizes Chayo has not arrived with the car yet. He checks his watch, grunts and wonders if he is collecting retribution for his previous unannounced departure. Just as he looks down from the window, he hears gravel crunching in the driveway, and there is the big blue car with the top down. Chayo is all smiles at the wheel. He is out the door, locking it behind him, and into the car in no time at all. Chayo is chattering away as he climbs in, asking about his night, what he did yesterday after she left him at the house, the usual small talk. Then she asks, "Did you go to the beach yesterday?"

"Why?"

"Just wondering. Louisa, a friend of mine, was there with her family, husband, and baby boy. And she told me about some gringo stranger who chased away some boys who were bothering the people. She said two boys did not leave so fast because they were on the ground and could not get up. I was just wondering whether you might have seen anything."

Her rendition of the events ends with a smarmy smile that says, "I know what you have been up to," but Jim doesn't bite and simply says, "No, I just had a quiet day of reading and listening to the radio. It has been a long time since I have had American radio to listen to. Don't know anything about it."

That brings a chortle from Chayo, who is relaxed and is driving with one hand on the steering wheel. They arrive at a chic two-story building where she pulls into the no-parking zone and turns off the ignition. "I am getting out here. My friends are inside at the spa and I agreed to meet them here to spend the day. I won't be finished until about 7 p.m. and they will drop me off at home. You can keep the car until tomorrow morning. Yes, you are welcome. Say hi to Marta, yes?"

Jim sits in his seat as she climbs out, not saying anything, just watching her in her pert summer outfit. Marta's allure mesmerizes him for a moment. Chayo is just standing there beside the convertible until Jim suddenly shakes off his reverie and scoots across to the driver's seat, offering his sincere thanks. Chayo looks long and hard at him, then leans over and gives him a peck on the cheek. "Adios, Jim, my friend."

"Adios, Chayo. See you in the morning. I will bring the car to Marta's restaurant, OK?"

With a wave and a small hop, Chayo responds, "OK." She is inside the spa before Jim can get the car in gear and pull it away from the curb.

The drive to the restaurant is only about 10 minutes and he arrives at five to nine. Stopping across the street, he can see everyone going into the restaurant. He is concentrating on the front door when the passenger door opens and Marta plops into the seat, startling him in the process. A wicked smile lets him know she is pleased at his reaction and he gives a warm smile back. Then he looks closer at her and realizes she is dressed for work in a blazing flamenco dress with spaghetti straps "Marta, are you going to work? I thought we were going to have the day together for you to show me all your favourite places."

Suddenly her expression changes from pert and saucy to sad and gloomy. She looks at Jim, then down at the floor. "Is this a bad dress? You do not like it?"

"No, no. The dress is fine, but I think you would have more fun in something not so formal, something we can go to the beach or wherever."

"I can go to the beach in this dress. No problem. The police will not bother me. I went before."

"Yes, I know the police will not bother you. But all you will be able to do at the beach - or anywhere else - is just walk or sit or whatever. Why don't we go to your place so you can changed into clothes that you can have more fun in?"

Marta is quiet for a moment. Then she looks straight at Jim, juts out her chin and says, "This dress is all my clothes. The cafe gives it to me for working, and I throw my rags away. This dress is beautiful, is it not?"

Jim sits and takes his time to respond. "Your dress is beautiful, and so are you. You should have more clothes for your life. We are first going shopping for new clothes for you, then we will go play. You must not worry about paying for the clothes. Chayo, your friend, will understand and she can explain it to you later. Let's go shopping!"

Off they went to a large department store with relatively inexpensive, but good quality clothes that emphasized her best attributes. Jeans, shirts, blouses, shorts, sandals and shoes, and two dresses. Once she got warmed up, she swarmed through the women's section, shoe department, casual clothing, and lingerie. Jim consulted throughout, smiling or frowning at her choices. She accepted his sense of fashion and taste in clothes, nodding her head each time, then buying exactly what she wanted.

Marta is an impressive woman who has the grace to accept each gift on its merits, with a smile and the absolute understanding that there were no strings attached in the process. Jim was not prepaying for her affections. It was a wonderfully freeing day of shopping then sightseeing around town. Marta's flamenco dress was neatly folded into a box provided by the store and placed carefully in the trunk of the car.

As it turns out, the flamenco dress gets used another month while the whirlwind romance plays out. Jim signs up with the merchant marines and takes an assignment that has him leaving from Long Beach in one week aboard a freighter heading to Panama with a load of wheat, and returning with bananas. He will be gone for two weeks. In the meantime he has rented his own apartment near the beach, purchased an inexpensive car, and started teaching Marta to drive. They are inseparable: each day he sees her at the restaurant or they drive north of Los

Angeles and into the hills, exploring, entertaining one another, getting into arguments that end in exciting resolutions, simply enjoying each other's company completely.

Before Jim leaves for his two-week stint at sea, he invites Marta to dinner at the seafood restaurant overlooking the harbor where his boat is being loaded. It is already evening. The sun has just sunk below the watery horizon and they are seated on the seaside porch, the perfect spot for watching the comings and goings of ships and small crafts from the nearby yacht club. They are quiet, listening to the music from the three-piece band that is playing inside. The music streams through the French doors that open into the restaurant. Their dinner was good and the wine excellent; Jim didn't even put an ice cube in his glass. It was white wine, nearly against his principles, but chilled and wonderful with the dinner. They are both feeling quite comfortable when the dessert arrives, American apple pie a la mode. Marta is concentrating on Jim as he takes a large forkful of his dessert, glancing out of the corner of his eye at her. While keeping her eye on Jim, she sinks her fork into her dessert and is about to place the forkful in her mouth when Jim suddenly stops her and says, "Wait! You should look at what you are eating, don't you think?"

Marta's hand stops in mid-air, pie dangling precariously on the fork and looks sternly at Jim.

"Why do you stop me eating? I am..." And with that, her eyes return to her fork and there a glistening ring is perched on top of her piece of pie. Slowly, she lowers the fork back to the plate, sets it down, and separates the ring from the dessert. Taking it in her fingers, she wipes it off with her napkin and examines it carefully. It is a beautiful Aztec design with one medium diamond in the middle of a yellow-gold band. Aztec calendar symbols encircle the ring. She recognizes the symbol that represents her birth month and sits and stares for a full minute, then simply puts the ring on her finger. She looks at Jim and smiles. He is as happy as he has ever been.

The End

David A. Rohe (Dave to most) is a retired physical therapist and teacher whose only other publication was a text book written in collaboration with his boss in the 80's. His experiences living in Central Africa, Asia and Egypt provided the perspective which drove the need to write about Jim Tuck. There is something about a larger than life existence that requires recording. As noted elsewhere, this writing project is in 4 parts with the first part published being book 2; inspiration from Star Wars duly noted. Starting to write for the public in one's seventies seems a tad foolish, but perhaps no more than planting trees whose shade will never be enjoyed by the planter.

Here's to Dave's foolishness, and his family: Wife Sharon, kids Jo Ellen, Jennifer, Adam, Sarah and Will. Go forth and prosper.

Dave and Sharon

www.ingramcontent.com/pod-product-compliance
Lightning Source LLC
Chambersburg PA
CBHW020915140626
46545CB00015B/56